CW01367875

12 Canary Greats

ISBN 0-7117-4026-7
© Jarrold Publishing and Norwich City Football Club. 2004
All rights reserved. No part of this publication may be reproduced, stored in a retrieval system or transmitted in any form or by any means, electronic, mechanical, photocopying or otherwise, without the prior permission in writing by the publisher.
Designed and produced by Jarrold Publishing
Text by Rick Waghorn
Edited by Peter Rogers
Pictures: Action Images, Archant and Roger Harris
Project Manager: Malcolm Crampton
Design: Kaarin Wall
Printed in Great Britain. Jarrold Publishing 1/04
www.jarrold-publishing.co.uk

JARROLD
publishing

12 Canary Greats

Rick Waghorn

Norwich City
Football Club

Contents

	page
Foreword by Ken Brown	7
1 **Bernard Robinson**	9
2 **Johnny Gavin**	22
3 **Terry Allcock**	32
4 **Dave Stringer**	48
5 **David Cross**	67
6 **Martin Peters**	84
7 **Kevin Reeves**	99
8 **Dave Watson**	116
9 **Jerry Goss**	131
10 **Bryan Gunn**	148
11 **Iwan Roberts**	165
12 **Nigel Worthington**	181

Foreword by Ken Brown

Norwich City Football Club has been blessed with some truly talented players over the years and during my seven-year spell as manager of the Club I was privileged to work with a great many of them.

But there is a marked difference between a talented player and a truly great player. This book celebrates the careers of some of the "greats" who have pulled on the yellow and green jersey. They are among a select group of people who are remembered with great fondness, not just by everyone associated with this marvellous football club, but by the city and the county as a whole.

The names of people like Dave Stringer, Martin Peters, Jerry Goss, Bryan Gunn and Iwan Roberts are familiar with far more people than just football fans. They are characters whose conduct off the pitch endears them to the entire community – role models for youngsters and a true credit to the game. And when you make friends with the public, it can only serve to improve your game.

I had that kind of rapport with the fans at Upton Park. When I was plying my trade as a centre-back at West Ham I felt like I couldn't do anything wrong. I could have scored three own goals in a game and the crowd wouldn't have moaned. When you are happy off the pitch, you are going to be far more effective on it. And the players in this book are clear proof of that.

As I said, I have been honoured to work and play with a number of great players during the 45 years I have spent in the game. Martin Peters was one of those during my West Ham days. He was a very quiet personality and kept himself to himself, but loved his football. He never went off the rails, but he would work hard: you could call him the ideal professional footballer. He was especially popular in this part of the world when he came here; the Norfolk public recognise quality and give players respect. Martin also demonstrates perfectly what it takes to get to the top of the tree.

He was extremely talented – but talent can only get you so far in this game. It's the saddest thing when you see a young lad with bags of talent, but isn't willing to put in the work. Talent will take you a long way in football, but not all the way to the top.

It was at West Ham that I had the honour of playing with a truly great player in the form of Bobby Moore. He was an unbelievable fellow. He would work and work and work. He wasn't the quickest player going, but his mind was very fast and his control and passing were unbelievable. I lost count of the amount of times I went round the back to cover for him

– but I never had to be there because he never made a mistake.

It would be unfair to the players in this book to compare them to someone like Bobby. But to Norwich City fans, they have one thing in common with him – they are true legends. I have some great memories of working with some of these players.

Bryan Gunn was a player we signed, relying on the testimony of a certain Alex Ferguson, and – as the football world now knows – Sir Alex has an eye for a decent player. After all, he took Steve Bruce off us! We had just lost Chris Woods and we badly needed a new goalkeeper. When Mel Machin went to see him he had nothing to do the whole game, but apparently he was brilliant in the warm-up! We signed him and the rest is now history. He has done tremendously well. He had the tragedy of his daughter Francesca dying and he won a lot of admirers for the way he dealt with that and managed to devote his time to his fundraising.

Another player I am very familiar with is Jeremy Goss. He was coming up through the youth ranks when I was in charge. You knew what you were going to get with Jerry. He was one of those players who were great to work with and never any trouble. It speaks for itself when you consider what he's achieved with the Club. He will always be remembered for his two goals against Bayern Munich in the UEFA Cup – possibly one of the proudest achievements of Jerry's career.

Dave Watson falls into that same category. We brought him here from Liverpool. I gave him his debut against Ipswich over the Christmas period. We had two games in quick succession, and Dave played against Ipswich and was brilliant. We felt that it was his type of game. But I'll always remember the following day, when I said I was leaving him out for the Spurs match. We didn't feel the Spurs match was his type of game and I explained this to him. All I can say is that, if looks could kill, I wouldn't be here today! But he took it in his stride and went on to become a great player, not just at Norwich but also when he went back to Merseyside with Everton.

Iwan Roberts is another City star who has left his mark on the people of Norfolk. I first spoke to Iwan when he was a young apprentice at Watford. He is proof of someone who has had to work hard in the game, and that's exactly what he's done. He is a nice fellow too, and that is a quality which means a lot to people who support Norwich City.

Ken Brown – October 2004

1 Bernard Robinson

Bernard Robinson is currently the oldest living ex-Canary, with 92 years' life under his belt and 17 of those spent plying his trade for the Canaries. He is able to recall playing at The Nest; the Club's move to Carrow Road and the effect of the Second World War on his footballing career.

One of the Club's greatest servants, Bernard was a member of the 1933–34 Division Three South championship-winning side and went on to rack up a total of 380 appearances for the Club. In all honesty only the war stopped him from going on to become the Club's record appearance maker.

A true Norwich City legend, Bernard took part in most of the Club's Centenary celebrations and the tales from his playing days offer a fascinating insight into life as a professional footballer in the 1930s and 40s.

> **Bernard Cecil Robinson**
>
> **Born:** Cambridge, 5 December 1911
> **City Debut:** 2 April 1932, Exeter City (a) 0–3 Division Three South
> **Final Game:** 12 March 1949, Ipswich Town (h) 2–0 Division Three South
> **League appearances:** 360
> **League goals:** 13
> **FA Cup appearances:** 17
> **FA Cup goals:** 1
> **Other appearances:** 3
> **Other goals:** Nil
> **Total appearances:** 380
> **Total goals:** 14

The memory probably isn't what it once was. In fairness, it is 55 years since Bernard Robinson last kicked a ball in anger for the Canaries. After 380 City appearances, split by the small matter of the Second World War, the 38-year-old wing-half turned full-back bowed out in the finest possible manner, playing in a 2–0 win over the old enemy, Ipswich Town, in a game watched by 35,361 people at Carrow Road on Saturday, 12 March 1949.

'I suppose when my career came to an end, it was my age, mostly,' said Bernard, now 92 years of age and living in quiet, dapper retirement on the northern outskirts of Norwich. 'I just couldn't keep up with them so I thought it best to pack up. And then I did the worst thing I could have done, went into running a pub. Because I was no drinker, you see, and that was all it consisted of...There were a lot of football people there. I must have had it three or four years. But I didn't look after the place. If it had been my calling I would probably have been in there for several years after that. But I didn't like the life for a start and I suppose I let things slide.'

For the record, the alcoholic hostelry concerned was the Ipswich Tavern on Westlegate. The days when Norwich had a pub for every day of the year and a church for every week are, of course, long gone. The Ipswich Tavern is no exception. It might even have given way to McDonald's or some other essential of 21st-century living. Notwithstanding the reluctant landlord, it was it seems a popular haunt for the city's football folk. After all it wasn't every pub in Norwich that had such a Canary legend working behind the bar; someone who knew exactly what it was like to play at The Nest. But it was never his calling, running a pub. Playing football, now that was a different matter.

Bernard Robinson was actually born in Cambridge in December 1911. The family were soon on the move – to King's Lynn, where his father was head postmaster. But by the time his young son was beginning to make his mark on the sporting field, Mr Robinson, snr, had already moved on.

'My father, he left mother many years before I played. I couldn't care less about him, but my mother, she used to come and watch me play for King's Lynn. So I'm told, I don't know how true it is, but during the match she used to shout: "Kick him! Kick him!"

'I guess I must have taken up football when I was 12 or 13. King's Lynn Schoolboys. I left school at the same time practically as seven or eight of the young players did and two brothers in King's Lynn, they formed a team and called us the King's Lynn Old Boys. We used to play the villages around and from there, of course, I played for King's Lynn. A schoolmaster at the grammar school where I was at, his father was one of the directors of Aston Villa. I was tempted, but after hearing that they had seven or eight internationals in the team I thought: "Not much prospect there!"'

'I was to have a trial with Aston Villa, but Norwich got to hear of this and they persuaded me to sign for them.' (As a full-back, not as the free-scoring forward who, by the summer of 1931, had become the hottest footballing property in west Norfolk.)

'We had a trial match at King's Lynn, I was playing in the forward line and one of the full-backs didn't turn up and they put me in his place. I'd never played there before.'

The athletic 20-year-old – then an office boy on seven and six a week – had still done more than enough to persuade then Norwich manager Jimmy Kerr that this was a lad with real potential. Alas, the canny Scot would not live to see his young protégé fulfil all that tender promise. Ten months after B Robinson made his full City debut away to Exeter City in the old Division Three South on 2 April 1932, Kerr was dead.

Bernard Robinson

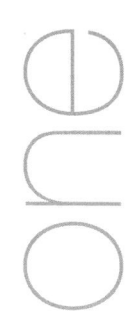

'Bronchial pneumonia, I think, while he was still manager, and it was a big shock,' said Bernard, now on four pounds a week as a professional football player.

If Kerr's untimely death was a shock, his successor – former Arsenal and England full-back Tom Parker – was about to inject one or two more shocks to the City system. Or rather to those who paid Norwich City's bills. The Pier Hotel, Gorleston, was about to strike it very rich.

Spend even an hour in the company of a player from that generation and one thing swiftly emerges. Football hasn't changed. Give young men four pounds a week in their pocket, the best digs in the city, an adoring crowd of fans every Saturday and a manager with a taste for the finer things in life and 60 years later you can still see some familiar beasts from the football jungle emerge, blinking, into the limelight.

Alongside Robinson and the quiet Scot Doug Lochhead in a midfield three that swept Norwich to the Division Three South title in 1933–34 was Tom Halliday – one of whose many claims to fame was the fact that he was the first Canary player since the First World War to boast a moustache.

From such a distance, it is difficult to work out who brought what to that half-back party. Robinson and Lochhead appear to be of a similar ilk either side of Halliday – footballers, if you get the drift.

'I think the half-back line we had then – myself, Lochhead and Halliday – was the strongest half-back line we had at the Club in my time there. I think so, yes,' said Bernard, whose chosen beat was the right. Lochhead took care of the left leaving Halliday, a former England Schoolboys star, slap bang up the middle.

'We worked very well together as a three. Lochhead was a very quiet chap; just a good, solid professional. He was one of my big friends.'

Bernard appears to have been the all-rounder, the player with that little bit of everything to his game – all underpinned by an in-built athleticism. As events were to prove, he would also prove to be a very quick healer.

'I don't know what I had as a player, I'm sure,' he would modestly protest 70 years later. 'I suppose I was a good passer of the ball – I always tried to be. I was quick. I think it would be fair to say I was a natural athlete.'

As for the third of Norwich's three pre-war musketeers, he was something else. Described as 'dapper' by one Carrow Road historian, 'resolute' by another, Halliday appears to have been a 5ft 11in slice of northern rock in the middle. Throw in the 'tache and a cross between Barry Horne and Graeme Souness starts to emerge. He certainly, it seems, had the latter's taste for the high life; a tabloid sports hack's dream.

'Tom Halliday, was he a character? Oh, my word yes,' said Bernard. 'He used to ride around in a huge car. I believe he used to hire it. A ladies' man? Yes, yes…One of the boys he was.'

For obvious reasons, it doesn't translate easily into print. But those two lines on Tom Halliday were interspersed with a delightful, soft chuckle.

The same knowing laugh would follow any mention of Tom Parker. There were some good times being had, if the flickering glint in an old man's eye was any guide.

Put it this way. If you thought big, flash footballers driving big, flash cars through the centre of Norwich with a flash woman in tow were a modern invention, think again. Ditto clubs living way beyond their means, as the Canaries found in ex-Gunners star Tom, the 1930s answer to "Big Ron" Atkinson, only perhaps without so much of the fake tan.

'They were certainly lovely days – especially when Tom Parker came.' And there was that chuckle again.

Follow Norwich City on their travels for any length of time and everyone will tell you the same story. You spend hour upon weary hour on the road. So the fact that over the years Norwich sides have always stayed at hotels overnight on the eve of away games comes as no surprise. Staying at hotels on the eve of home games, however, is rather more unusual.

'Tom Parker – what a chancer he was. How he didn't bankrupt the Club I'll never know. He sort of carried on where he left off with Arsenal…We used to go away to several towns on a Friday afternoon when we wouldn't have done otherwise. Even if we were playing at home we'd go to the Pier Hotel. Before home games we'd stay in a hotel, yes.

'He was a shocker. I don't know whether anyone actually said: "Excuse me Tom, I don't think we should have been spending this money…" I suppose someone on the committee might have done.'

Or maybe not. Those running football clubs tend not to question the destination of every penny when things are on a roll. As any long-suffering Leeds United fan would willingly attest, success on the pitch can all too easily lead to excess off it and besides, Parker's managerial nous was not solely limited to the art of having a good time.

For come the summer of 1933 and Parker was returning to Highbury to steal the services of right-winger Billy Warnes. As well as digging the colourful Halliday out of Darlington, Parker was also raiding Sunderland for a centre-forward – Jack Vinall. In the historic title season that followed, Warnes and Vinall would grab 21 league goals apiece as the Canaries finished the season seven points clear of Coventry City. With record attendances filling The Nest, everyone was having the time of their lives.

'Oh, it was a wonderful time, absolutely. Wonderful times. I can't say there was anything I didn't like about it,' said Bernard, whose afternoons were now devoted to the golf course at Eaton after Parker had persuaded the Club to make the players members.

What those who didn't fancy a round in Norwich's leafy suburbs were up to, we may never know. Perhaps it is just as well that time has cast something of a veil over Norwich's 1933–34 championship side. Besides, whatever they were on, it obviously worked. City lost just six games in the course of that extraordinary season.

Bernard Robinson

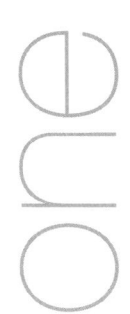

'I can't remember any big parties. Or having drinks. Mind you, I'm speaking for myself. Whether one or two of them did, I don't know,' said Bernard.

It is equally possible that we may be doing Tom Parker a huge disservice. The thought that the Canaries rode off with the Division Three South title on the back of fast cars, champagne and parties doesn't sit easily with his memories of City's pre-match routine. Watching what a player eats is again, it seems, nothing new, nor is the idea of early nights at away-day hotels or home-day hotels, for that matter.

'If we went away to stay away, everyone had to stay together. We couldn't go out separately. I mostly shared with Jack Vinall; we didn't that often, but if we did it was Jack,' said Bernard.

As for their pre-game menu, fish and chicken are straight out of football's 21st-century rule book.

'I think before a game we'd either eat lamb or fish. There was a restaurant near the station, on Riverside, I can't remember the name of it now. That's where we always used to go for meals…People used to pay attention to what we ate, oh yes. Especially Tom Parker when he came. He used to get us to eat mostly chicken. And vegetables.'

Bit by bit, line by sketchy line, the picture begins to clear – the hows and whys of Parker's title triumph. First and foremost, he bought well. Secondly, he looked after the players. In accommodation, diet, pre-match routines, he injected an obvious sense of professionalism into the Canaries. And somewhere within that "treat-them-right" mix, he found the characters and the talents he needed to bond a promotion team together.

'It was team-work,' said Bernard. 'I think we had strength right through the side. As I say we had two or three ex-First Division players who were great assets. Stan Ramsey, Spud Murphy, Thomas Scott. Billy Warnes – he came from Arsenal.

'And there was a real mix of backgrounds. Tough lads who'd come down from the North-East, from pit villages to rural Norfolk. Although we were pretty much all working-class men.'

Not that they were all whiter than white. If Halliday had an eye for the ladies, Murphy it seems might perhaps have made a better publican than Bernard.

'One or two of them couldn't care less,' said Bernard. 'Old Spud Murphy. Well, he was a funny lad…I used to get on with my job and let him get on with his,' added Bernard, as he raised an imaginary pint glass to his lips and saluted the one-time Derby County star, whose prowess on the ball was firmly on the wane by the time he arrived in Norfolk in May 1931, aged 35.

'There was a bit of this for a start; as I say, he was about 35, 36 when he came down here. I think he gave people the impression that he was taking the money but not really trying his hardest. I don't think there were too many like that. They were all a good lot of lads, really.'

Now let's throw another team-building factor into the pot. Everyone was on the same wages. The abolition of the maximum wage in football was still a long way off. Everyone got the same. No petty financial jealousies to split that dressing room asunder.

'We were all on the same money. They weren't allowed to pay any more – the Football Association put a limit on it,' said Bernard, more than happy with his little lot…I don't think anyone ever went in and actually asked for more money – not that I know of. Eight pounds a week was very good. I know I thought at the time how lucky I was to be paid so well for doing something I loved. Well, I know I did anyway.

'We say eight pounds a week, well you could get jolly good digs for 30 shillings a week.'

And where did the up-and-coming footballer of the 1930s find his 'jolly good digs'? 'I was on Unthank Road, near the cathedral.'

There is, I would suggest, one other factor that may have been at work that memorable season – something perhaps borne out by the figures. For the Canaries lost just once at home that year. To Torquay United, 2–0, in the October.

Look at their FA Cup record of the time and a similar case can be argued. City's 1931–32 cup adventure ended away at Brentford in the second round; a year later they fell at the first hurdle – away at Folkestone. In 1933–34, the title year, Norwich again came unstuck in the first round – this time at Crystal Palace.

It was only in 1934–5, with Parker at the helm, that the Canaries enjoyed any sort of cup run. Their new-found Second Division status gave them a ticket to the third round where they beat Bournemouth 2–0 at home. In the fourth round, they drew First Division Leeds United at home. And in an epic duel, the minnows forced a replay via a 3–3 draw – and all after being 2–0 down at the break.

A fabulous 2–1 win in Yorkshire booked City's place in the fifth round hat where, on 16 February 1935, they met Sheffield Wednesday at The Nest. They lost, narrowly, 1–0, to one of the then strongest teams in the land in a game watched by 25,037 people.

'That was one that we should have won – Sheffield Wednesday. They were a good First Division side in those days,' recalled Bernard, as cup fever gripped the city of Norwich and the county of Norfolk in the same way it would in that epic spring of 1959. Or again en route to the First Division play-off final at Cardiff in the early summer of 2002.

'There was a lot of excitement in the city when we did well in the Cup. And beating Leeds in the round before was a shock, absolutely.'

What is interesting is Bernard's lingering memories of those glory, glory cup days. For 60 years on, the one thing that stands out is the noise – of those record-breaking crowds squeezed tightly around a pitch carved rather bizarrely into a steep Norwich hillside.

Bernard Robinson

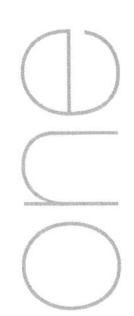

'I can't remember much now, but I do remember the crowd, the noise. Oh yes. They really had a full house for those two games.'

For the moral of this tale is quite simple. The Nest – built out of an old, high-sided chalk pit off Rosary Road – was a truly wretched little place to play football. As if the trip to Norwich itself were not bad enough, what lay in wait for visiting teams must have made the sternest heart skip a beat. For not only were the fans packed so many flat caps deep on the touchline, there was the added frisson of knowing that there, behind the far byline, was an ugly great wall of concrete, rearing up 50 feet high, seemingly designed with the specific intention of splattering the first forgetful opposition forward that chased the ball in its general direction.

'It was a shocking ground – never a professional football ground,' said Bernard, dispelling one or two of the more romantic myths about Norwich's former home. 'At one end of the ground, for instance, about five feet from the touchline, there was a concrete wall. As a matter of fact when I became half-back and had to take throw-ins I used to go back in the afternoon and practise throwing it in by throwing it against the wall.

'I think it must have been very intimidating for teams that weren't used to it – especially wingers. They were probably only about five feet away from the crowd. Did people swear at them? Oh my word, yes.'

Little surprise, therefore, that Norwich's home record provided the platform upon which Parker would take the Canaries up. Brick by brick he'd got a team of decent players together; by treating them as both adults and professionals, he'd bound those bricks together with team spirit and managerial respect – that crucial willingness of players not only to play for the paying punters, but more importantly to play for each other and to play for the boss.

But the rock upon which Tom's house was built was The Nest. A nasty, little, uninviting ground that would, several generations later, find common cause with Rotherham's home at Millmoor. The Millers merely have a scrapyard for a backdrop, nothing as good as a 50-foot slab of concrete with the odd row of supporters desperately clinging to the steep, chalk hill-face above.

In the end, it was that FA Cup clash with Sheffield Wednesday that brought matters to a head, as a concerned Football Association fired off a warning letter to the Club, suggesting that it may have out-grown its chalk-pit home. Time for the Canaries to fly their unloved nest.

The FA's letter arrived on 15 May 1935. On 1 June a deal was struck with J and J Colman Ltd for Norwich City Football Club to take out a 20-year lease on the Boulton & Paul Sports Club. Before the summer was out, the terraces at Carrow Road were in and on 31 August 1935, the Canaries' new home was officially opened.

How was it paid for? In the same way that Norwich has always paid for ground improvements. Twenty years to the month later, £17,500 and

Johnny Gavin's signature would seal Maurice Norman's departure to Spurs, where the one-time Mulbarton farmhand would write himself into White Hart Lane legend as a formidable member of the 1961 Double side, not to mention the 1958 and 1962 England World Cup parties.

His exit after just 35 senior appearances – or rather the big, fat cheque that came the other way – would in a time of dire financial difficulties part-fund the club's £9,000 investment in floodlights a year later.

Likewise, Kevin Reeves' departure for £1 million in March 1980 would build the Norwich & Peterborough Stand.

Roll the clock back to March 1935, and the player making the big-money move down to the Smoke was a 21-year-old winger with a sharp eye for goal and a smart line in footwork – Alf Kirchen.

The mighty Arsenal reached for the cheque book and coughed up the then healthy sum of £6,000 for the flying Norfolk boy whose 18 Canary appearances had yielded 10 goals – including six in a seven-game spell at the turn of 1934. 'Alf Kirchen was my best friend,' said Bernard.

Again, so much water has passed under Carrow Bridge since the lad from Shouldham was making such a mark on City's first-ever season in Division Two. But one wonders whether the hand of Parker was not at work again as the former Arsenal full-back gave the traditional "This lad's a bit special" call to his former employers.

'I wished him all the best and I'm sure he would have done better than I would have done,' said Bernard, with Kirchen's illustrious Highbury career yielding 39 goals from 96 Arsenal league appearances before the war and injury brought an untimely end to his chapter of legend.

'Right from the start you could tell he was going to do well,' said Bernard. 'He was a big, strong chap. But he had the ability as well. He was a good player. Moving down to London and joining a big club like Arsenal was a big thing at the time. That was the tops that was.'

The obvious question followed. Did the lad from Lynn not want to spread his wings and follow his pal Alf to a big city club?

'I don't think anyone tried to sign me – not that I know of,' said Bernard, with perhaps the first flicker of regret passing across his well-worn face.

'I wouldn't have minded going to one of the bigger clubs, of course. Arsenal, Aston Villa had interest. I kept in touch with Alf. He told me what a wonderful life it was playing for such a big club.'

Besides, there was little or no time to ponder the what-might-have-beens as Bernard and his team-mates headed for pastures new.

'When we moved from the old Nest, we thought Carrow Road was a palace. Absolutely. Oh yes. Well it was a palace compared to the old Nest. Oh yes.'

And, of course, every palace needs a king. Cue a little spot of history in October 1938, when King George VI became the first reigning monarch ever to attend a Second Division football match. All too predictably,

Bernard Robinson

the Canaries managed to fluff their lines on the big occasion – losing 2–0 to Millwall.

'A lot of people thought it something to even see him in those days,' said Bernard, who went one better by actually being asked to shake the King's regal hand, in the appropriate manner, of course.

'We were given explicit instructions not to shake his hand, but let him shake yours. I suppose somebody had given him a bit of a hard one – a Mason's squeeze, or something. I don't know.

'But it was a terrific occasion. Terrific. I don't think I was nervous at all. I just sort of took it in my stride.'

The fact that by this stage in his City career Bernard was still able to take both ball and a non-squeezy handshake with the King in his stride brings us to another remarkable aspect of this Canary hero's career – his injury record.

'I was very, very lucky because during the time I was playing I had two cartilage operations and got over them whereas my brother – who I think was a better player than myself – it finished him. Because in those days it was looked upon as a serious operation,' said Bernard.

For the record, the big brother in question was Frank. Football's loss was, it seems, the bus company's gain. 'Frank just played village football. He worked in the office of the bus company. In fact, I think he thought more of his job than he did playing football.'

As ever, the passage of time makes the interpretation of events slightly fraught with peril, but Bernard's recollection of his first brush with the surgeon's knife is fascinating.

If his name was Craig Bellamy or Alan Shearer, in these days of a global sporting community the football club concerned would think nothing of jetting their stricken striker off to sunny California for a date with the world's best knee man – someone whose surgical skills had been honed to near-perfection on the ruptured limbs of an American footballer.

Turn the clock back 70 years and the Canaries were equally anxious to get the best cartilage man in the land to repair Bernard's troubled tendon. Only they sent their star north, to Newcastle Royal Infirmary, where – one suspects – the accomplished surgeon involved had probably mastered his trade on the shattered joints of local pitmen, growing rich and famous on a steady diet of colliery accidents.

'The first one I had to go up to Newcastle – they sort of specialised,' said Bernard, still agile enough to demonstrate how and why his injuries came about. 'Just one of those things. I was probably nudged and instead of catching the ball there, caught it there.

'I was probably out for about a month. When I had the operation, I was still quite young. About 23, I suppose. I suppose he just used to do knee cartilages, but he used to do quite a few. He might have had a lot of mining accidents, I don't know.'

It would be interesting to know what had changed by the time history repeated itself and Bernard had to undergo a second cartilage operation. Perhaps Tom Parker's way with money had left City short of the train fare to Newcastle – or rather the price of a decent surgeon. Perhaps the Norfolk and Norwich Hospital had just caught up. Either way, the second operation was performed rather closer to home. Once again, Robinson, jnr, emerged with his professional career still intact – unlike his brother, whose promising amateur career had been cut so short by what then was a serious injury.

'The second operation I had at the Norfolk and Norwich. They were both tackles – mostly you get the injury when you don't get your foot on the ball, just the toe. It twists you round, you see.

'My brother had already retired by then, but I never gave it a thought that it might happen to me.'

By the time royalty descended on Carrow Road in the autumn of 1938, the Canaries' grip on their prized Second Division status was fast beginning to loosen. Parker had long since moved on – heading for the bright lights of the South Coast to become the manager of Southampton in the middle of the 1936–37 season, as Norwich start slowly to founder. In tow with Parker went a young City reserve, Ted Bates, who would write himself into Saints legend over the following years.

City trainer Bob Young and Bernard's midfield pal Lochhead stepped into the breach, with all the success that John Deehan and Gary Megson brought to a similar role in the wake of Mike Walker's exit from Everton just weeks after the Club's European adventure ended one afternoon in Milan.

Once again, it was a slow and lingering death as Norwich's Second Division fortunes ebbed away over the course of the two pre-war seasons. With a return to their Division Three South roots beckoning, the then chairman, Jimmy Wright, played his last card in the January of 1939 by appointing the 1938 FA Cup final referee – Jimmy Jewell – manager.

Bernard, it seems, was less than impressed. As too – if the results are any guide some 70 years on – were his team-mates, as Jewell's arrival coincided with a five-game losing streak, including a miserable 5–0 FA Cup third round exit at Carrow Road at the hands of First Division Manchester City. Even Norwich's famed cup prowess was on the wane.

'Jimmy Jewell? I hardly ever used to see him. He was never a manager. Fairly good referee, but not a manager,' said Bernard, with a neat line in irony still intact. 'I guess the manager I had most respect for was Dougie Lochhead. He was a friend of mine; he was the same age.

'But I got on with all of them really. Was I ever tempted to go into coaching or managing myself? No, not really. I've not got the top piece for that!'

You suspect that Bernard was doing himself something of a disservice there. For by the time Adolf Hitler's designs on the playing fields of Europe put his Canary career on hold for six years, the one-time Lynn Schoolboys star had matured into a genuine Carrow Road hero with far more to his game than natural athleticism and an eye for a simple pass and a crisp tackle.

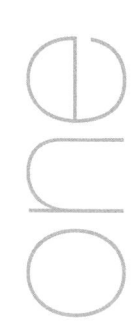

He was, courtesy of that infamous concrete wall at The Nest, a dab hand at the long throw, having stayed behind many an hour after training to practise – heaving those old, leather balls against that famous City backdrop time after time.

Bernard had, however, another string to his bow. From 12 yards out, he was also developing into the Club's penalty king. The secret of his success was all in the technique – one that would, these days, provoke a degree of controversy.

'Whether it did any good or not, I don't know, but I used to stand with my back to the goal, turn round and "Whoosh!" All in one movement, with no run up at all,' said Bernard, whose unique style would probably find charges of ungentlemanly conduct lobbed his way by today's armchair pundits – not to mention a chorus of boos from the opposition fans.

'I don't think many other players did it at the time. I don't think so. I didn't take a lot but I don't remember missing one,' said Bernard, without a hint of apology. He also had a chosen side to aim for – one based on the simplest of logic. 'I used to think that most people are right-handed so I always used to try and hit it to the goalkeeper's left. I don't think there were as many penalties given as there are now. As I say, it was very rare for me to take one.'

Three games into the 1939–40 season and Bernard's supply of competitive penalties dried up altogether with the outbreak of the Second World War.

On the day that Germany invaded Poland and set the wheels of world conflict in motion, Bernard Robinson was 28 years old and had 272 Canary appearances to his name. He was at the peak of his playing powers; an old-fashioned Norfolk hero for whom even greater league glory would surely have beckoned, were it not for Hitler.

Typically, Bernard makes light of the rude interruption. Like so much else in his City career, he took it all in his stride.

'There you are, that is what happened. One of those things. I never gave it a second thought really. Like everyone else I just got on with it,' said Bernard, who would still go on to make 160 City "appearances" over the next six years, as the Canaries somehow scrabbled together various friendlies in the midst of the chaos of war. The Anti-Aircraft XI were just some of the many unusual visitors to make their way to the banks of the wartime Wensum.

'Had it not been for the war then, quite possibly, I would have finished as Norwich's record appearance maker, but I don't regret the fact that it didn't happen. Not really. If it wasn't for me, it wasn't for me.'

Unofficially, the games and the performances continued to flow.

'We used to play a lot of friendlies. Almost every Saturday. We were amateurs then but we played other league teams, RAF teams, that sort of thing,' said Bernard, by now skippering City when he wasn't building electrical motors for Carrow Road's long-standing neighbours, Laurence & Scott.

'I used to shout out a bit, yes. I never got booked that often – I was a good boy. I didn't give away too many fouls – not if I could help it,' said Bernard, who would emerge from the war as fit and able as when it started – even if he was four months short of his 35th birthday by the time City's reacquaintance with Division Three South started, at home to Cardiff City, on 31 August 1946.

Cyril Spiers – a man who had worked war-time wonders with Norwich's opponents that day – was the man entrusted with rebuilding the debt-ridden Canaries. Interestingly, of the team that got relegated at home to Nottingham Forest on 6 May 1939, one world war later five would start against the Bluebirds – Robinson, the 'keeper Fred Hall, John Church, Jack Taylor and the inside-forward, Billy Furness.

Hewn from tough, north-east mining stock, Furness arrived in the summer of 1937, as City's board of directors splashed the cash in the hope that the one-time Leeds United favourite could halt Norwich's seemingly inexorable slide back to whence they came.

In the event, despite hitting 11 goals from his 39 appearances in his first season, seven from 42 in Norwich's relegation year, the task proved beyond Furness. He does, however, still command a special place in Bernard's affections.

'The best player? Billy Furness,' said Bernard simply. 'Very good inside-forward. Made clever runs, good control, quick feet, he had everything, Billy. I think his height stopped him from going on to bigger and better things. He wasn't very tall.'

Nor did he figure very large in Spiers' post-war rebuilding plans. For while Bernard would make 33 league appearances in City's less than impressive return to Division Three South life – they would finish one off the bottom, having conceded 100 goals en route – Furness was slipping into gentle retirement. Times were a-changing. A 21-year-old wing-half called Ron Ashman was completing his service with the RAF before embarking on a career that would span 17 successive seasons with the Norfolk club as Spiers trawled his old, South Wales haunts for the next generation of Canary stars. Ken Nethercott, Noel Kinsey, Don Pickwick and Les Eyre would soon be the names on everyone's lips.

'You could see that they were going to be good players. Ron Ashman was always a good player. Noel Kinsey, he was a good player mind, but he always gave me the impression that he was playing under duress. But a good player,' said Bernard, as time finally started to catch up with the long-standing City favourite.

Bernard Robinson

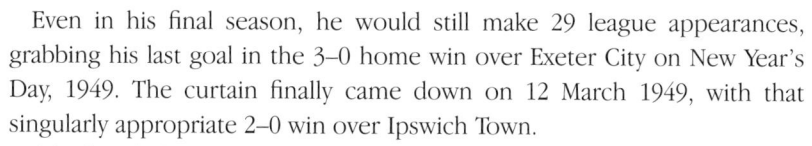

Even in his final season, he would still make 29 league appearances, grabbing his last goal in the 3–0 home win over Exeter City on New Year's Day, 1949. The curtain finally came down on 12 March 1949, with that singularly appropriate 2–0 win over Ipswich Town.

'The big derby games against Ipswich were very special, oh yes. I don't know if there was any great animosity in the crowd, but let's say they were the enemy,' said Bernard, with a degree of understatement.

So, what would he have changed – if he was able to have his time again?

'If I did have my time again then, of course, I'd like to be a footballer in this generation – particularly when you look at what they're paid, well, that's almost natural isn't it?

'But I don't really have any regrets. We were always treated well here – especially as I say, when Tom Parker became manager.'

(chuckle).

2 Johnny Gavin

Imported from Ireland by then City boss Doug Lochhead in 1948, Johnny Gavin is Norwich City's record marksman with 132 Canary goals to his name.

Johnny racked up his 132 goals in 338 appearances for the Canaries, a goals to games ratio that also sees him up there with the very best of City's goalscorers. He is one of only four players to have had two separate spells with the Canaries. An ill-fated 13-month stint at Spurs halted his goal-scoring antics at Carrow Road.

Like every player that has been chosen to feature in this publication, Johnny is an inaugural member of the Club's Hall of Fame and always receives a special reception when he returns to Carrow Road.

John Thomas Gavin

Born: Limerick, 20 April 1928
City Debut: 30 April 1949, Bristol Rovers (a) 2–2 Division Three South
Final Game: 21 April 1958, Coventry City (a) 1–2 Division Three South
League appearances: 312
League goals: 122
FA Cup appearances: 26
FA Cup goals: 10
Total appearances: 338
Total goals: 132

With his boots long hung up, Johnny Gavin followed another Carrow Road legend, Bernard Robinson, into the pub trade. Having seen out his footballing days with Cambridge City and Newmarket Town, for seven, memorable years Johnny was the landlord of The Rock Hotel, Cambridge.

Turn the clock back 40-odd years and there was, it seems, a great "crack" to be had at The Rock – particularly on a Saturday night when the live music sessions drew in punters from miles around. Horsemen from Newmarket, travelling fair people, country folk and even the odd local, they all made their way to The Rock.

'It was a great success,' said Johnny. 'You couldn't find a parking space it was that packed – not on Cherry Hinton Road. From the top where the cattle market was, going the other way out into Cherry Hinton itself, there wasn't a space to be had.

Johnny Gavin

'And I used to have the fair people in. They loved it. They were entertained and they never caused an ounce of trouble, not in my time. I'd do anything for them and they loved it. Not an ounce of trouble. They used to come in from the county, Newmarket and all around. They came in every Saturday night.'

And as the music played, so the beer and the stories flowed.

'I did extremely well,' said Johnny, now 76 years old and still living just off Cherry Hinton Road. 'When I was landlord at The Rock we used to sell 21 and a half barrels of beer a week – that's bottle beer as well included. And that was a record for Greene King.'

But then breaking records was nothing new for the proud, Irish landlord of The Rock Hotel, Cambridge. He had, after all, made a career out of it at Norwich City. To this day, Johnny Gavin remains the Club's record goalscorer. And with 132 goals from his 338 Canary appearances it is a record that is unlikely ever to be broken.

John Thomas Gavin was born in Limerick, in what is now the Republic of Ireland, on 20 April 1928. From an early age, the young Gavin displayed many of the athletic traits that would later serve him so well across the Irish Sea. The nimbleness of feet and mind and the sinewy strength that underpinned a fierce competitive streak all came with the territory – those of weak will and faint heart would, after all, have never survived the hurly-burly of street football and hurling – as the future Canary hero first began to keep a crowd entertained.

'Sunday morning used to be really enjoyable for the neighbours,' he recalled. 'We'd play in the streets on Sunday and when I used to go home they'd say that they'd really enjoyed that Sunday morning session on the road.

'As a kid I was always active and where we lived we had plenty of ground in Limerick to play. It wasn't all built up then, there was plenty of space. And we used to go hurling, of course. That was a hard game. I used to love that.'

His first football medals would soon follow and by the time the teenager had left Jamesborough United for Limerick, word was fast spreading of the free-scoring talent on the banks of the River Shannon.

News had certainly reached Norfolk. For in the summer of 1948 Norwich manager Doug Lochhead travelled to Limerick to meet the city's bright young prospect, by now working as a painter for the local railway company.

Lochhead certainly made a favourable impression on the young Irishman, who had barely left County Limerick before the Canaries came a-calling. Not that Norwich were Johnny's only suitors. West Ham United were also in the running for his signature. In the end it appears that Lochhead's fatherly approach and the fact that another Limerick prospect, Kevin Holman, was also due to sign for Norwich persuaded Johnny to put pen to paper and begin a new life as a professional footballer in Norfolk, in the old Division Three South.

'I was surprised to hear that an English club were interested in me, but I was very pleased,' said Johnny. 'At the time I had, I think, to make my mind up whether to go to West Ham or Norwich. In the end I went to Norwich because Kevin Holman had already gone and I thought: "I'll go there, I'll have company." It was my first time out of Ireland you see.

'I was 20 and very, very nervous, but Doug Lochhead was terrific. Like a father. When I first met him in Limerick, he was a gentleman. So I packed in where I was working at the local railway as a painter and signed for Norwich. It was a hard job leaving, but I never thought about turning them down.'

First impressions of his new home helped persuade Johnny that he had made the right move. 'I liked Norwich, I thought it was a nice clean place and I got lovely digs. Telegraph Lane, I think it was, and they were very good.'

Kevin Holman would never actually play a first-team game for Norwich. But in making Johnny Gavin feel right at home in his new surroundings, he deserves his place in the Club's history.

'I really was very shy. But, as I say, with Kevin there he gave me more confidence. All the questions, he answered them.'

It would, however, be another eight months before Johnny would make his first-team debut – ten days after his 21st birthday, in the penultimate game of the season away at Bristol Rovers on Saturday, 30 April 1949.

'It took me 12 months to find my feet at Norwich. I was more or less playing in the 'A' team, then I got into the reserves – in fact I've still got my first programme that I received with the 'A' team,' said Johnny, in no immediate rush to be playing with the big boys. He was still learning his trade and, for now at least, was happy to wait for opportunity to knock.

'Playing was all I wanted to do. I wasn't forcing myself to get into the first team. I just carried on and really enjoyed myself. From the 'A' team to the reserves, I was getting confidence and eventually my chance came.'

By now the goals were starting to flow as Johnny's effortless ability to drift in off the right wing and hit the far post on cue was winning him many friends and admirers – not least in the reserves where Yarmouth-born centre-forward Roy Hollis was also busily making a name for himself.

The City striker would smash home 54 reserve goals in only 88 games and the two young guns appeared to be tailor-made for each other as they swept forward with deadly effect. Though they would play only a handful of first-team games together in the 1949–50 season, by the time Norman Low succeeded Lochhead as manager in time for the start of the 1950–51 campaign, the Gavin-Hollis combination was very much part of the Low thinking – particularly once the early season experiment with Les Owens at centre-forward came to nought.

At the back, Canary 'keeper Ken Nethercott would set the ball in motion courtesy of his pin-point distribution. And with the likes of Don Pickwick,

Johnny Gavin

Les Eyre and Noel Kinsey ready to play ball too, Norwich were in business as Johnny pinged one-twos this way and that before bursting beyond the final defender, invariably to score.

'Ken (Nethercott) could always find me on the halfway line; I'd come in; meet nearly every ball he kicked. I was sure to flick it on to Hollis and then I'd double around into Roy's place.

'I was always closely marked, yes, but I'd stay back enough to make space for myself to come and meet the ball,' said Johnny. 'I'd come back, receive the ball and then play it off. Play it back into Pickwick, then "one-two!" and that was me away. That was my game – I used to play that a lot, the one-two football.

'Of course, Noel Kinsey was quite clever and he'd thread the ball through to me too. Or he'd play it through to Hollis, then Hollis to me, in my run. That's how I was getting scoring opportunities; that's where the goals were coming from.'

Low would introduce another string to Johnny's bow when he went shopping in Lincoln that summer and came back with a left-winger named Tommy Docherty.

All of a sudden, a whole new supply chain opened up in front of Johnny as the two became the best of pals – on and off the field.

'Tommy and myself were very good mates – he was left wing and we understood our play. He was feeding me more than anybody else with a fairly long ball down the middle. And that's where my speed came into it.'

There was, it seems, a little of that sixth sense going on; two players who knew just what the other was thinking – in the manner, perhaps of a Cross and Paddon, a Crook and Bowen.

'I wouldn't be in there, in the area. I'd wait outside and then I would go through a gap and Tommy would know I'd be somewhere around the area. He had a beautiful left foot, Tommy, and I got most of my goals from his crosses.

'I'd be waiting there; I'd have the distance; he could picture me going in and, as I say, I scored a lot of goals from Tommy's crosses.'

Docherty was nigh-on ever-present that season and yet grabbed just one goal from his 45 league appearances. His moment of lasting glory came in a famous 3–1 FA Cup third round victory against Liverpool on 6 January 1951, when – in front of 34,693 fans – his two goals and glorious wing-play booked Norwich a place in the fourth round.

Legend will always remember that game as "Docherty's Game" and no doubt it figured large over a jar or two later. John Duffy – the one-time Clyde welder who would become a fixture at right-back that season – was another one up for a wee drink; as, it seems, was Ken Nethercott.

'Ken was a terrific lad,' said Johnny. 'There was me, Ken, John Duffy and Tommy Docherty – we four used to stick together. We used to have a pint, the four of us.'

In keeping with this lasting image of the "gentlemen players" of that era, there would still be the rounds of golf against the Norfolk Constabulary or Yarmouth beauty pageants to be judged. But away from such formal, possibly slightly stuffy affairs, the working-class Irish boy still lingered and found common cause with Docherty, the former colliery footballer from the North-East, and Duffy, the ex-Glaswegian welder.

'Oh God, I sure loved a pint. Too true – still do,' said Johnny, whose favourite Thorpe Hamlet haunts still trip off the tongue 50 years later.

'There was The Quebec and then there was one coming down the hill, The Jubilee, that was my local. I had plenty of friends in there. I wouldn't be out drinking during the week, but I called in and had one. I wanted it and there was no offence to go into a pub and have a pint. There was always good banter between you and the supporters. It was all very good natured – we were never pulled up for drinking or anything like that.'

Likewise, the one-time pub landlord is not too far away either. For his chosen tipple at the time wasn't a drop of the black stuff.

'No, I was drinking bitter at the time – not the Guinness. It all depends on whether it was a Bullards pub I went into.'

Whatever Johnny Gavin was on, it was a powerful brew that put some serious lead into his shooting boots. In that 1950–51 season as the Canaries finished second – six points off an all-conquering Nottingham Forest – the 22-year-old winger would finish with 18 goals from his 51 league and cup appearances, one more than Roy Hollis (17), two more than Les Eyre (16).

For if sheer pace and bright football got him into shooting positions, confidence, wiry strength and a right-foot hammer of a shot would do the rest. That and the sheer, bloody-minded determination gleaned from his early days hurling back home in Ireland.

'If the gap was there for me to go, I was there,' said Johnny, well aware of the limited number of tricks up his sleeve. 'I wasn't very clever with the ball, beating a man; I'd only beat him by speed. But, yes, I was quick off the mark to get into a position and when I got there I'd probably shoot. Although there were quite a few goals I scored with my head. I was quite good at climbing; I had a very good leap.'

Whether he scored or not, the first and foremost aim was to win the game. At a time when players were bound to a maximum wage – £18 a week in the case of Division Three South – the £2 win bonus made a difference. Or it certainly did to Johnny.

'Winning the game is the whole thing – I never thought about taking the glory over scoring a goal. That wasn't the policy at all – it was all about the wage packet at the end of the week, £2 extra.'

The shame of it all was that Norwich should run into a Forest side that oozed goals at one end, shut up shop at the other. The 1950–51 Division Three South champions would hit 110 goals that season; concede just 40.

Johnny Gavin

City may have finished seven points clear of third-placed Reading, but it counted for nothing in the face of such Forest fire.

'That Norwich side was a great team,' said Johnny. 'It had everything. It was solid, confident; everybody knew what was going on; we knew how to play. I was fit as a flea and I'd run people into the ground.'

A year later and City would finish third – level on points with Reading, but five short of Plymouth Argyle. Roy Hollis would just shade the season's top-scorer contest, his 22-goal total boosted by a fabulous five in the 8–0 thrashing of a hapless Walsall side on 29 December 1951. Johnny would bag a mere 20 goals from his 44 league and cup appearances.

Having already thrown another centre-forward into his potential promotion brew with the arrival of Alf Ackerman in the summer of 1951, a year later and Low would bank on Tommy Johnston as the frontman to deliver the Holy Grail of an exit out of Division Three South – all with Johnny's goals in tow, of course.

And for the first ten games of the 1952–53 season, Low's judgement appeared to be spot on as the big Scotsman drilled home ten goals from his first ten starts. Once again, however, the Canaries were to be denied – this time by four points as Bristol Rovers stole the title, with Millwall and Northampton Town relegating Norwich to fourth. If the Club's league standing was consistent – so near and yet so far – Johnny's scoring record was running like clockwork as he finished that season with another 20 goals to his name, second to the 22-goal Ackerman.

By now the shy, young Irishman was long gone. He was, it seems, a driving force in the dressing room, never afraid to make his frustrations plain as the Carrow Road side struggled to go that final, extra mile promotion-wise. He could, after all, put his medals on the table; season after season, game after game, goal after goal, he delivered.

'Oh yes, I was terrible for having an opinion – especially against the managers. I took my shirt off a couple of times and threw it at them,' said Johnny. 'I'd stick up for myself and if I thought I was right, I was right. I was hot-headed in the dressing room. It came back to the old cash box. The win bonus – that's what we wanted. Of course I was so dedicated they had no reason to get on to me – I was always pulling my weight and scoring goals.'

The 1953–54 season found Low unveiling yet another potential ace in his pack as Northern Ireland international Bobby Brennan was signed from Fulham for a then record fee of £15,000. Though Brennan would weigh in with 15 goals in his first season in Norfolk, promotion appeared more distant than ever with City finishing seventh. The only real highlight was a notable cup scalp as the mighty Arsenal were felled 2–1 away at Highbury in the fourth round of the FA Cup, with Johnny adding a notable assist for one of Tommy Johnston's two strikes, before Leicester City ended Norwich's cup dreams for another year with a controversial 2–1 win in the fifth round at Carrow Road.

Johnny's unstinting efforts in a team seemingly intent on going nowhere were not going unnoticed and in October 1954, he made the big move down to the Smoke, to White Hart Lane, to Spurs.

The move had a lot of logic to it. At 26 years old, Johnny's best years were still ahead of him and having been brought up on playing the one-two way at Norwich, he was deemed to be tailor-made for Tottenham's own footballing needs.

'That's why Tottenham came in because that was their policy – to play the one-two. And I fitted in,' said Johnny, blissfully unaware at the time of his impending move.

'I only became aware of Tottenham's interest just like that. After some game somebody came into the dressing room and said Arthur Rowe wants to see you from Tottenham. That was the start of that and of course he offered a couple of pounds more in wages – which was £20 in those days – and I said I'd chance it.

'It was a big move from Norwich and I never really settled down there at all. It was a big place. I didn't settle. I got injured and I tore a muscle or something in my ankle and it took me a long time to get back.'

Despite the fact that he'd score 15 goals from his 32 Spurs appearances and, by many an account, looked the part, Johnny's hopes of a return to sender were answered in November 1955, when he returned to Norfolk. For that he had a young, Mulbarton farmhand to thank – Maurice Norman, who would go on to form the defensive bedrock of Spurs' legendary 1961 Double side.

Johnny became the makeweight in the deal that took Norman to north London after just 35 appearances in a City first-team shirt.

Normal service was swiftly resumed as he grabbed 15 goals from his 26 league and cup appearances. Indeed, little more than a month after his return, Johnny was racking up four goals in the 7–2 dismissal of Southend United. All the old faces were there – bar the manager Norman Low who had made way for Tom Parker's second spell in charge of the Canaries.

It was a fresh face that came to dominate that season – Ralph Hunt. Signed from Bournemouth, he grabbed 33 goals in his 48 City outings that year and immediately met with Johnny's approval.

'Oh yes! A great goalscorer. He was one of the best goalscorers I played with. We used to really work well together. He understood my way of playing and we got on very well,' said Johnny, as Norwich's slick, one-two football found the likes of Gavin, Hunt and Brennan switching this way and that – one moment dropping deep, the next flying beyond the final defender as a team-mate dropped in to cover. All in all, fairly flexible stuff. He was, he readily admits, 'a roamer' on the field of play. And a hustler – chasing and harrying anything that moved.

'We were playing modern football, yes. And to swap positions like that you've got to have common sense and know what's going on. If anybody

Johnny Gavin

saw me doubling in, someone would always drift to the wing to make room for me and take the full-back or centre-half out of the way.

'That team had good footballing brains, of course they did. I've seen Norwich play over the years, but they wouldn't compare with the team in the 1950s. You had great players: Kinsey was good, Hollis was good, Johnston and Hunt were both good centre-forwards. You had Bobby Brennan – a brilliant player. But it was a team – that's all I can say.'

And, of course, it had Johnny Gavin's goals.

The big 100 arrived on Saturday, 15 September 1956, in a 3–0 home win over Plymouth Argyle. It was a rare bright spot in a season of unmitigated gloom – the lowlight of which, aside from finishing bottom of the table, was the unfolding financial disaster engulfing the Club and threatening its very existence.

'When I scored my 100th goal it wasn't in my mind at all – I don't think I realised that it was my 100th goal,' said Johnny, seemingly not one to keep records.

'No, I never thought of it. Never. Never thought: "Oh, that's number 96!" That's the gospel truth. I never reckoned on how many I'd got. I wasn't looking forward to reaching a number or anything like that. Afterwards I was told it was my 100th, too true. I think I had to go over on to the microphone. I wasn't thinking about it. But when I found out, I was as pleased as punch, anyone would be. But I don't think it was such a big thing as it is now.'

The goals and the games still kept coming. In his final season in a City shirt before he left for Watford in the summer of 1958, Johnny would make 45 appearances and add another 22 goals to his extraordinary collection.

Take aside that strike rate, the man not only scored goals, but played games – week in, week out. Quite an achievement for someone who undoubtedly would have been a marked man in Division Three South.

'I was kicked all over the place, but it never really hurt so much that I had to miss a game. I think I had this natural, wiry strength. I had enough in me to stay on my feet, put it that way. And I didn't mind a tackle. I could take it. Just get up and walk away.

'I wouldn't say I'd walk away with a smile on my face – I more or less cursed most of the time after the tackle, but that's the game. And if they're going in with a sliding tackle, you're not really going to get hurt from a sliding tackle.'

In the 50-odd years since Johnny Gavin's departure, only Terry Allcock has really come close to threatening his goalscoring record. Iwan Roberts would finally fall four short of the magic 100-mark, and that after seven years of hard slog at the goalmouth coalface.

It is hard, if not impossible, to see someone ever threatening Johnny's tally, given the fluidity of the modern transfer market. Six or seven seasons of hitting 20-plus goals a year? Norwich might be a Barclays Premiership club with an income to match, but such a strike record would inevitably find the big boys beating a hasty path to Norfolk. It would take a fairly unique set of circumstances – and involve a fairly unique individual – for the player concerned to stay at Carrow Road.

'Iwan Roberts, he tried very hard, and got to 96,' said Johnny, well aware, despite the passing years and his own growing infirmity, of how his nearest rivals are faring.

'He was trying very hard – he was hoping. Now he's gone somebody else has got to try and get it,' said Johnny, an old man's pride still very much in evidence.

'I am proud, yes, in a small way. I never go shouting my mouth off or anything like that, but I know it's there.'

And if, somehow, it did happen, how would he feel? 'I'd be disappointed. I hope I'm dead and gone if it does happen, put it that way.'

At 76 years old, life is starting to take its toll on Norwich's greatest-ever goalscorer. Now confined to a wheelchair, even a trip to the Abbey Stadium to watch Cambridge United play is getting beyond a challenge. An electric buggy provided by the Professional Footballers' Association's benevolent fund takes him down the road to his club, for a quiet jar, a smoke and a chat.

'I'd been fairly regular at the United. I was more or less guaranteed a ticket there by the chap that washes the kits. I know him, you see, so he used to have a ticket for me every Saturday.

'But, of course, now with my buggy I'd rather use that to go anywhere. But then it's too awkward for me going in there with that and then, of course, there's getting up the steps.

'I am finding it very hard at the moment because of my feet and my leg. I go out every morning, I go to the club and have a couple of pints, but I don't have a pound to spend above my usual weekly do for the missus and I.'

In such circumstances, it would be a hard heart indeed who would begrudge an old man a few, wry "if onlys…"

For if only Johnny Gavin had been born 50 years later, what on earth would he be worth now as a player? He would be 26 years old, approaching the peak of his playing powers. More pertinent to him perhaps is the next obvious question: what on earth would he be earning as a 20-goal-a-season striker?

He has little doubt that his natural sporting gifts and fierce determination to get on would have served him equally as well today as it did Norwich in the old Third Division South. Only then, of course, under the maximum wage ruling no one was allowed to earn more than £20 a week – even the most prolific striker of them all.

'Twenty pounds was the highest I got,' said Johnny, and even then he had to wait for his move to the top flight before he hit the ceiling of his earning potential.

Johnny Gavin

'That was at Tottenham, that was the first time I got £20. And when I went back to Norwich they were still on £18. But I said: "No, I'm not coming back for lower wages!" so they then paid me £20 at Norwich.'

Could he cut it now? Of course.

'You see Norwich now in the First Division, in the Premier League, and it will be hard for the players to score. But I found it very easy to knock a few in. I wasn't in any way lacking.'

Above all he had pace, real pace. And pace kills defenders. Did then, does now. People pay big, big money for players with pace. Or rather they do now, didn't have to then.

It was not until football's own winter of discontent in the midst of the 1960–61 season that the PFA, led by its chairman Jimmy Hill, finally managed to get the maximum wage ruling abolished. Hill's former playing pal at Fulham, the England skipper Johnny Haynes, would become the first player to earn £100 a week. In April 1961, Johnny Gavin would have been 33 years old. It was all too little, too late for the players of his generation.

'When you see what they're getting today, my God above, you wouldn't believe it. It's impossible to believe. If I scored the goals I did now, oh my God, you'd be made.'

'Do I think I'd have done all right? Yes, I do, I think so. I had pace, determination – that's the whole thing, yes. And appetite and attitude. Yes, attitude. That's it. I would, I think so, anyway. I missed out. And, yes, I am very disappointed. I wish I was 50 years younger. Yes, that would be nice.'

He did, at least, have a club and a city to call his own – and some very special memories courtesy of being a very special player.

'I enjoyed every moment, every minute of it, I enjoyed it at Norwich. And for me it is a special club. Of course, these days my connections are not with the Club itself, but the friends I've got up there. I'm always more than welcome and it's a pleasure for me to go up there. A pleasure.'

3 Terry Allcock

With 127 Canary strikes to his name Terry Allcock's name is etched into Canary folklore. He stands second in the Club's all-time scoring charts and to this day remains the Club's record FA Cup goalscorer.

He learned his trade at Bolton Wanderers alongside the likes of England internationals Nat Lofthouse and Doug Holden. With first-team football far from guaranteed at Burnden Park he made the move to Norfolk in March 1958 and became one of the best signings made by manager Archie Macaulay.

Terry went on to play an influential role in the famous 1958–59 Cup run as the Canaries put themselves on the footballing map. He played a total of 389 times for Norwich between March 1958 and April 1969 before joining the Club's coaching staff.

Still a firm favourite at Carrow Road, where he now works as a matchday host for corporate clients, Terry was voted onto the Club's inaugural Hall of Fame in 2002.

Terence Allcock

Born: Leeds, 10 December 1935
City Debut: 15 March 1958, Walsall (h) 2–1 Division Three South
Final Game: 23 April 1969, Blackburn Rovers (h) 3–1 Division Two
League appearances: 339
League goals: 106
FA Cup appearances: 33
FA Cup goals: 12
League Cup appearances: 17
League Cup goals: 9
Total appearances: 389
Total goals: 127

There are many ways into these interviews – some, no doubt, work better than others.

In the case of Terry Allcock, whose 389 appearances and 127 goals in an illustrious Canary career have long made the Lakenham funeral director a sure-fire candidate for inclusion in this book, the best starting point seemed to me to be the simplest. For as the years pass and the '59ers slip ever more into the mists of Carrow Road legend, so the fact remains that fewer and fewer people can actually envisage what sort of player Terry was.

Terry Allcock

One glance at that scoring record suggests he had an eye for goal. Throw in the point that for much of the latter part of his days in a City shirt, Terry was more cultured defender than stylish striker and his final goal tally – second in Norwich's all-time list behind the master marksman himself, Johnny Gavin – stands out even more.

But even then the picture is far from complete. After all, goalscorers come in all shapes and sizes. Was he a Bellamy? A Roberts? A Huckerby? A McKenzie? Just what kind of player was Terence Allcock? To borrow from a Barclay chant, "Who are ya'? Who are ya'?".

'I would have thought the person who seems to play a similar game to me is probably young Chris Sutton,' said Terry.

'He's about the same physique, heads the ball well and can play in more than one position – he's not just a striker.'

As a reference point for all that follows, it is hard to beat. Think Sutty. Strong in a tall, supple and wiry way. With two good feet and a smart footballing brain at his disposal; a player who will spot either a pass or a tackle with untutored ease; a footballer who, through little more than simple ability, can play with equal effect at either end of the pitch. What both lack in straightforward speed, they gain in swiftness of thought.

There is one other interesting aspect to the two players' respective sporting abilities. For as anyone who has wandered up to Drayton Rec on a summer Saturday will attest, Chris Sutton – along with father Mike and Brother John – is no mean cricketer. Likewise Terry was a first-class cricketer. Literally almost, had Yorkshire persuaded the sporting youngster in their midst to stick to the county of his birth, rather than swapping white rose for red as he pursued his early footballing ambitions with Bolton Wanderers on the other side of the Pennines.

'I was one of the youngest-ever boys to play for Leeds Schoolboys,' said Terry, about to tread a well-worn path to a football apprenticeship as both county and country honours beckoned. 'From there I graduated to the Yorkshire Schoolboys – I was captain of the Yorkshire Schoolboys, I think – and from there to the England Schools set-up.

'I was playing for England versus The Rest at Watford and when you get to that standard all the best clubs in the country are looking at you. I was approached – indirectly or whatever, I can't remember the exact circumstances now – by Bolton. They had a very good record of promoting youngsters. They were one of the top six clubs in the country at that particular time, but what really influenced me going there was my father, who was being moved work-wise to Blackpool.

'And Bolton said they were prepared to let me commute from there to Bolton, which was just 40 minutes or so.'

Even at that early age, the young Allcock had every confidence in his own abilities with a ball of any size or shape – just as well given the illustrious company he was about to keep.

'It was just natural – any sport. I wouldn't have said it was in the family. My dad played football, but only local amateur stuff, and my brother played, but nothing to any quality. It's strange how it develops. I was playing very, very young in the school team because I was always tall – so I was in the senior team when I was a junior – and it just progressed from there on.'

The fact that Terry's first-team debut went with something of a bang also helped.

'I was lucky enough to play in the first team when I was 17,' Terry said, recalling events of October 1953. 'It was a local derby against Manchester City and I scored a couple of goals in the first 20 minutes so I got off to a good start!

'But then I think I've always been very self-confident; I was confident of my own ability; I could kick with both feet; I could head it reasonably well.

'It's strange. Throughout my career I've never felt inferior to anybody on a football field and I think that's stood me in good stead – even when you were playing, in the later stages, against the likes of Best, Charlton and all those other players. I never felt overawed by any of them. It's probably been an overriding factor throughout my career.

'And I could always score goals, which is always a tremendous asset.'

It certainly helped the young teenager sleep well at night. 'The amusing thing was that my first away game was at Sunderland and I was marking Len Shackleton of all people.

'But the evening before they'd put me with the goalkeeper at Bolton who was just coming up to 40 years old – Stan Hanson. They thought it'd be a good idea for me to room with him. And he was up half the night, nervous as a kitten, and I slept like a log!'

There were one or two other players in that particular Bolton side made of rather sterner stuff – above all, the "Lion of Vienna", England centre-forward Nat Lofthouse.

'I had plenty of quality players to learn from,' said Terry. 'Of the three inside-forwards, one was Willie Moir, the captain of Scotland, then there was Nat Lofthouse, the great England centre-forward, and Harold Hassall, who was then the other England inside-forward. They were all quality players.'

The Wanderers' manager at the time, Bill Ridding, could see strengths and weaknesses in his young, teenage charge.

'The manager thought I was like a wet lettuce,' laughed Terry. 'I've never been particularly heavy. And when I played I was very much the same weight as I am now – just under 12 stone. I was probably a little bit firmer then – but I was still developing. And the game was quite physical, to be honest with you. Probably much more so than now.'

It was, in hindsight, going to take a minor miracle for the teenage inside-forward to shift any of that illustrious trio out of Ridding's first-team thinking. Nor was there much hope of them moving on in a hurry. It wasn't the done thing in those days. The young Allcock was obliged to sit and bide his time in Lofthouse's imposing shadow. Besides, what was the point in moving whilst the maximum wage stayed in force?

'That, throughout my career, was a leading factor in why you stayed at any one club,' said Terry, with the run-up to Bolton's victorious 1958 FA Cup final campaign against the post-Munich Busby Babes proving something of a turning point for the eager, young inside-forward.

'I'd played in three of the rounds the year that they won the FA Cup and I played because Lofthouse was injured,' said Terry, as he switched to a more central, forward role in the absence of the England bull.

'I'd been playing centre-forward and that was one of the first occasions I'd played there,' said the reluctant striker, happier being the box-to-box boy that the role of the old style inside-forward entailed.

'I didn't actually like playing centre-forward. I enjoyed the involvement of the inside-forward much better. And it was only because I was tall that if we were ever short of a centre-forward I stepped in.'

Come the spring of 1958 and Allcock had stepped in to some effect. He was, however, only keeping someone else's place warm.

'I scored a couple of goals in the earlier rounds, but I knew I wasn't going to play in the final because Lofthouse had been injured with a dislocated shoulder.

'He'd got back into the team, but because I'd done so well they played him on the right wing. And he was England's centre-forward.

'He only played one game there and he obviously made a song and dance about it – though he was a brilliant fella' – so consequently I was left out and he went back into his old position.

'I made a song and dance about that – very much so – and then I went into work one morning and the manager said we've got an offer from Norwich and they'd like you to go down to see them. And my first reaction was: "Where the hell's Norwich?"'

His first trip to the wilds of Norfolk was particularly memorable – if only for the man then Chairman Geoffrey Watling despatched to meet Archie Macaulay's transfer-deadline target.

'At Bolton we'd not come across them in the First Division and so when I came down I said: "How do I do it?" and they said: "Meet us at Peterborough station."

'And so I said: "Who'll meet me?" and they said: "Oh, it'll be all right. They'll recognise you!"

'And strangely enough I was met by a midget. A fella' who ran a garage business in Yarmouth was very friendly with Geoffrey Watling and one of his drivers was a midget…Norwich were playing Coventry that night and he said: "Do you mind if we drive a little bit quickly?" And I said "No!" – until I saw him get behind the wheel and he had blocks on the pedals and a cushion to sit on! But we did get back to see the second half.'

Terry would make his Canary debut in a 1–1 draw at home to Millwall on Saturday, 15 March 1958; his first goal in City colours would arrive three weeks later in a 2–1 win at Swindon Town, as the Canaries booked their place in the new-look Division Three proper by finishing the 1957–58 season in the top 12. The old Division Three South – the Canaries' natural habitat for so much of their life thus far – was consigned to the history books that summer.

By then, the 22-year-old striker had long since settled into his new surroundings. In Terry's case the grass was definitely greener on the other side of the fence. So, too, were the trees.

'When I came to Norwich the thing that impressed me was obviously the environment. Coming from Leeds, which is industrial, and having played for Bolton, which is exactly the same, and you drive from one city to the next without realising that you've crossed the border, to come into Norfolk and see trees in the street, well, I'd never seen trees in the street in my life.

'The Club provided me with a good house and all the things you'd require at that stage. I'd only been married about two and a half years; my wife came down with me; my eldest son was about 18 months, I think, and that was another influencing factor – living in this environment we, as a family, were going to have an expansion of life. Because every day it was winter in the north of England, with the coal fires they had in them days and all the smog. You went to work and you were in fog. Coming here was an entirely different world and it was a culture shock really. But I was made so welcome.'

Not everything was entirely new. Bolton was, after all, a top First Division side.

'They tried to impress me with things like the floodlights, which in those days were very new, and the quality was measured by the amount of bulbs.

'And Geoffrey Watling was saying: "We've got brilliant lights here – there's 12 bulbs on each pylon…" And in actual fact at Bolton there were 54 on each pylon…'

The City chairman may have been better served by actually running through who and what Norwich had on the pitch. Or else leaving the manager, Macaulay, to do the talking.

For as the 1958–59 season loomed and the Norfolk side made their debut in the all-singing, all-dancing Third Division and made their first acquaintance with the likes of Bury, Rochdale and Accrington Stanley, the Canaries were about to embark on a cup adventure that, as an emotional ride, would not really be equalled for a generation – until Mike Walker's UEFA Cup side packed their bags for Munich in the autumn of 1993.

Before then, however, there was just time to unpack his whites for a game of cricket on the playing fields of Gresham's.

'As well as my football, I was opening bat for Yorkshire Schoolboys and played for Yorkshire Seconds. So when I came to Norfolk that summer I was offered the job of cricket coach at Gresham's,' said Terry, about to win his first county cricket cap long before he ever started to grace the local club game.

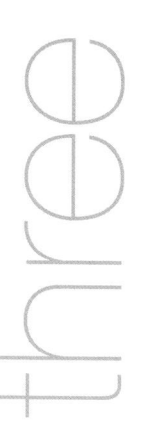

'I played for the masters against the boys, got a hundred and there were two people there who were county cricketers and they obviously must have recommended me. And my very first game for Norfolk was the day Bill Edrich came back to skipper the county. And I got 50 not out in both innings.'

Cue pre-season and the really good times were set to roll.

'You'd had a full, pre-season training with the boys, you got to know them reasonably enough and from there on in everything from my point of view – and from the Club's too – everything was successful.'

High time to introduce the Class of '59 kicking off with the manager – Archie Macaulay.

'I thought he was a very good manager,' said Terry. 'Quiet – a very calm man. Very concerned that everybody had an input.

'We used to have team meetings that went on for hours and on Fridays he was a menace because the team would go up and those that were playing would go into the boardroom, sit down with the manager and go through all the details of the opposition – who'd pick up who. He was just very, very thorough. And a great reader of the game.

'Very often we'd change things around in the second-half and, as I say, he encouraged players to have an input.

'One of the famous things was that Jimmy Hill was not the bravest of players, but a very skilful player. And we would all be critical of him at these team meetings – sometimes he was in tears – but we all still wanted him in the team for the contribution he gave. At home he was brilliant. Away, sometimes you wished you had someone else there, but that was the type of guy he was – mentally and physically. But he had great skills.'

Macaulay's skill – precise preparations apart – was to usher in the age of the thinking manager; the one who went beyond simple instruction and physical well-being, to look at what made an individual player tick, what went on between his ears just as much as what was going on below his hips.

'He made you feel better than you were,' said Terry. 'He was one of the first people I came across who worked a little bit more on the psychology. He always told us that we were as good, if not better than the opposition. Even when we were playing Manchester United or Tottenham.

'Certainly in the cup run I don't think anyone in the team went on to the field with an inferiority complex. And that stood us in good stead – or it stood me in good stead.'

So much for the manager. Run through the players that were about to figure large in Norwich's glorious run to the FA Cup semi-finals that season and you could sense that something might be afoot – not that you would notice 45 minutes into City's first round clash at home to lowly Ilford Town. A goal down at the break, two goals from Bobby Brennan and one from the aforementioned 'homer' Hill rode to Norwich's rescue.

'If you looked at the nucleus of the side, it was Ken Nethercott, Roy McCrohan, Ron Ashman and Bobby Brennan who were the senior members – all of those had years and years of experience and were good pros.

'I mean Bobby was an international prior to that – his quality was there for everyone to see. But he was played in a wide position where he could conserve his energy and his passing was magnificent.

'Roy and Ron had both got a tremendous work ethic and Kenny, in my own opinion – and I've played with all the good goalies that Norwich have had and they've all been good – he was the top one. Number one without any doubt.

'His positional sense, his use of the ball, his handling of the ball was immaculate and he was so quiet,' said Terry, reaching for a ready example of Nethercott's calm assurance.

'The best I can explain it is that we played at Tranmere once under atrocious conditions and he virtually played them on his own. And when we came in the dressing room he went round and shook everybody by the hand and said: "Well played!" That was Kenny; he's a marvellous guy.

'So we had those four as a nucleus and then there was Barry Butler, myself, Jimmy Hill, Errol Crossan, Matt Crowe – and he'd been playing regular First Division football in Scotland before he came to Norwich. Barry had been playing the equivalent of Premiership football with Sheffield Wednesday; I'd been playing Premier football at Bolton; Errol Crossan had been at Manchester City. The only two people who'd really not experienced anything like it were Bryan Thurlow and Terry Bly.'

Not that they exactly let the side down. Quite the reverse. Bly was on fire in front of goal, bagging seven goals from his nine FA Cup appearances that year. More remarkable still was his league tally – 22 strikes from 23 appearances.

'Terry had been in the reserves as a wing-half and just came in at centre-forward and just seemed to hit it off just like that. Everything he touched flew into the back of the net. Bryan Thurlow was one of the hardest, physical players for a slender frame that you've ever seen in your life.

'He was actually nicknamed "Unconscious",' said Terry, himself nicknamed "The Count" thanks to his own, immaculate dress sense.

'In every game, Bryan never saw any danger, any bodies in his way; he was never intent on hurting anybody – but most games he'd run into somebody and they'd both fall down. And that's why he got his name, "Unconscious."'

He was not the only person who could look after himself.

'Bobby (Brennan) was very placid, very frail, but Bobby could be the

Terry Allcock

nastiest thing on two feet. I've seen him crucify a defender – and intentionally do it. You can't be a good player without being able to look after yourself. At any level.

'Barry was a strong, physical player; Ron Ashman was always very physical. We could mix it with anybody. But we could play, that was the beauty.' (As the likes of Manchester United and Tottenham Hotspur were about to discover once Crossan's lone goal in the second-round replay against Swindon Town had booked Norwich's place in the third round.)

'Throughout that cup run and the amount of what were then Premier League teams that we beat, not one did we kick off the park.

'We actually played very good, solid football. And I think that came over in all the recordings and the press cuttings. The only time that the physical thing came into it was when we lost in the semi-final against Luton Town because they made a point of physically destroying Errol Crossan. Every time that Errol went, he was violently taken out.'

The flying Canadian winger was, it seems, the nearest the '59ers had to Darren Huckerby. He was the spark.

'Errol was the release; he was so quick. If there was any pressure we could just knock it over the full-back and he would beat anybody there. He used to make me look a good player because I played inside-forward to him, I could over-hit a pass but he could catch it every time!

'He had tremendous ability; more like Kenny Foggo than Ruel Fox – only quicker. He had finishing ability too. He could shoot. And he ran like Michael Johnson, the 400-metre runner; he sort of sat up – a very unusual gait.

'But he was a tremendous team man; the humorist of the team; a real comedian.

'He was just a tremendous asset. He was like Darren Huckerby is now – if you look at his pace, how it frightens defenders. Well, Errol was like that – but more direct. Much more direct. He was the fastest thing I've ever seen on a football field. And his crosses, well, with the old ball you had to strike them rather than just float them in and he was exceptional.'

The next trick up City's sleeve was rather more tactical. For as talented and committed as the manager and the 11 players undoubtedly were, through luck or design, they were also posing new questions to the opposition in terms of their starting line-up.

Consult the history books and Norwich went into that famous '59 FA Cup run in a then orthodox, 2–3–5 formation – Thurlow and Ashman were the two full-backs, in front of them Butler was the lone centre-half, with Crowe and McCrohan being the two wing-halves alongside him. The five came in the shape of two wingers, Crossan and Brennan; two inside-forwards, Allcock and Hill; and the centre-forward, Bly.

So much for the theory. In practice, 2–3–5 slipped into something far different as the 33-year-old Brennan – 34 on the day of the first semi-final clash with Luton – dropped back, Hill moved forward and Butler and McCrohan sat back between the two full-backs, Thurlow and Ashman.

'What we didn't realise at the time was that probably, without knowing it, without the intent, the formation we played was probably the first time ever anyone had played 4–4–2.

'I played as a very withdrawn inside-forward; Bobby (Brennan) also played in a very withdrawn role and Roy McCrohan slipped in alongside Barry – so we had a back four with Thurlow, McCrohan, Butler and Ashman.

'Then there was Errol Crossan, myself, Matt Crowe and Bobby as a four across the park; Jimmy Hill and Terry Bly then played more like the twin, attacking forwards. So we played 4–4–2 without realising it and that was one of the advantages we seemed to have over the other opposition.'

Nor did the opposition feast on a sherry-and-egg concoction the day before a game – another one of Macaulay's little ways that would pass into '59er legend.

'If it was a cup game, we'd always go to Gorleston, play a round of golf and have a steak lunch – that was the ritual.

'And then, of course, there was the famous sherry and eggs. It was on a Friday lunchtime when we were having one of these meetings. It was always provided for us.

'A raw egg in sherry, beat up, as a cream. It wasn't very nice to be totally honest with you, but again it was a psychological thing. You felt it was doing you good, so you did it.'

The 3–0, third round win over Manchester United on a snow-bound Carrow Road really set the Canaries in motion – certainly as far as the national newspapers were concerned. By the time Cardiff City, Spurs and Sheffield United had fallen prey to Macaulay's nous and Bly's goals, the Division Three side had captured hearts and stolen headlines way beyond the boundaries of Norfolk. They were, much like in the autumn of 1993, national property. Closer to home, Norwich was in the mad grip of cup fever.

'The city virtually erupted with the Manchester United result and from there on in it was just a snow-balling bandwagon,' said Terry, whose lone cup strike away at Tottenham Hotspur in the fifth round would earn yet another replay.

'All the away games, we travelled by train and whenever we came back to Thorpe Station there were huge crowds – we're talking thousands – waiting to welcome us back.

'They used to stick us on the luggage trolley and wheel it down the platform,' he recalled. As for tickets, cue further bedlam – and the boys out to make a fast buck.

'When we drew games away and there was going to be a replay on the Wednesday, on Sunday the queues for replay tickets used to form out of

Terry Allcock

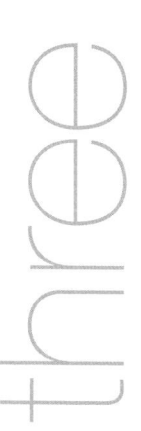

Carrow Road, over Carrow Bridge, down past County Hall and that was for every game.

'The majority of those had travelled away on the Saturday; they'd not go home, but just started forming a queue ready for Sunday morning.

'Tickets were at a premium. The top spivs from London came down and they were dealt with rather harshly by the local guys. I believe two or three of them were thrown into the River Wensum.

'And then these press boys came down and they effectively lived with us for the next two months; they followed us about; got stories – like the one about the ticket spivs and various others – and there was coverage all week, every week, for that sort of limited period.

'I think it was all down to the fact that we were this Third Division side, but also the quality we provided, the standard we played at and the number of games that we played – I think the 11 games we played that year is still a record for the number of FA Cup games played in a season. In fact a lot of those reporters built their names out of our cup run.'

His favourite moment? 'I think from an emotional point of view – which doesn't usually affect you too much as a player – I think the atmosphere when we played Sheffield United at Carrow Road, that was my favourite moment,' said Terry, as Norwich won their quarter-final replay 3–2 in front of 38,000 fans.

'It's the only time I've felt affected by the noise. Prior to the game starting when we were just having a limber-up. The crowd were singing the old anthem and it did, virtually, make your hair stand on end.'

The dream would die in the semi-final replay with Luton Town on Wednesday, 18 March 1959. The writing, however, was on the wall in the first game when City had what, 45 years later, Terry still cites as a sure-fire winner ruled out by the referee. The game duly ended 1–1. Luton went to Wembley on the back of a narrow, 1–0 win in the replay.

'There was definitely a feeling in the dressing room that our name was on the cup that year; in fact, we still believe that we actually won the first game,' revealed Terry. 'I was pulled up for an infringement on the goalkeeper, which I'm convinced wasn't, and Errol Crossan scored a goal that was then disallowed.

'I jumped with the 'keeper – or rather I jumped before the 'keeper – and he tried to come over the top of me, missed the ball and Errol knocked it into an empty net. The referee gave the foul and it was nonsense.

'But we didn't feel we played very well in the first match; as a team we didn't play to the standard that we had been.'

Four days later and Billy Bingham – the future manager of Northern Ireland – scored a 56th-minute winner at St Andrews – to take the Hatters, not the Canaries, to Wembley.

'The dressing room door was shut for half an hour after that game and I think that was down to the emotional strain on everybody.

'Once we started to go back on the train everybody let their hair down and let their emotions run riot and we all, as a team, went through every carriage on the train between Birmingham and back to thank the supporters for the support we'd received. I believe the actual train was drunk dry by Peterborough and they had to re-stock it at Peterborough.'

It is an extraordinary image of a long-gone age – an FA Cup semi-final team passing down the corridors of "The Top Brass Special" chanting: "You sang for us, we'll sing for you!" as they sang their hearts out for the fans in a joint rendition of "On The Ball, City!"

Quiz Terry now on the relationship that the '59ers side enjoyed with both the city of Norwich and the football club's supporters and that gesture comes as less of a surprise. It was an altogether more gentle age; of almost gentlemen players who were still very much part of their community. They knew – and respected – their roots. They knew who paid their wages and they knew how best to repay the fans' support – on and off the field.

'Players were on the same level as the supporters,' said Terry. 'We had this great camaraderie with all the supporters in the city and in the county and that's why I think it's been a legend from there on in – the '59ers.

'I know we weren't getting much, but we were better off than the man in the street. We'd walk down from Thorpe Station, along Riverside Road and you'd be walking with the crowd that were going to watch you. They had an affinity with you. And that still applies…People come in here who I've never seen before and they immediately come in and they're talking about those years – 40 years ago, which is a long time.

'And there was this social side – very much so. We used to go round and judge beauty contests, play in darts matches, bowls matches, golf matches. The routines we got into were habitual and that stayed throughout – even when Ron Ashman took over as manager later.

'There were no clubs and most pubs closed not much past 11. And when they did close, they closed. As regards to the lifestyle of the present players, it's completely different. We had the rule book and the all the restrictions that you would expect – no dancing after Wednesday night, no drinking, no riding motorbikes, all the restrictions were there. I'm not saying we always stuck to them…but it was a very enjoyable period.'

More success was to follow. Come 1959–60 and virtually the same Canary side that had got within a referee's whistle of Wembley was booking its place in the Second Division – helped, in no small part, by Terry's 16 goals from his 44 league appearances. No mean feat for a midfield player.

'These days if you're a midfield player who gets double figures then everyone thinks they've had a great season.

'In those days, as an inside-forward, you were expected to be back in your own penalty area defending and also in the other penalty area scoring goals. And if you didn't average 15-plus a year as an inside-forward you were a failure.'

Terry Allcock

A season later, as City made their debut in the dizzying heights of the Second Division, Terry not only hit 16 goals from his 26 league appearances, he was the only Canary player to reach double figures.

Goal scoring is an art and Nat Lofthouse's one-time understudy was proving a master. A natural athlete with a great engine, a smart footballing brain and two good feet, he'd looked and learned. Mother Nature had also blessed him with the ability to heal quickly. For Terry would suffer the first of two broken legs in the autumn of 1960. Typically, he'd be back with a bang.

'When I broke my leg against Plymouth it was my first major injury. I remember I just went past the wing-half, he accidentally clipped my ankles and I landed very awkwardly. The leg broke and I was carried off.

'But I was lucky. I'm a good healer. I recovered pretty quickly and the first game back I scored a goal – I went straight back into the team which was very fortunate. I think they were quite keen to get me back. I finished top scorer that year having broken my leg, still playing inside-forward.'

Goals followed Terry around. Only when he reverted back to centre-half following a second broken leg did they finally start to dry up. Take 1962–63. As well as bagging 26 from his 42 league appearances, he grabbed six in five FA Cup appearances – memorably four in a fourth round 5–0 romp against Newcastle United – and five from five in the League Cup, including a history-making hat-trick against Carlisle United in another 5–0 cup success at Carrow Road, this time a third round replay in October 1962.

'I've still got the record of getting a hat-trick in the FA Cup and the League Cup in the same season,' said Terry, as he looked back on some remarkable goal-scoring feats. A game against Bury was normally a cue to fill his boots, while a hat-trick at Anfield in an extraordinary 5–4 defeat against that year's Second Division champions on 13 January 1962, must rate as one of the great individual scoring displays in the Club's 102-year history. Two goals in an FA Cup derby clash with the old enemy, Ipswich Town, in a 2–1 fourth round replay win in January 1962 – away against a Town side on the eve of winning the Football League championship under Sir Alf Ramsey – would prove another sweet moment.

And all from a man, who still, to this day, doesn't consider himself an out-and-out striker.

'I always scored goals – right from being a teenager – but I never regarded myself as an out-and out-striker,' said Terry.

'Most people talk to me now, and see the goals that I scored and think I was a centre-forward all my life.'

The goals do, at least, bring back some glorious memories of a player in his predatory pomp.

'My memories are probably more about scoring goals than anything. I remember the most famous ones – like scoring four against Newcastle United in the FA Cup.

'In fact in that week I scored seven. I scored on the Saturday against Stoke; Wednesday we played Newcastle and I scored four. Funnily enough that day, at lunchtime, I'd taken my preliminary FA coaching exam – prior to the game and that wouldn't happen in this day and age – and the chap who was assessing me obviously came to the match and must have thought I was good enough!

'And then, on the Saturday, we had another FA Cup game against Manchester City and I scored two goals at Maine Road and so I scored seven in the week. That was a great time.

'And then the other occasion that sticks out in my memory is scoring three at Liverpool, which was the record for a long time.

'The one team that I liked playing against was Bury. Bob Stokoe was the player-manager there, centre-half, he was a nice fella' and every time I played against them I scored a hat-trick. I scored three hat-tricks against them – so there are teams that you seem to do well against and others that you seem to struggle against.'

There was, it seems, a knack to it all. A very happy knack in Terry's case.

'You accumulate goals. I know that if I'd scored early in the game, you were never content with that; you felt that you'd score every time you got in sight of goal. It was just an attitude of mind.'

There was also an appliance of science to the goal-scoring art; that and having an in-built instinct for being in the right place at the right time.

'The lads used to laugh at me because I used to pick a lot of goals up when the goalkeeper's deflected things. Or getting on the end of other people's shots that have been saved.

'But that was by intent and forethought. That if anybody was shooting, I always ran across the angle of the shot. There was a lot of premeditation about scoring – or I think there is.'

Cue the thought process at work once opportunity knocks.

'When you get through on your own you've got to have a set plan in your mind and I always used to try to hit the goalkeeper's feet because they'd always try to dive one way or the other and the most difficult area for them to get to is just by their own feet.

'And, of course, many of them would end up going through the goalkeeper's legs. If you try to pull it across them you invariably miss the goal as well.'

In amidst the endless goals, times were changing at Carrow Road. The manager for one, as the increasingly erratic Macaulay moved to West Bromwich Albion in October 1961.

'It was definitely time for a change because he'd lost the plot himself,' said Terry, as Macaulay's now legendary Friday team meetings became a cross for everyone to bear.

'He became very ill-disciplined in terms of his own time schedule. He'd be late and we wouldn't know what time we'd get home because we were waiting for him to come. But prior to that he was very successful and he was a charming man.'

Ill-starred spells under first Willie Reid and then George Swindin would follow before stability finally reigned under Terry's long-time team-mate Ron Ashman.

'He was a strong character. He was well-liked by both the public and his colleagues and it was a natural progression, really. It's never easy coming from within the dressing room, but he wasn't the first one.'

The brief, of course, was quite simple – to get Norwich into the First Division for the first time in their history.

'We were confident that we were good enough to get promotion. It didn't work out, but every year we had a very good cup run.

'It was very unusual if we didn't get to the sixth round of the Cup – whether it was the FA Cup or the League Cup.'

Ashman – as he subsequently proved with a certain K Keegan at Scunthorpe United – could spot a player. Under his watch, Dave Stringer and Kevin Keelan would arrive at Carrow Road as well as a player who, in 1963–64, would steal Terry's goal-scoring thunder, Ron Davies.

'Ron had exceptional ability. He was bought because he destroyed Ron (Ashman) playing at centre-half when he scored four goals against him – and three of them were headers…Ron (Davies) was an out-and-out centre-forward. He had the right physique. For in those days to be the out-and-out striker you had to be a big, strong fella'. He was also exceptionally quick; an excellent header of the football and very determined.'

Davies' arrival would also coincide with Terry's second broken leg – away at Halifax Town, in November 1963. With Gordon Bolland arriving the following March, first-team opportunity was about to knock elsewhere for Norwich's regular goal-machine.

'When I came back from breaking my leg for a second time they'd brought in Ron Davies and Gordon Bolland and the manager asked me if I'd play at wing-half.

'The words he actually used were: "Go play at the back like Bobby Moore!" So I did. Whether it was any repetition of Bobby Moore, I don't know – but it was an easy job.

'The one thing I lacked was pace, but then if you've got a good head on you you can overcome that because you're thinking two yards ahead of other people.

'So when I played as a sweeper at the back, it stood me in great stead because I could stroll into position.

'In fact I thought the last five years were the easiest five years of my whole career. Everything's facing you; if you're reasonably tall you'll win the majority of high balls. I probably had to become a little more aggressive as a tackler, but invariably you'd cut balls out and you wouldn't need to tackle hard.'

It wasn't the same, however. 'I was disappointed really – I went and played at the back too early.'

There is another major event in the history of Norwich City Football Club that also played a part in the management's thinking. For by the start of the 1966–67 season there was a huge gap to be filled in the heart of the City defence.

The name Barry Butler is now primarily associated with the big piece of silverware dished out at the end of every season. For many, Barry Butler is just a name. For Terry, Barry was a close friend and a hugely-respected team-mate. His death, in a car accident on 9 April 1966, aged just 32, carries a poignancy and a pain to this day.

'By strange coincidence, that was the first time I was ever involved in carrying a coffin – I was one of the pall-bearers that carried his coffin,' said Terry.

'Barry was a very close colleague. We lived in the same road; we both came from the north of England; we'd played against each other in the old First Division. Most people even thought we looked very much alike. In actual fact when he'd had his road accident, people thought it was me.

'He was also an exceptionally good centre-half. Apart from being a tremendous tackler and header of the ball, he was also quite competent in controlling the ball and using the ball.

'Very much a leader – along with two or three others in that team – and, I feel, all good teams need two or three leaders on the field who can make decisions to change what's happening and can support other players, encourage other players and make others play. Barry was exceptional in that direction.

'I was very proud to be the first recipient of his Memorial Trophy. And I honestly couldn't say anything wrong about the guy.'

As for the night itself, some memories never fade. 'I remember the night – very much so. Barry was very fortunate regarding injuries. He never had a serious injury in his life; he played a tremendous number of games consecutively. And then he had a minor break, a training accident, and he never really overcame it.

'He'd just started playing again in the reserves. The first team were playing that day away up north. It was Huddersfield Town, we came back, and when we got back usually we'd be dropped off and have a casual drink in one of the pubs. And Barry was always normally there.

'The next I knew was that I was woken very, very early in the morning to be told that Barry had been killed. It was a very tragic occasion.

'There was tremendous sense of shock about the place. Barry was one of the most popular players – it's as if the likes of Adam Drury or Craig Fleming had a road accident today, it would be headlines throughout the local press. It was just a tremendous shock to all the supporters, the players, everyone connected with the football club.'

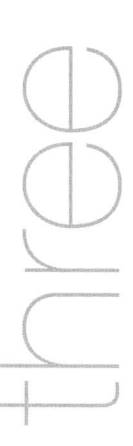

Terry would, of course, see City into the old First Division, but only as a coach under Ron Saunders. His last competitive first-team game came at home to Blackburn Rovers on Wednesday, 23 April 1969. At centre-forward.

By then the Canaries were back in the managerial mill again after Lol Morgan's exit. Saunders' arrival – and all that followed – would lead Terry, briefly, in a new direction. Back to where it all began, as that two-goal Bolton teenager, to Manchester City.

'The two regrets I had probably was that I got to Wembley twice as a coach and I would have much preferred to have got there as a player and, as a coach, you don't get the same satisfaction. There's nothing like playing,' said Terry, uneasy at handing over his professional fortunes to 11 other men, however good and true.

'It's a funny life, really. When I went to Manchester City with Ron Saunders, my hopes and desires from there would have been to go on into management on my own, but when you've sampled all the problems that are involved in it, it wasn't really my scene.

'You could be a good coach, the best technician; but those 11 people, when they go on the field, if they don't perform to expectation, it's you that's going to lose your job over it. And that's not a very nice scenario.

'As a player I felt my destiny was in my own hands; it was always down to me whether I gave 110 per cent and what performance I gave. You could only blame yourself. When you're a coach or a manager, your destiny is in the hands of 11 other individuals and I found that very unhealthy. That's why I came out of the profession, basically.'

His memories of his time as a player and, indeed, of his time at Norwich would, in any case, serve him well as the years passed.

'Overall, how was my time at Norwich? Brilliant,' said Terry, now part of Bryan Gunn's matchday hospitality team at Carrow Road.

'I've no regrets whatsoever. From a personal point of view, from my family's point of view, it was the best thing I could ever have done.

'At the time, I thought coming to a Third Division club from one in what was then the Premier was going to be a step down, but from the '59 era onwards Norwich were always on this pendulum going up and the strange thing was that Bolton went the other way.

'Indeed within three years I'd passed them – so from a personal satisfaction point of view, that was great.

'Plus I loved the area, my family were very settled, my children – who I'm all very proud of – have grown up in the area and now I'm a businessman in Norfolk and everything's down to the football.'

And his happy knack of scoring goals.

4 Dave Stringer

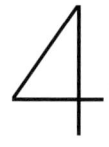

Norfolk-born Dave Stringer progressed through the ranks at Carrow Road to amass 499 appearances for the Canaries between 1965 and 1976. A figure that sees him sit proudly third in the list of the Club's all-time appearance makers.

Player of the Year in the 1971-72 promotion-winning season, Dave also played in two Wembley finals for City during his impressive playing career.

However, Dave didn't just play for Norwich, he went on to manage the youth and reserve sides before enjoying a successful four-and-a-half year tenure as manager at Carrow Road.

Under his leadership the Club achieved record league finishes and twice reached the FA Cup semi-finals. It is fair to say that Dave Stringer has just about done the lot at Carrow Road – and done it very well.

David Ronald Stringer

Born: Great Yarmouth, 15 October 1944
City Debut: 10 April 1965, v Coventry City (a) 0–3 Division Two
Final Game: 21 August 1976, v Liverpool (a) 0–1 Division One
League appearances: 419
League goals: 18
FA Cup appearances: 24
FA Cup goals: Nil
League Cup appearances: 42
League Cup goals: 4
Other appearances: 14
Other goals: Nil
Total appearances: 499
Total goals: 22

Run down the cast list for this book and one thing stands out – that for a club that prides itself on being so near to the heart of Norfolk life, how few of the big, big characters contained within these pages actually come from this little corner of the country.

There's the Essex boy done very good in the shape of Martin Peters; there's Johnny Gavin, who would learn his football on the back streets of Limerick before going on to become Norwich City's greatest ever

Dave Stringer

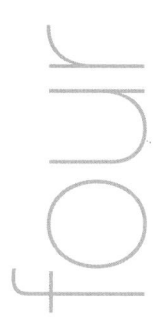

goalscorer; plus the traditional clutch of northern lads who left their hard, industrial roots to carve out a name for themselves with the Canaries – from Leeds came Terry Allcock; from Rochdale David Cross; and from Scotland Road, in the heart of working-class Liverpool, came Dave Watson. Even Bernard Robinson, the darling of The Nest, was born in Cambridge before the family moved on to King's Lynn.

Dave Stringer is the one exception. Born in Southtown, Great Yarmouth, 60 years ago he was, and firmly remains, very much of this parish. And that's important. For, after all, the vast majority of Dave's adult life revolved around Norwich City Football Club. Be it as player, youth-team coach, manager, or the man who helped to put the Club's Colney training HQ on the map, Dave never strayed very far from the heart – or, indeed, the soul – of his local professional football club.

His Norfolk roots also serve another purpose: to bury the widely-held notion that, lacking a tough, urban ghetto to get out of, East Anglia's finest somehow lack the desire to get on; that within their mental armoury, the competitive edge has been lost; the fire in the belly of a Cardiff-born Craig Bellamy is more likely to be the odd, glowing ember in anyone born on the banks of the Wensum or the Yare.

'I would challenge that – people say that. That Norfolk people are quiet, they're a little bit withdrawn and everything else. I suppose I was quiet, but that doesn't mean you're not competitive.

'There's been a lot of good sportsmen come from the Norfolk area and what we have to remember is that the Norfolk area hasn't got such a large population as some of the bigger cities, the towns and those surrounding areas.

'But if you look at cricket, athletics, swimming, all the different things – there are people coming from this area. At that time I can remember the England cricketer Peter Parfitt coming to watch us train when he was injured; he was a Norfolk man. Bill Edrich and people like that were all top sportsmen.

'And I've only named a few from my era. You also had Barry Bridges who was from Norwich and went to Chelsea, played for England; you had Terry Butcher, from Lowestoft, played for England – he's only just down the road.

'And in terms of competitive spirit, you can't have anyone more competitive than Butcher; Bridges – he used to compete. I consider myself a competitor. And then you had people like Edrich – great batsman, a top competitor in the world of sport.

'To me it's a little bit of a fallacy. No, we compete. We want to win as much as anybody. Perhaps it's the way we are; the accent that we have here; it's a little bit slow, drawn; that gives the impression that people are not as forward as people in the big cities. But when it comes down to it, you've got some crafty boys among the Norfolk and East Anglian people and they've done well in life.'

And therein lies the bedrock of all that follows. Dave Stringer is indeed "a good ol' boy" of Norfolk legend. But more than that, from day one of his 13-year playing career at Carrow Road he proved he was a fierce competitor and, as his subsequent managerial spells would prove – be it en route to a famous FA Youth Cup triumph in 1983 or steering the Canaries to their then highest-ever league finish and two FA Cup semi-finals in the space of three, memorable years – he was more than a little crafty when it came to the inexact science of football management. Put simply, he was damned good at it.

There are two other influences on Dave's formative, teenage years which, in part, help explain the drive and the determination that lay beneath the surface of that quiet Norfolk man. One was an early rejection. The other was something he would share with Dave Watson – a working knowledge of what lay on the other side of the coin, what exactly it meant to earn a living in a dockyard.

'When we got to the last year at school one of the teachers in particular – Barney Gibbon – took a very big interest in the football and ran the football team,' said Dave, as the old Alderman Leach secondary modern school turned itself into a regular little footballer factory.

'There were some scouts in the area. Some for Charlton and people like Mike Bailey and Eddie Stone went to Charlton on trial and actually got signed by them, but when I was leaving school we had an Arsenal scout in the area and he came to watch us and took several boys from the area – from the Yarmouth Schools team – to go to Arsenal for trial. Me being one of them and another of them being Peter Simpson who actually played in the Double winning side for Arsenal. And he actually sat next to me at school.

'We were great pals coming up through school, but there was quite a rivalry. He went down to Arsenal just before I did and I learned that they were very keen on taking him on and, of course, that made me want to try even harder. But unfortunately having played three trials for them they sent me a letter to say that I wasn't up to the required standard. And Peter was and had a very good career there.

'I then went for other trials at places like Crystal Palace and played local football for Gorleston at the age of 15 – my first ever game in the FA Cup was at The Wellesley against Yarmouth – and I still wanted to be a footballer. That was my main object in life, but I went into industry, into ship-building. My father was a shipwright, my brother was a shipwright,' said Dave, whose father was about to wear another hat – as his son's agent.

'So I was doing a job as an apprentice fitter and turner, but I still kept playing and when I got picked for England Youth I was asked by Ron Ashman to sign professional forms for Norwich City.

'That knock-back I got from Arsenal made me more determined – without a doubt. In some ways it was good for me because it taught me a few values: in particular, going out to work and knowing how life was outside of the football sphere. The fact that it's a nine-to-five job and you have to dig in there to make sure that you're there on time.

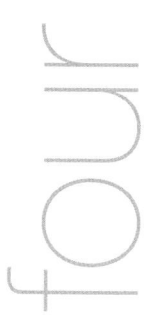

'But being a footballer was a privileged life in many ways: hotels, going abroad at the end of the season and earning good money. I think when I was down the shipyard I was earning about three pounds, three pounds ten shillings a week – something like that, as an apprentice.

'I still remember my first Norwich City pay packet being £15 a week and I thought I was earning a fortune because my father was a tradesman and he was on about £12 a week – flat rate. He'd actually gone in with me to negotiate my contract with Ron. I think they offered me £12 to start with and he said to them: "Well, he can earn that on the shipyards!"

'He was trying to do his best for me – he was my agent. And they said: "OK, we'll give you £15 a week."'

For it is worth remembering that playing senior football for Gorleston at the age of 15 was no mean feat. These days things ain't quite what they used to be on the coast. Witness an FA Cup tie between Yarmouth and Crystal Palace at the time.

'I can always remember going to watch Yarmouth play Palace in the Cup and 11,000 people watched the game. And they were sitting on these fish boxes. For at that time the fishing industry in Yarmouth was at its height and they didn't have that kind of capacity in the grandstand, so they made the fish boxes so that you could sit on them. And that's how the thing was at that time.'

Playing at that level not only introduced the young Stringer to the experience of playing in front of a crowd, but it also gave him an early insight into the more physical aspects of the game – just as it would a 15-year-old Iwan Roberts in the amateur leagues of North Wales some 20 years later.

'It taught me to look after myself. You had to be either quick or strong – if you were quick you got out of the way, if you were strong you mixed in. And I tend to think that I was able to do a little bit of both at times.'

Waiting at Carrow Road to take Dave under his wing was someone who should, by rights, have gone on to play a major role in the Club's future, first in a coaching capacity as his influence as a player slowly waned and then – in every probability – as manager. Fate, however, would decree otherwise.

'For me, it was a dream come true. I was doing what I wanted to do and I was amongst these people who I looked up to. I didn't want to be too forward and brash in their company because of what they'd done. But as time went on I found they were just as amiable as anybody else and they helped you as much as anybody else.

'It was people like Barry Butler – someone who was destined to be one of the coaches at the Club and maybe a future manager somewhere.

It was people like that who helped me early in my career, taught me a few things, to think: "Yeah, I've got to give something back to other people…" And, in fact, the things I enjoyed most after playing was dealing with younger players and teaching them; trying to give them a little of my experience and hope that that would help them along the way.'

Dave was just 21 years old when Butler died in April 1966. 'I was actually in the team at that time,' said Dave, who would make his first-team debut for the Canaries in a 3–0 defeat at Coventry City on 10 April 1965.

'When he died it was a big, big shock. I remember we must have been playing early in the next week because we went in early on the Sunday for training and Barry had been killed on the Saturday night and I hadn't heard because I lived in Yarmouth. I got to the ground quite jolly and happy – it wasn't like there was local news on the radio or anything at that time – and I met Phil Kelly and he said: "I shouldn't go in there with a smile on your face."

'And I said: "Why not?"

'And he said: "Barry was killed last night in a road accident…"

'It was like hitting me with a brick. He was thought so much of at the Club at that time that it hit everybody. I suppose you could say, in today's terms, it would be like Darren Huckerby in terms of his standing within the Club. But then there was a whole group of players there that were held in similar high esteem – any one of them, if anything had happened, each of them would have had the same sort of respect.

'The funeral was at the St Peter Mancroft Church and the senior players – Sandy (Kennon), Terry (Allcock) and the rest of them – were pall-bearers. And there was a big gathering at that time of supporters – everyone wanted to go to the church for the service. And I think that showed how much esteem he was held in.'

Come that difficult summer and change was in the air as Ron Ashman made way for a new manager, the 35-year-old Lol Morgan. If the Norwich board were hoping that the bright young man at the helm was going to add that mystery ingredient that would lead to the Club's promotion to the First Division for the first time in City's history, they were to be disappointed. Norwich flat-lined – stuck fast in the middle of the Second Division as Morgan found himself with little alternative but to preside over a period of change as, one by one, Ashman's older guard made way for a new generation.

Ashman, in all fairness, had started the process: in Allcock and Butler, he would have had two able lieutenants at his disposal on the coaching front, had time and fate allowed. Instead, the board opted for a fresh face and new ideas. The continuity that comes from appointing a manager from within the dressing room was lost.

'Under Ron it was more of a family club; more intimate in terms of the manager having been one of the players, one of the group and being very good friends with the people that were playing at the time. And with Terry Allcock being captain and Barry Butler, who would maybe have been one of his coaching staff, there would still have been that family atmosphere to take it on, which has always been a big feature of Norwich.

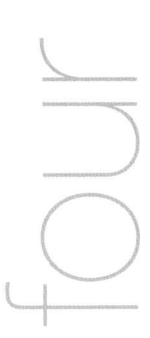

'Lol (Morgan) came in and though he worked as hard as every manager does to get success, it didn't happen for him. He brought in players that he knew from his north-eastern days – Bryan Conlon and Albert Bennett – and others like Mike Kenning, he was a winger, and Lol tried to mix it and it didn't work. We weren't successful. They were quite lean and disappointing years. The crowds started to wane; people were losing interest. It wasn't quite right – there wasn't the same sort of family atmosphere.

'I think the board realised that it needed a shake-up, it needed sorting out, it needed a particular person and Ron Saunders had just gone to Oxford. And Oxford were in relegation trouble round about Christmas and he pulled them right out of the mire – he did very well with them. And at the end of that season they appointed him manager of Norwich.'

Saunders, married with four children, was only 36 at the time. From the day that he was officially unveiled on 10 July 1969 he made a big impression. Pre-season training was never going to be the same again. From the moment he gathered the players around him on the first day of training that summer, change was afoot.

'It was what the Club needed at that time – somebody as strong and as tough as him in terms of standing no nonsense from anybody and wanting people who were going to graft for him and do it for him on the pitch. Every one of them did; those who didn't just didn't stay. They were gone.

'I thought that was exactly what was needed. I was getting a bit fed up at that time – I wanted a bit of success for myself. I'd worked hard; I'd been at Norwich for about eight seasons; I was beginning to think: "Well, are we going to get this success? Have we got the ambition here?"'

'And Ron looked as if he was going to shake it up and take it in the right direction. He brought that togetherness back through the fact that we all had to scrap together. Anyone who was out of line would either be out or let known in no uncertain terms that he wasn't doing the right thing. We worked hard off the pitch; we worked hard on it.'

If the appearance of someone in the ilk of Graham Paddon in their midst suggested that the Saunders style was not all kick and rush, there was no doubt that the Canaries grafted as if their lives depended on it. Press, press, press; chase, chase, chase. The opposition never got a moment's rest when City were in town.

'We were probably the forerunner of people like the Wimbledon team – that sort of steam-roller football, if you like. We were taking teams apart by the fact that we just out-worked them. We ran the legs off them on the pitch. And those teams that were good footballing sides, we had the work-rate to stop them playing and perhaps sneak results against them.'

All the Mousehold madness, the Trowse sweat box – it was all a heaven-sent opportunity to get on, out of the Second Division doldrums as far as Dave was concerned.

'I loved it. I did, really. I used to like training. I was 27, 28 at that time. I was in the peak of my career and I loved training. I liked to be fit and I couldn't stand anyone not doing it or messing about in training. When you're working, you're working. He had the same attitude; he had the same outlook.

'I always remember when he first came in, the first day he stripped off – it was sunshine, pre-season – and his upper body was like chipped out of bleeding marble. He was this really strong-looking fella'; really solid. He sat on the ball in the middle and he's said: 'Right, I want to go to the top – I want to get promotion. Anyone who doesn't want to come with me, I'll see them in the office at 12 o'clock and you can go.'

'And I thought: "You'll do me!"'

And just as Dave had welcomed a kindred, competitive spirit in the new manager, so Saunders saw everything he was looking for in the 28-year-old defender.

'He did respect somebody who gave that back and I felt that was coming from him to me.' The hard man act – as good as it undoubtedly was – was still just that. Saunders' heart wasn't pure stone.

'When we got promotion we were coming back and the families were on the bus. And I remember his daughters were there and one of them was sitting on his lap. I think she was singing something to him or saying something to him and he started to do the same and I thought then: "He's a family man as well."

'He had to be hard, but I think he had a side to him where he was as human as anyone else. He wouldn't very often show it. He would do something for you, but it wasn't in a way that he'd be all over you gushing. It would just happen.'

By now, of course, Dave came as something of a pair. He had a sidekick in that City team who, for the better part of seven seasons, would barely leave his side – Duncan Forbes.

'It was actually Lol (Morgan) who put us together in the first place. Because for the latter part of the time that Lol was there I played a few games at centre-half and I felt I took to it like a duck to water. I always felt I was a good tackler – I could tackle well and tackle clean. Most of the time.'

And almost from the moment that Forbes made his Canary debut, following his £10,000 switch from Colchester United in September 1968, the pair clicked. Watson-Bruce, Fleming-Mackay – Stringer-Forbes is right up there at the top of the tree with the very best defensive partnerships the Club has ever produced.

Neither gave an inch; both would give everything in the City cause. The two would also develop that mutual sixth sense that underpins every great sporting partnership. Who picked up, who dropped off, who mopped up – as the years and the games went by, it all became second nature. Like, for example, who picked up who.

'It just happened,' was Dave's simple response. 'Normally, what they would do is fight for everything through the air – the bigger one. And then they'd try and use him as a target and hit him, so Duncan would challenge and battle him and I would like to read off where that quicker one was going to run – as well as where the ball was likely to go.'

There were, on occasions, horses for certain courses. Malcolm MacDonald was one. 'When we played against someone like Malcolm MacDonald who was quick – he wasn't that tall but Duncan was quicker than me and I'd say: "Well, you sort him out Dunc and I'll pick up the bits and pieces."

'It worked well. Normally, one plays left, one plays right, but we didn't use to do that. If this lad is going to go wherever he wants to go, Duncan just used to follow him. A lot of centre-halves would allow forwards to switch and you can understand that – why run with him if you just end up getting yourself into this confused state? So let him run on to you. Switch.

'But Duncan always used to want to follow these players, so I had to read – if he was coming into my area, I'd have to pull out into maybe a left-sided area while he went right. Duncan wanted to do that marking job. He felt more comfortable doing that and putting someone out of the game – which he did in more ways than one.

'It did all become second nature. When we finished playing and then went to play in testimonial games and friendlies, we'd just pick up where we left off.

'Duncan would do his bit and he was no less competitive in those games. Same as if you ever played him at table tennis. Stonewaller. He'd bore you to tears. But that's how he was – he'd stick at his job. He was like a terrier with a bone – he wouldn't let it go. It must have been murder to play against him because he'd never let you go. He'd be inside your shirt; always be there; kicking the ball away; nudging you; heading it. Just awkward – nobody liked playing against him.'

Throw City keeper Kevin Keelan into the whole Forbes-Stringer mix and 30 years on it is still easy to sense a fierce determination within that little trio. Particularly once the Canaries hit the dizzy heights of the old First Division for the first time, the three men were in their element – backs against the wall and telling anyone that would listen that they shall not pass. A third round FA Cup draw against Leeds United in that 1972–73 season provided a classic case in point.

'Leeds in particular was one – we played them three times in the FA Cup. Drew at home, drew away and played the replay at Aston Villa and lost 5–0. They tore us apart that night.

'But up until that point you had Kevin (Keelan) in goal making miraculous saves and Duncan and myself and the rest of the back line. And while everyone defends when you defend, you were the last ones – the ones that had to make the last-ditch tackles and efforts. Sometimes it was just a case of throwing your body in.

'Arsenal away was one – when Duncan punctured his lung in the League Cup – the quarter-final when we beat them 3–0 and Graham Paddon scored three. Peter Simpson was playing for the opposition, plus Alan Ball, people like that and it was one of those that we really wanted to win. And I wanted to win for a different reason because all those years ago Arsenal had given me the heave-ho and I probably wanted to prove a point – and the fact that Peter, my best mate from school, was on the other side. I just didn't want them to score at all.

'And there was one occasion when Kevin was grounded and it was either Radford or whoever had a point-blank shot at goal and he was only, what, two feet from the line and I actually dived at his feet and put my body in the way and he hit the ball against me and we saved it. It's that sort of thing – like the Alamo that night.

'I can still see it now – I must have been mad. Because he was going to blast it and I just threw my body in the way. Like diving on a grenade.'

It was, of course, through such defensive will and sacrifice that Norwich not only got promoted for the first time in the Club's history, but also survived their first season in the top flight – if by the skin of their teeth. On both occasions Dave would also pop up on cue in the opposition area, grabbing the goals that secured the Second Division title at Watford on 29 April 1972, and a year later – on Tuesday, 24 April 1973 to be precise – snatching the goal that helped preserve Norwich's top flight status for another year with that tumultuous 2–1 home win over Crystal Palace.

'I hadn't really been put in a position to score goals in my career until Ron (Saunders) came there. And then he put both me and Dunc up for corners,' said Dave. And while promotion may have already been secured ahead of his title-grabber at Vicarage Road, the goal against Palace was a big, big strike as the Canaries fought desperately to avoid a swift return to the Second Division, once everything had started to unravel following the League Cup final defeat against Tottenham Hotspur that spring.

What is fascinating is the way that Dave backs David Cross's memories of that time: that not only did the whole Wembley experience leave the Club running on empty for the rest of that season, but perhaps the years of sheer, unremitting graft doing it the Saunders way was finally catching up with City. People were on their knees as that final, fraught fortnight loomed. Norwich were holding out for a hero like never before.

'We had a big challenge after the final and by Easter time we had West Brom who were in trouble as well, Wolves on the Easter Monday and Palace on the Tuesday – you used to play three games over Easter at that time. We beat West Brom away which was great because that then allowed us to steal a march on them; Wolves beat us 3–0 at Molineux and we were still reeling from that when we had to go into this game against Palace, who were in trouble as well.

'We had that one and the last game was away at Stoke and we knew we had to win one of those to stay in. Palace, being at Carrow Road, was the one we were more likely to get a result from; going away to Stoke would be more difficult. They had quite a good side at that time – we're talking Geoff Hurst and people like that.

'I can remember feeling out of sorts, shattered really. I think most of the players did – emotionally as well as physically.

'I don't think I had a particularly good game. We went into the lead – Colin Suggett scored. They equalised and it was 1–1 right to the end. And with a minute or so to go, we got a corner and I thought: "I'll go up!" So I went up and I just kept running. And funnily enough I arrived in the area as the ball was coming across, Duncan went up for the ball, took the 'keeper Jackson out, I arrived behind and just hit it and it flashed into the net. And that was it. The game was virtually over. Everyone was on their feet; grown men were in tears.

'That was nice – to do that. To score the goal that actually kept us up.'

At least one person in the crowd of 36,688 that night would put that Palace clash in his all-time top five City games – an evening when the Norfolk boy did very, very good.

There was one other lesson that Dave learned that year as the end of the Saunders era started to loom. For less than a fortnight before City's big day out at Wembley, Jimmy Bone – the man who put the very spring into Norwich's step – was sold to Sheffield United for £30,000. In his place arrived Trevor Hockey and Colin Suggett with Hockey, in particular, brought in to do just one job – to ensure that by hook, crook or flailing rugby boot the Canaries stayed in the First Division.

It was the act of an utterly practical manager as the flamboyant Bone was sacrificed for the more agricultural virtues of Hockey – a brave, brave move given Bone's place in the fans' affections. Equally, it also taught Dave a valuable lesson in that Bone was probably one of only a handful of sellable players Saunders had. And he had to get one out to get the one in that he needed.

'Understanding it a bit more now than I did then – Norwich couldn't afford at that time to go out and buy players. And I don't think players understand this. When you're playing you're just thinking: "Why don't you just go out and buy a player?..." But they had to sell someone first before they could buy, to balance the books and be able to then bring players in. And that's what Ron did. Jimmy Bone went to Sheffield United and we brought in Trevor Hockey and Colin Suggett.'

Hockey may have grabbed all the headlines in terms of the change he made to Norwich's style of play, but it was Suggett who scored the opener in that crucial clash with Palace. As ever with Saunders, there was real method to his apparent madness.

Within three months of the new season starting, however, Saunders had gone as Norwich scrabbled around near the foot of the First Division table, with the manager trading verbal blows with the new chairman, Sir Arthur South. The new man in charge was about as far removed from Saunders as you could get – John Bond. About the only thing they shared in common was a dislike of losing and a short fuse. After that, be it in personality, dress sense, press relations and, of course, style of play, they were worlds apart.

'They were chalk and cheese. Ron wasn't what you'd call the flamboyant type – more a hard, firmer type.

'John was completely flamboyant. Ron would keep the press at arm's length, there was a wall there – nobody talks to the press unless I get to know about it. And then John, when the press asked him, and they'd say: "Is it OK if we talk to whoever…" And he'd say: "Yes, of course, it is! No problem…" He was so open about everything. It was – chalk and cheese. There was a different atmosphere altogether.'

Not that the new manager came alone – half of the Bournemouth first team were soon hot-footing it up the A11 to join Bondy in the First Division. And they were there to play football – not to run up and down Mousehold Heath for a living.

'We had to go the next step,' admitted Dave. 'We'd got the fitness, we'd got the work-rate, the team spirit and everything else that went with it, but to play in the First Division you had to have a little bit more.

'And John came in to add that little more spice to the mix. Teams were coming then and they didn't know what to expect of you – you were hard to read because you had individuals who would do their little bit of individualism on the day that would probably get you the win or the result, whereas before we were perhaps a bit easier to read because we were a little bit straight up and down. People knew what to expect.

'But playing against John's teams you had every aspect of the game – you had your Jimmy Neighbours, your Ted MacDougalls, Phil Boyer, Kevin Reeves and, of course, Martin Peters who was a world-class player at the time. He lifted the whole scene in terms of his play.'

Certainly as far as the Dave and Dunc show at the back was concerned hitting Row Z on a regular basis was not the be-all and end-all of a centre-half's life. All of a sudden you could look up and pick a pass.

'As far as we were concerned under Ron, it was a case of thump it away – get it out. With John it was a case of get the ball down, have a look, have a touch and pass it out if you could,' said Dave, a task made infinitely easier by the players now arrayed in front of him.

'Players would always make themselves available. Instead of seeing people turn away from you and go forward – because they know it's going to go forward – with John you had people looking for it.

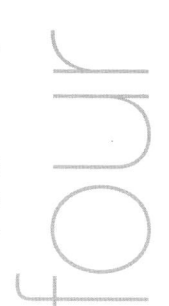

'But I think John liked us, myself and Duncan, in terms of the fact that we were quite strong; hard to beat; disciplined as defenders. And people around that were given the licence to go forward because they knew they had that foundation.'

Suddenly, as Peters in particular would appreciate, the whole West Ham way of doing things – as first preached to Bond by Ron Greenwood – gained a new twist. City had this defensive hard core that traditionally was West Ham's Achilles heel. All Bond did was to bolt a bit of football on to the front.

It was a shift that was repeated in training as the old Trowse sweat box disappeared. 'You always trained with the ball – I enjoyed that part. Whereas with Ron we knew what we were going to do – same routine, every week.'

Again, the nagging thought returns that the Saunders way – as effective as it was – had a sell-by date. It was a short-term wonder.

'I suppose in the end it does wear itself out – people want to be stimulated a bit more. And again that taught me a few things – to have someone like Dave Williams, when I was manager, to have someone there that would give you plenty of variety. Plenty of ball work with the fitness work as well – and that's the modern way that they train. And that's right – that's how it should be. If you're going to play with a ball on a Saturday you've got to train with it.

'But fitness, for me, has always got to be high on the agenda. You cannot play the game without being fit. The fitter you are the more able you are to perform to your highest ability. That is a big thing that I emphasised as manager and when I was in coaching – that is what I wanted.'

And, in all fairness, he got it. To nigh on perfection. To marry the very best of Ron with the very best of John. Do that and you'd have a team. Particularly if you could unearth that final Holy Grail of management: a striker who can score you goals. In the case of the team that Dave built, he found two. And with them, the silverware duly followed.

Given all that followed, it would be easy to dwell too long on Dave's illustrious playing career – and, indeed, the one that followed initially under Ron Atkinson, at Cambridge United. Suffice to say that Bond's openness with the press left Dave less than impressed when he only discovered through the newspapers that he'd been dropped. His final outing in a senior City shirt came, away at Liverpool, on the opening day of the 1976–77 season – his farewell gift from the management was the chance to make his 499th and last appearance for the Canaries in midfield, man-marking Kevin Keegan.

In 1980, Dave returned to Carrow Road as the Club's youth team coach. He had, in many ways, never been away. He still trained regularly with the Canaries. He just played his games at the Abbey Stadium.

Once back in the fold, he inherited a set of players who would prove a young coach's dream. He had round pegs for every round hole he needed – including the two big holes up front. No one was ever asked to do something they couldn't. Above all, at the age of 15 and 16 the likes of Jeremy Goss, Louie Donowa and Tony Spearing were still young enough to be moulded into that middle way: the best of Ron meets the best of John. It would be a philosophy and an outlook that stuck with Dave as he worked his way up the Norwich coaching ladder.

'My real philosophy is that you blend players; you get the balance right; you then allow them to play. Don't ask players to do things that they can't do. Get them to do what they're good at – but within the team structure.

'And you build your team on defence. There's no point in having a team that goes forward to score goals if they're letting them in as fast as you can score them at the other. So you've got to have a good, compact unit – a base to play from.

'They feel secure in that; they feel confident in that; confident enough to go forward knowing that that unit will make up for anything that might happen, mistakes or whatever, the majority of the time. It's simple, but for me, that's the right way to do it.'

Time to introduce the team that Ronnie Brooks spotted, Keith Webb nurtured and Dave led to the 1983 FA Youth Cup final where, after three epic games against Everton, Norwich finally lifted the biggest prize in English youth football.

What is more remarkable still is the fact that of the basic 12 that featured, only three would really make a name for themselves in the higher reaches of the professional ranks – Goss, Spearing and Donowa.

The likes of the keeper Andy Pearce, the two centre-halves – Mark Crowe and Brendan McIntyre – and, above all, the two free-scoring strikers – Paul Clayton and Jon Rigby – got lost en route to a lasting place in the professional game. And yet their achievements that season were phenomenal. For not only would they win the FA Youth Cup after three final games watched, all told, by over 40,000 people, but they would also complete the League and Cup Double that silver-laden season in the South-East Counties League.

For the better part of 18 months they barely lost a game. It was – and remains – a remarkable feat of arms that has possibly never gained the recognition it deserves. Certainly not by history.

'When I got them they'd already been playing together in local leagues for a year,' said Dave, as his new charges graduated from Sunday schoolboy football to the world of a Youth Training Scheme trainee and the next challenge in their young, footballing lives: the South-East Counties League.

'In that first season I had to then emphasise what had been done before but also put in what I wanted – a certain strict discipline and fitness. And for six months of that season they didn't do a thing. They were absolutely rank. They went out of the FA Youth Cup in the first round; they struggled to get results; they were getting wound up because it wasn't happening for them when it was all happening before for them when they were playing

Dave Stringer

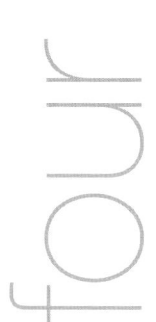

Sunday league football and they were beating everyone out of sight.

'The full-time training was hitting them hard and they didn't know how to handle that; got to January – now you could start to see them grow – and for 18 months we didn't lose a game.

'Well, we may have lost one in a Mickey Mouse cup competition, but we went right through without losing a game, winning the FA Youth Cup, winning the President's Cup and that team was the best team – in terms of football – that I can remember youth-wise.

'They were a good team. They passed it. The two strikers, Rigby and Clayton, I think scored 30 goals each; the two wingers were Louie Donowa and young Neil Riley – so we had a flyer on one side and a Tricky-Dicky on the left. We had a good midfield in Austin O'Connor, Mark Metcalf and Gossy – three good players there, though Mark was one of the younger ones and didn't get in as often that year.

'And then we had a back line of Mark Crowe and Brendan McIntyre at centre-half and Tony Spearing and Daryl Godbold, with the lad Andy Pearce in goal. We had a good squad, we passed it so well and they just took sides apart. It was great – I could just sit back and relax!'

Few could honestly have guessed what thrills and spills awaited over the next fortnight as that young Canary side began their final assault on the FA Youth Cup at Carrow Road on Monday, 25 April 1983. City would beat Everton 3–2 in that first leg; in the second, back on Merseyside, Norwich lost 3–2. The venue for the third and deciding leg was made on the toss of the coin. Everton won the toss, but lost the game 1–0 – and all in front of 20,000 people.

For all the highlights of his subsequent career as first-team manager, watching that young side lift the FA Youth Cup remains one of Dave's proudest moments.

'It was brilliant – I think I enjoyed that as much as anything. I really mean that. Just the way they were playing – you always had confidence that they were going to go out there and do it. The problem was keeping them together.'

Try as he might, it was one particular circle that neither Dave nor, indeed, the football club could ever actually square. Handed professional contracts en masse as reward for that Youth Cup triumph, Rigby, Clayton, Donowa, Goss and Co ran their little hearts out – straight into the brick wall that was reserve-team football.

Suddenly there were first-team players coming back from injury in their midst; worst still, first team fringe players whose careers – and attitudes – were going backwards.

'They were such a close-knit bunch that they were getting players coming in that probably didn't have the same outlook as them – they had different motives, different reasons for being in there: being injured, being out of favour, whatever. And in some ways that broke it up.'

Today, some clubs might have given that team a chance – stuck with them as City's new, youthful reserve side and arranged the odd, friendly game to keep the more senior professionals on side. 'In hindsight, I think had we given them two years, then, for me, we might have got more players out of them.'

In the event, Rigby would make just ten senior City appearances without ever scoring a goal. A spell with Cambridge United would follow before a niggling pelvic injury cut short his professional career. Clayton, who like Rigby would score twice in the course of that great FA Youth Cup final adventure, made 15 City appearances. Again, he never scored a senior goal. His travels would take him to Finland, Darlington, Crewe and Macclesfield. Mark Crowe, youth team skipper and Player of the Year in 1983, would make just one City appearance – as a 17-year-old substitute against Brighton and Hove Albion in December 1982.

Rigby and Clayton, in particular, were the big loss. For thereafter, as Dave climbed the managerial ladder at Carrow Road – first as reserve-team chief and then, following the exit of Ken Brown in such poisonous circumstances in November 1987, as the first-team boss suddenly left to hold a then screaming baby – his quest to unearth another 20-goal-a-season striker in the Clayton-Rigby mould would be unending.

Robert Fleck – the man who in terms of being the team's brightest spark was the Jimmy Bone and Darren Huckerby of his day – came closest when he bagged 19 goals in Dave's final season in charge. In 1988–89 when Dave's Canaries were at the peak of their Division One powers – topping the table for three, glorious months – Fleck would finish with just 15. Iwan Roberts' best pal Malcolm Allen would hit 12.

It was only when Chris Sutton came fully to the fore under Dave's successor, Mike Walker, and smashed home 28 goals in the season of Munich and Milan that Norwich found a man who made the goals flow. Sutton, of course, was alas still a raw, gangly teenager under Stringer. And having matured and blossomed under Walker, there was another huge problem to overcome: how to resist the big, fat cheque that invariably accompanied the sight of a young striker hitting such heights at a selling club like Norwich.

The chairman Robert Chase couldn't. Nor could his successor Bob Cooper, when Coventry City came a-calling for Craig Bellamy.

Therein lay another big frustration for Dave as he first successfully steadied the Brown ship and then set sail for the upper waters of the First Division. Having finally found the round peg to fill your round, striker hole – and only then by carefully and lovingly nurturing two precocious teenage talents in Sutton and Bellamy over the course of five or six years – as soon as they started to deliver, they were off. And it was back to making do and mending; back to fingers crossed and hoping as square pegs were squeezed into the wrong-shaped holes.

Dave Stringer

To this day, Dave still believes that in Rigby and Clayton the Club might – just – have had two round pegs.

'Perhaps it's a bit stars in my eyes, but I think they could have gone on to play very, very well together. It was like telepathy those two. They were both big lads. Not physically huge – just a nice size. Six-footers. They worked very, very hard for each other; their movement and everything else was terrific.'

Look back now on those two, FA Cup semi-final defeats – against Everton in April 1989, and Second Division Sunderland in April 1992 – and it's City's basic bluntness in front of the opposition goal that stands out a mile. What is equally telling is that on both occasions, the one person whose absence and injury would do so much to dictate what happened on each of those two, disappointing days was the one person that gave Norwich that extra edge – Robert Fleck.

Telling the City striker that his beloved father had died suddenly of a heart attack the day before that first semi-final at Villa Park remains the hardest job Dave ever had to do in management. Arguably the biggest piece in his jigsaw that day was missing.

'It is like a jigsaw. We've got big Robert (Rosario) up front and Flecky – a good pair because he can hold the ball up, he can play off him. Dale Gordon – he can play down that flank. We had Trevor Putney playing on the left – a right-footed player on the left – but because he was playing with that right, he held as a player.

'Didn't get forward and weaken the midfield with everyone going forward. So he sat in that position. We had Mickey Phelan in the centre of the park who'd run for fun; we bought Andy Townsend who had an abundance of ability – skill and running ability. Big Andy Linighan playing as a big, central stopper. You looked at him and thought: "Well, we've got a chance today…" Ian Butterworth who could pass and play a little bit off the back of him; Ian Culverhouse and Mark Bowen who were Tottenham; Ian Crook who was one of the best passers of the ball you could think of.

'We bought Malcolm Allen who could score for fun. Wasn't quick but could score – that group of players, you just had to blend them. They're all comfortable; they're all playing in the position they want to play in. They've just got to perform there.'

But it was Flecky that everyone wanted to see perform. 'The character of Flecky was something – he had the rapport with the crowd. And they loved him. He was a good player, scored goals, but also had that little bit of devilment in him as well.

'And the crowd took to that. I knew he was going to get up to some sort of antics. He was never, ever frightened of anybody – he'd get embroiled. The bigger they come, he'd have a go at them. He wouldn't shirk a tackle; he'd work back.

'He was a breath of fresh air for us – and for the players. They all wanted to show him what good players they were when he went into training.

So the first training session it sharpened – it went up another ten per cent. And that then encourages the coaches as well. They're getting players that they think: "Yeah, we can work with these." and they're brightening everybody up.

'He did that, Flecky. To be fair to him, he did that.'

And then that light went out. Or at least flicked off briefly the night before the trip to Villa Park.

'We'd been training. Robert had even phoned his father – there was one of those old car phones on the coach, one of those that was as big as a car battery.

'And I'd actually said to him: "Oi, what are you doing using that…" And I thought: "Oh, let him get on."

'And then in the afternoon we got the phone call to say what had happened and I had to call Robert in and give him the bad news. That his father had just collapsed and died of a heart attack.

'And I said to him at the time, because he said: "I want to play tomorrow…" and I said to him: "You must go away and phone your sister and your mum and have a chat with them and then come and tell me whether you feel you can still play tomorrow."

'He came back and said: "No, I'm going to have to go home" and I think that was probably the right decision for him.'

'We'd also lost Mickey Phelan through injury – he was out of the side. And they were two influential players in the side – the captain and Robert, who was the spark if you like. The heartbeat of the team. And we did lose something.'

When Norwich returned to the last four of the FA Cup to face Sunderland, Fleck was again centre stage.

'That one was, without a doubt, the more disappointing. We were favourites to go through – Sunderland were the Second Division side. Everybody must have thought the same thing, that: "Well, we've got to have a chance of going through this time…"

'Flecky's injury didn't help. We got him back and though he was physically fit, he wasn't match fit. He'd give you everything anyway, but he would have probably have said that he would have wanted more games to lead into it because he would have been at his sharpest then – there's that little half a yard, half a second difference in being tip-top.'

Without a fully-fit Fleck – without that Rigby, Clayton figure at the head of the team – City's dreams of a first-ever FA Cup final appearance were dashed. John Byrne scored the game's only goal.

'That is the difference in any team, between being really successful and being an also-ran – that ingredient of somebody who has the ability to just put the ball in the back of the net. Who are the most fêted players through time? Always the strikers and the centre-forwards that score goals – they've got that knack.

Dave Stringer

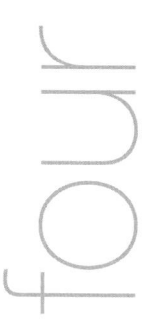

'And not everybody's got it. They have that something different. An edge of some sort that gives them the chance and they take it.

'Had Sutty been a year older? Well, he proved himself to be a goalscorer and they paid £5 million for that ability. At that time he hadn't developed. The ability was there but it was an ability that he had to develop through becoming more mature physically and mentally to be able to do it. He had it – he had that knack.'

The Sunderland defeat wasn't the only reason why Dave resigned as Norwich City manager on 1 May. For one thing he was tiring of constantly having to find other round pegs for round holes as one success after another left. Steve Bruce set that trend when he left for Old Trafford within a month of Dave's arrival as caretaker boss. Having identified John O'Neill as his possible replacement, it was back to square one again once a collision with John Fashanu on his City debut ended O'Neill's Canary career just 34 minutes after it had begun.

The search resumes; in comes Andy Linighan; in comes Arsenal; the search begins again.

'I was filleted to be honest – it had taken its toll on me,' said Dave, as he looked back on his sudden and largely unexpected exit.

'They say if you can't change the players, you change the manager, and I thought it needed someone else to take it on. It gives them a different voice.

'I'd probably had enough myself by that time in terms of being manager. I didn't want to move anywhere else. Norwich was my club – always has been. So I said to the chairman: "I'm going to resign."

'I don't think he wanted it to happen, but there you go. I did come close before – over Andy Linighan.

'When he left – because I thought he was a big part of the team – and I said to the chairman: "Well, I'm resigning!" But he talked me out of it. So I stuck with it. I suppose I wasn't so tired and filleted by that time.

'It was total frustration – I'd come to that realisation. However much I did, it would always revolve around to the Linighan situation again and again. And I wondered how I would handle that – you'd build something up, then it's destroyed, then you've got to build it up again. Having to maintain that, and still keep the quality, I was thinking: "Do I still want to put myself through that?"'

'If you get a decent player his own ambitions are going to say to him: "I want to go on, go out and play for bigger clubs, get the bigger prizes and everything else". And I thought this is never, ever going to change. The supporters are getting frustrated with it and I thought I'm going to be on the rack here all the time.

'It's always going to happen; it's always going to come up. And I'll always be the one in the middle. So do I want all that?'

He didn't. Mike Walker did and the rest was UEFA Cup history. In the event, it was the luckless John Deehan who was left to watch as the bricks that he, Dave and Walker had put into place were, one by one, sold to the highest bidder. Walker, perhaps sensing that history was about to repeat itself once Norwich's European dream had ended in the San Siro, jumped ship before the inevitable happened.

'I made the decision and actually recommended that Dave (Williams) should take over, but the board didn't see it that way. Dave left, Mike took the team on and they did what they did for the Club and perhaps, in a way, vindicated my decision to get out.'

Regrets? He has two. 'We'd win the semi-finals.'

Winning the League that year, when City flew so high for so long, in the end only to finish fourth, was possibly never really within their grasp. Not quite. Winning the FA Cup – that was.

'We were inches away from actually winning the League. From actually doing it. We'd beaten all the big sides, we were on the home stretch, but we just didn't have the depth in our squad, the quality to go on and win it. We didn't have that player that we've been talking about to stick the ball in the back of the net, to give the side a lift. Who knows? Perhaps we didn't play Malcolm Allen often enough. You just don't know.'

One final postscript. Due to the utter, technical ineptness of a certain author, a two-hour chat featuring all the above was never actually recorded onto the tape. We had to do the whole interview again. And being that "good ol' boy" of Norfolk legend, Dave never uttered a hint of protest. He was a different class.

5 David Cross

David arrived at Carrow Road during the Canaries' historic 1971–72 promotion-winning season. Signed by Ron Saunders from Rochdale for a fee of £40,000, David went on to notch up eight vital goals in his first season at Carrow Road.

A powerful centre-forward, David forged a great understanding with Jimmy Bone as City won promotion to the top flight for the first time in the Club's history. His eye for goal continued in Division One, where he scored 17 goals in the 1972–73 season, 11 coming in the League.

After life with the Canaries, David enjoyed successful spells with Coventry City and West Bromwich Albion, but it was at West Ham where he played possibly the best football of his career. During his time at Upton Park he scored 97 goals and played in FA and League Cup finals as well as tasting the success of another promotion to the top flight.

David was an extremely popular player at Carrow Road and along with his fellow 1971–72 promotion-winning team-mates, he received a wonderful reception when he returned to Carrow Road for the 30th anniversary reunion in February 2002 as part of the Club's Centenary celebrations.

David Cross

Born: Heywood, 8 December 1950
City Debut: 9 October 1971, Sunderland (a) 1–1 Division Two
Final Game: 10 October 1973, Stoke City (a) 0–2 Division One
League appearances: 84
League goals: 21
FA Cup appearances: 4
FA Cup goals: 2
League Cup appearances: 9
League Cup goals: 6
Other appearances: 9
Other goals: 1
Total appearances: 106
Total goals: 30

To some David Cross may seem a strange choice for inclusion in this book. After all, his Canary career lasted little more than two years.

And while his final goals' tally of 30 strikes from 106 appearances was more than respectable, it still pales beside one or two others.

But talk to the generation that stood on the Carrow Road terraces and watched City finally achieve their First Division dream in April 1972, and the then 21-year-old centre-forward still commands huge respect and affection.

'I remember when he left it was the first time that I really felt upset at a Norwich player leaving,' said one.

Leaf through old editions of the city's Saturday night football paper – the *Pink 'Un* – as the *Evening News* did last summer and the name of David Cross again figures large in one of the classic *Pink 'Un*s that the paper reproduced for old time's sake. (That and a few extra weekend sales.)

The game in question was a thrilling 5–1 home win over "a punch-drunk" Blackpool on Saturday, 25 March 1972. Coming on the back of a 2–1 away defeat at Portsmouth the previous Saturday, that thumping success sent the Canaries flying down the final straight as the finishing line loomed.

Read Bruce Robinson's final verdict that night and it is Cross's influence that shines brightest. "Almost everything City did today turned to gold," wrote the reporter. "They produced their most sparkling attacking display for many weeks, with David Cross, in particular, having an outstanding match.

"There was menace in their every movement...This was a sweeping City victory, which should put them in great heart for the important Easter programme."

A week later that same Easter programme opened with an away trip to Charlton Athletic. And for the second week in a row David and his new, attacking sidekick Jimmy Bone were both on the scoresheet as the Canaries won 2–0.

That night's *Pink 'Un* proved another classic – its front-page headline would become part of Carrow Road folklore as Norwich took another big step towards bringing top flight football to Norfolk for the first time in the Club's 70-year existence. "Hot Cross Bone Day!" greeted the supporters from the news-stands as they returned to Thorpe Station that night. History was being made; legends were being born.

'What I hadn't realised when I first got down here was the significance of my signing to everyone else except me,' said David, as then City boss Ron Saunders unveiled the final piece in his promotion jigsaw – the one man who would make all the difference to the Canaries' dreams of hitting the big time.

A 20-year-old lad from Rochdale. A player, it would later emerge, that Saunders had never even watched before he persuaded the Club to part with the not inconsiderable sum of £40,000 for the young man's services in October 1971.

'It all kind of hit me after a couple of weeks when I realised that this had been going on for some time. That apparently they'd been looking for a

David Cross

striker; Ron Saunders had been promising and promising the supporters that they would sign a striker and that striker would be the final piece in the jigsaw which would take the team up.

'And I was that final piece. It was that – when are we going to sign a striker? Oh, here he is…And it's me. Who's played 60 games for Rochdale.'

David has long since returned to his Manchester roots and lives in leafy suburbia in the rolling hills above Bury – no distance from where his footballing career all started at the Spotland home of Rochdale.

'I'd been with Rochdale since I was a young boy of 15; playing in the reserves. I wasn't even certain that I was going to be a footballer. It was actually quite a surprise to me when I signed full-time.

'I played a handful of games in my first season, played another full season, started my third season and kind of hit pay dirt, if you like.

'Everything just came together in the '71–72 season – the beginning of that. And after about ten games I think I'd got about a dozen goals.

'At the time we had a good winger called Norman Whitehead and a couple of other players – and it was always them that were going to be on the move in the local press – Norman Whitehead is interesting Everton, Manchester City…

'We had an idea that somebody would be on the move because they were desperate for cash. They'd just put floodlights up and they needed to pay for them. And I just went in one Wednesday morning and the manager said: "Oh, you're not training today. Just hang on here – don't go with the others."

'And I'm stood there thinking: "What have I done now?" I'm racking my brains thinking: "Was I in a pub somewhere? Was I doing something I shouldn't?" And my best mate, a lad called Bobby Downes, he was injured that particular day and he came in to see me. And he said: "What are you doing here? Why aren't you going with the lads?" And then he said: "Oh, I bet you're on the move! I'll find out…" So he sort of sneaked off and came back about five minutes later and he said: "You're on the move!"

'And I said: "Right, where to?" Because I knew he'd seen the forms. Anyway I had a couple of guesses and I said: "I honestly don't know!"

'I was shell-shocked because I'd lived at home for the first 20 years of my life and I guess I was hoping it was someone local. There were stories that Manchester City and Liverpool were looking at me and I just said: "Oh, it's probably going to be some out of the way place like Norwich!" And he said: "Have you been in the office yourself?" And I said: "No!" And he said: "Well, that's where you're going!"'

With a clutch of A-levels to his name, up until that point David's life was very much up for grabs. He was happy to give football a go, but if it didn't happen, then university would.

But that Wednesday morning, opportunity knocked like never before. 'I was 20, approaching my 21st birthday, and it just suddenly hit me that this was my chance. That maybe I was, after all, going to be a footballer.

'To think that I was going to go to a club like Norwich with their history – and I was well aware that they were top of the League at the time – it was a case of: "Wow…if I go down there and we get promotion…I'll be in the First Division!"

'So it was just excitement, really. There was no way I was going to turn it down. Money wasn't a factor. I got down, met Ron Saunders, he told me what I'd be on and I just nodded.'

News of City's new signing was broken to the supporters over the tannoy at Carrow Road during the half-time interval that night, as the Canaries powered past Carlisle United 4–1 in the third round of the Football League Cup. David's arrival as the answer to Norwich City's centre-forward prayers was made more remarkable by the fact that he'd been born and bred a winger.

'I'd never actually been a striker before I signed for Rochdale; before I became pro I was a right-winger. I knocked it past people, went to cross it or cut inside to score. I'd scored a lot of goals at junior level. But when they saw I was six foot two, when I signed for Rochdale they played me up front. I didn't really know how to do it. So I learned as I went along, really.

'I had a good first touch; I was a good back-to-goal player; I had very good pictures of play; I was brave; I was mobile.

'I wasn't quick, but I was mobile – I worked hard. Probably my biggest asset – and obviously the one that would have attracted Ron Saunders – was the fact that I worked hard. I never stopped working hard even in the back end of my career – 700 games later, I still worked hard. And that slotted straight in with what Norwich wanted at the time.'

In fact, run through the list of David's youthful attributes and he ticked virtually every Saunders box there was. Above all was that ability, that willingness to graft – to run himself into the ground time and time again. But a knack for scoring goals also helped. The two, it seemed, went hand-in-hand.

'However badly I played – and I know I wasn't the prettiest player ever – whatever else I did, my goal record was always good. Even if I played poorly, I'd seem to score. I've played in games where I haven't played particularly well, we've won 2–0 and I've got both. But I always felt that was a result of working hard. I always wanted to get in the box. I didn't mind missing; I didn't like missing, but it didn't faze me to miss. I'd go back for more.'

Even if it hurt, he'd go back for more. 'People used to say I was brave – I wasn't really brave, I just didn't see danger. So in that respect I can't claim to be brave. Maybe I'd score a goal, a diving header in the box, and people would say afterwards: "You were brave, diving in there.."

'And I'd be surprised because all I'd ever seen was the ball. It wouldn't have worried me to get my head kicked, been knocked unconscious if I'd have got my head to the ball to score – it wouldn't have worried me.

I never, ever felt that there was danger out there.'

What else was out there in the wilds of Norfolk, David had little or no idea.

'I knew of Kevin Keelan and I knew of Graham Paddon, but really I knew very little about them. I talked to the Rochdale manager on the way down and said: "What sort of side are Norwich?" And he said: "Oh, they'll be a good side, they'll work hard, be a good team. They've no real stars in the side – that's the key to it."

'And it was really. That was what Ron Saunders had buttoned down – there were no real stars, no one became real stars. The only one of us who really got to that status – and then got his come-uppance – was Jimmy. Jimmy Bone.'

At this point, if anyone is starting to see parallels between the team that Ron Saunders built and guided into the First Division that season and the one that Nigel Worthington led back into the Premiership last summer, carry on. For if promotion was the puzzle, both men put together the same kind of pieces to make that jigsaw fit. To borrow one of those ghastly American management phrases, there was no "I" in the word "teamwork" as far as Ron Saunders was concerned. Nor was there for Nigel Worthington.

Honesty, endeavour, togetherness, workrate – the two men sang from the same managerial hymn sheet. Both, however, would make one exception to their no-star rule. Both would find one player that lit the blue touchpaper en route to promotion; that had the supporters either on the edge of their seats or out of them as a new Canary hero was born.

In Worthington's case, his star was Darren Huckerby. In Saunders', that role went to Bone – as the 22-year-old former electrician, signed for £30,000 from Partick Thistle on Leap Year's Day, 1972, added the final spark to City's promotion drive.

Mix Huckerby's pace and trickery with Robert Fleck's instant rapport with a crowd and that was Jimmy Bone. He lit up that side that spring and in so doing, left Peter Silvester's striking contribution at the start of that season to remain in the shadows. Silvester hit 12 goals before a serious knee injury sustained in the home game against Preston North End that January ruled him out for the next 18 months. Likewise Ken Foggo top-scored with 14 goals, but it was the "Hot Cross Bone" show that would come to dominate the memory.

'Jimmy and I played up front after Peter Silvester's injury and what one or two people overlook is Peter's contribution. I only got eight goals for Norwich that season; Jimmy got four. Peter got 12 before his injury. But Jimmy kind of took the limelight with the way he played. He was a bouncy character; he livened us up when we needed to be livened up. He came in, dazzled for 12 months or so and then was away.

'But he was a catalyst for us, really,' said David, as Saunders' attempts to make do and mend in Silvester's long-term absence came to nought. 'With Peter's injury, we were struggling to find someone who would play up front with me. No one was really partnering me until Jimmy came in and he was refreshing. He kind of got us all going a little bit.'

So much water has now passed under the bridge that it is difficult to be wholly sure on the matter. But if only for the fact that Bone was on his way no more than a year later suggests that the City showman was not a natural Saunders signing. He was a short-term fix that – on the pitch at least – fitted the manager's needs to an absolute 'T'. Needs must when a promotion race drives and Bone delivered in spectacular style. Playing-wise he was – as Saunders had undoubtedly spotted – David's perfect foil.

'What Jimmy had – and the reason that we worked together – was the fact that we were different,' said David. 'I was the stock-solid battering ram centre-forward. I was never a big fella'; I was never a Iwan Roberts. But I became a nasty piece of work, I have to say. Because I learnt that was what I was going to have to do, if I was going to make an impact.

'I was that kind of a player – back to play, keep the ball, blend it back to the midfield or touch it on to my co-striker. But Jimmy was a "face them up, go at you!" player which is exactly the opposite to me. It was a fantastic blend, really. If I could win it, give it Jimmy and he ran at them and then I went in the box and if Jimmy didn't score, I got the rebound.

'I mean Huckerby would be good for me to play alongside now, for instance. I'd win stuff for him, he'd get on the end of it with his pace and while they're all watching him, I'd be nicking in at the back post if his shot came off the 'keeper – it was that kind of thing with Jimmy and I.

'But we didn't know that straight away. It kind of evolved. Jimmy became the instant star attraction for the fans with his electric pace. He'd go at four people, Jimmy, and somehow come out with the ball out the other side. And I don't think Jimmy really knew how he did it.

'In fact when I spoke to him afterwards, at the end of that season, he said: "I never used to do that. In Scotland they'd be amazed if I did that. I wasn't really that kind of player…" But he just came down and did it. And it came off.'

It came off because Bone, like everyone else in that Saunders side, worked. Be it in training or in a match, they worked. Boy, did they work.

'We worked hard. We worked long days with Ron – two sessions a day, most days of the week. No days off. You could usually expect to have one day off during the week just to recuperate, really. There was none of that with Ron. We worked and worked and worked.

'The Mousehold runs, the Trowse sweat box – I was involved in all of that. But I didn't mind all that because that was me. It was exactly what I wanted. I knew I had to be fit to be an effective player.'

What is equally fascinating for those who like to draw their parallels between the promotion side of 1972 and that of 2004 is the dressing room mix that greeted David's arrival that autumn. For like the team that ran away with the First Division title last season, it too had all manner of people with all manner of points to prove. Whether they be young or old, local or incomer, amongst that particular group of individuals there was an instinctive hunger to do well – a desire that Saunders, ever the shrewd cookie, fed and nurtured.

'The dressing room was good in that respect in that all of us, for one reason or another, had something to prove,' said David.

'He'd signed myself from Rochdale – relatively unproven. Pete Silvester from Reading – relatively unproven until he came to Norwich. So you got lads like me and Pete from lower division sides who had never really done anything; you'd got Doug Livermore and Graham Paddon from First Division sides, from Liverpool's reserves and Coventry's reserves – lads who hadn't done anything yet, but were probably disappointed that they'd been released and again felt they had something to prove.

'And then you had the old stagers like Foggy, Duncan, Dave Stringer – lads who had probably gone through a plateau in their career and thought nothing was ever going to happen to them.'

Management, football or otherwise, is essentially a very simple business. Find, hire and encourage people who want to do well, be it for you or themselves, and that's half the battle won.

'He was a very clever man, Ron Saunders,' said David, as another shared managerial trait emerges – that neither Saunders nor Worthington had any time for bad apples. The first whiff that someone was going 'off' and they were away.

'Ron delved very deeply into character, I know that. He didn't like bad characters. I found out a lot later that he'd done a lot of homework on me, my background, what kind of a lad I was. Did I like a drink? Did I go out? He was big on bad people being bad footballers and to a certain extent he was right. He was very hard on us if he found out we'd been out drinking.

'There was nothing you couldn't do that wouldn't get reported back, but we were good lads. We'd go out, go to a pub, have a couple of halves of lager and maybe drift to another one, but it was never a nightclub sort of night. We were never, ever going to be like that. I think we all knew that we had to do it on the field; that this is our chance.

'Certainly that was my experience. This is my chance; my chance to be a footballer; I'd been given that chance and I wasn't going to let other people down who had put faith in me.'

What also swiftly emerges is Saunders' ability to know precisely the type of piece he needed to complete his promotion jigsaw. Not just in terms of their character, but also in their whole style of play. Thus, from day one, it appears that David and Graham Paddon clicked; two bright, young footballers who were, first and foremost, players. They could play; they could move; they could pass. And, above all, they could think.

'Graham was a player,' said David simply. 'He and I struck up an immediate relationship on the field because he was a Manchester lad as well. Like I say, I was a good one and two-touch player and I think it was even on my home debut that Graham and I had a couple of little interplays, little one-twos.

'For what I'd learned in my three years at Rochdale was that midfield players love to have the ball so if they gave it to you and you gave it to them back, they liked you. And if you gave them it back, they'd give it to you again. What creative players don't like is giving you the ball, moving into a different hole and you ignoring them and them not getting the ball back. Do that too often and they tend to give it to someone else.

'I was always bright enough to realise that if you gave them the ball back, they'd probably give it to you again in the later stages of the game or, if not, the game next week.'

Not only would they give you the ball back, the likes of Graham Paddon at Norwich – and, subsequently, Trevor Brooking at West Ham United and Asa Hartford at Manchester City – would add the icing on the striker's cake by putting the ball just where any smart forward would want it – in the gap, in the space, in the channel.

'If I made a run, bang! The ball was there. Brooking was one step ahead of me. Graham was like that; Asa Hartford was like that. They were such clever players that whatever I thought was on, they'd seen the space, the hole or whatever even before me and were just waiting for me to go in it. So I got good service off him.'

So much for the players up front. At the back it was a slightly different story where big Duncan Forbes ruled the roost. Pretty, pretty football was not really his thing and for David – who loved a centre-half who liked to dally – the Canaries were that much stronger as a result.

'I'd always liked playing in sides that had good centre-halves; good, uncompromising centre-halves. I didn't like playing against them. I liked playing against footballing centre-halves because they'd always give you a chance. Duncan and Dave (Stringer) probably wouldn't give you a chance because they didn't want to dwell on the ball.'

Forbes, in particular, had another big string to his bow – presence. Again, much like Malky Mackay, for all that heart-of-oak, no-nonsense leader-of-men stuff, he'd also weigh in with the odd, crucial goal in that promotion season – successive 1–0 home wins against Sheffield Wednesday on 8 April and Swindon Town on 22 April were both down to Forbes winners as the Canaries powered their way across the finishing line.

'Duncan's persona was such that he was in charge of the dressing room, in charge of everything, and I liked Duncan,' said David.

'But he was strange, really. Because in terms of technical ability he was probably the worst one of us out there. He wore these massive, big boots and he'd boot it half the length of the field. He'd roll his sleeves up and show the crowd he was rolling them up even more and sometimes I'd look at Graham and say: "Look at Duncan again…"

'But he was such a big, big presence for us. That ball went in the box and Keelan might save it, but Forbesy would get his head to it – and that's what you want. We missed him for the period when he had his hamstring injury and when he came back he scored a couple of goals in big, big games.

'He was larger than life in more ways than one. And it taught me never to underestimate someone just for their technical ability. He had something. He got us all at it. I can't emphasise enough what he had then. It's a big thing.'

(The same thing that Billy Bonds would have at West Ham and Dave Watson, first at Sunderland and then Manchester City.)

'I remember when I went to West Ham and Billy Bonds was there and we went down in my first season. And I said to Billy: "Look, you kick them at the back and I'll work hard and kick them up front and if we can get someone in midfield, at least we'd have something down the middle, Bill…"

'For I always felt that if you were strong down the middle, good solid centre-half, good keeper, good striker who worked hard, then you've always got a chance.' And if you have a good manager to boot, the world is almost your oyster.

For the Saunders influence didn't end with the players he bought or the players he nurtured. And nor was Norwich's success that season simply an issue of fitness. There was, it seems, real method in all that Mousehold madness – methods that, 30 years later, still have their place in the modern game.

'That team was probably years ahead of its time in terms of what we did,' said David, whose subsequent role as a coach at Oldham Athletic brought him into contact with one of this generation's brightest managerial thinkers – Crystal Palace chief Iain Dowie.

'Iain came to Oldham three years ago and was working on various 'new' kind of techniques and I showed him the videos from that year and we were doing the kind of stuff that he was trying to tell the lads to do. We were doing it 30 years ago – bounding, stick work, the kind of hurdles they use now.

'But I don't think anyone at the time thought of him as such a forward thinker. I didn't. I just thought of him as a bloody hard taskmaster who was going to get the best out of every situation he could. He would drain the last ounce of blood from you to get a result on the Saturday; from you personally.

'He was relentless, really, in what he wanted, but to me – and I was 20 years of age – he was someone who was going to give me a chance. If you bear in mind how I started that season with Rochdale, unsure of whether I'd actually be at Rochdale at the end of that season, and nine months later I was coming off the field at Orient having got promotion to what is now the Premiership – in nine months he'd given me all that.'

As for the man behind this iron mask, there was far more warmth and humour to the real Ron Saunders than history probably ever gives him credit for. The fact that the man himself might have gone out of his way to build and cement this forbidding persona in the public's mind merely adds another ingredient to a potent and beguiling mix.

'He was a hard man. He was a hard footballer – I know that. But I always got the impression with him that there was some sort of front, some kind of act, this hard man act. He was a big family man. He liked his quiet times; he liked his game of golf; liked to get away from football when he had his day off. And I always suspected there was something beneath that.

'For deep down Ron did have the lighter touch; he could relax. He could be very humorous. He and I had decent banter between us. He'd say: "How do you think you're playing?"

'And you're not going to say you're playing well. So it was: "Could be doing better, gaffer, yeah…"

"You got a girlfriend?"

"No…"

"Well, get one."

'Or: "Have you got a girlfriend?"

"Yeah…"

"Well get rid of her…" So you could never win. All he was really doing was drawing attention to the fact that you're not doing that well. I'm not going to steam into you, but you've got to do better…'

Whether the good gentlemen of the press ever saw Saunders' lighter side is probably a moot point. "No" would appear to be the general impression. 'He came across to the press as this very hard, very stern man. But he would want that. "Miserable, horrible bastard," would be what Keith Skipper might think. But he wasn't.

'He would do that with Skipper, have an interview with him, give him nothing and then come away and just wink at me. So you knew he was just winding him up. He didn't have time for the press. He just wanted to get on with his work. When you see the video of that season and you see the interviews he gave, it's laughable really. His whole PR was ludicrous. Hopeless.'

The method to his madness was just that – that Saunders' teams had this hugely methodical approach to games. Specific patterns of play that were drummed into individuals time and time again. If through nothing more than sheer repetition, little passing triangles would become second nature. Everyone – to a man – knew their job. Nine times out of ten, they knew everyone else's too.

'That is one thing that as a coach I've always tried to get into the players. If I have to ask a player at five to three: "What's your job today?" and if he doesn't know it then I've let him down,' said David, currently coaching for his old Rochdale pal, Bobby Downes, at Blackburn's FA Youth Academy.

David Cross

'Under Ron, I knew what my job was. We had a framework that we played to; a method that we played to. If Graham had the ball, I would make a particular run. Then Dougie (Livermore) would come in from where he was, Foggy (Ken Foggo) would stay wide and if the switch was on, I might get it out to Max Briggs or whoever was out on the right side. If I went one way, Peter (Silvester) would run the other.

'If I went short, Pete or Jim (Bone) would go long. If Jimmy went short, I would go long. All of that we worked on every single day.'

Not that individuality was wholly frowned upon.

'He didn't mind me trying to do a bit of a turn or having a piece of skill or whatever, but we knew our jobs. And we each knew each other's job. And so when we went on the field and someone didn't do it, we didn't need Ron to tell us.

'I coached at Oldham for a few years and you almost felt that you've got to move the players around like Subuteo men, you know, on sticks.

'Ron liked bright, intelligent people. He liked intelligent players. But the way he worked there was no equivocation about what you were going to do. "You know you should go there, we've worked it all week…"

'If you did a little bit of a fanny on the ball and it came off, fine. He wouldn't mind that. But if you did bit of a fanny and lost the ball he wasn't so happy.'

Put the whole package together and Norwich's success that season – crowned by a First Division title won courtesy of a 1–1 draw at Watford on the final day of the season – all starts to make perfect sense. And for all Saunders' genius, it was getting the basic ingredients right that served him and the Club so well.

'We had good players. Graham Paddon was a top class player; Dougie Livermore was a top class player; Terry Anderson had fantastic pace down one wing; Foggy had pace, ability and a great goal-scoring record on the other. And then you had myself and Jimmy Bone up front who ran and ran and ran.

'And good players working hard are a fantastic ingredient. That was our team. We worked our nuts off; we worked so hard.'

The rewards arrived in the course of that summer as the young City centre-forward finally let his hair down. Armed with a new sports car and, presumably, a spot of up-to-date sartorial advice from the dapper Mr Paddon, David had a ball that blissful summer.

'The local boys knew how much that promotion meant to everyone locally – Max, Clive Payne, Dave – they had that deep down. For me, it was only as we came nearer to promotion – only then did it become apparent to me what it meant. But when we did get promotion, that spring and summer it was really incredible.

'We could have done anything. I seem to remember for the first time in my life I went out and when I got home it was daylight – I'd never done that before. But then it was the end of the season and we had all that summer. It really was a magical time.'

The next big question was, of course, whether that same City formula could work its magic in the old First Division as the Canaries made their long-awaited debut in the big time the following August.

'There wasn't the same gap as there is now between the First and Second Divisions – the Premiership and the Championship as it is now – but people had a perception of us that we were just workers. People were saying: "Oh, they won't win a game because they're just not good enough…"

'But we were bright people, we spoke about it and we realised that we had to work even harder,' said David, with one or two facts of life in the top flight still holding true 30 years later. Like how you actually have more time on the ball far from the madding crowds of the lower leagues.

'What we actually found when we got up there was that whereas in the Second Division you never got any room anywhere, I found – certainly as a striker – defenders would give me respect. That, in certain areas, I could have the ball; that in certain areas the job was easier.

'Taking it on my chest on the halfway line, getting it down and blending it back – Mike England, Colin Todd, Roy McFarland would let me do that but the nearer you got to goal the harder it was. And that's where I had to be cleverer.'

And harder, as Saunders encouraged his young centre-forward to make his presence felt more than David's natural instincts might otherwise allow. Time to wind a centre-half up.

'There was some you couldn't; some would take it. I learnt that at Norwich – that when you played against what you'd call the hard men, they were the ones that I became hard against.

'I wasn't going to bully a weak, 18-year-old left-back, but I'd pit my wits against someone like Tommy Smith. I'd give them a smack early on – on the basis that they're used to it.

'And they'd say: "Right, you're in trouble for the next 90 minutes…"

'And I'd say: "Right, I'll be here until twenty to five. I'm not going to go anywhere, let's see what happens…"'

In fairness, it was a steep learning curve for all concerned – a 1–1 home draw against a fancied Everton side on the opening day of the season helped enormously. A 2–1 away win in the derby clash at Ipswich Town three days later then found real belief surging through Norwich's nervous limbs.

'We didn't know what would happen,' admitted David. 'As we approached the Everton game, the first match of the season – the first game Norwich had ever played in the top division – we were like everyone else. We were there thinking: "Let's just hope we don't make fools of ourselves! Let's hope that fantastic year we had last year doesn't blow up in our faces!"

David Cross

'Jimmy scored – I think Joe Royle equalised in the second half – and we finished 1–1. And we were absolutely delighted. We'd matched a First Division team. First game in the history of the Club where we'd played a First Division team on a level playing field, not a cup game, and we'd matched them. And Everton had won the Championship two seasons earlier with that very same side – Kendall and Harvey were still around. So we came off and thought: "That's good – we matched them!" We had – it wasn't a fluke. Then we went to Ipswich on the Tuesday and beat them.'

A 3–0 defeat at Manchester City would follow the next Saturday, but come the back end of September the Canaries were beating the mighty Arsenal at home as they rose to the challenge of top flight football.

'It wasn't about individuals – it wasn't about me or Jimmy Bone, whether he could take people on. We worked together as a team. If Boney lost the ball, I wasn't too far off him. And Graham Paddon and Dougie Livermore weren't too far off either. We worked so hard together. We never had any fear of taking anyone on and we took them by storm, really.

'And what we did find was – and I always have this now with players – that the players who we'd looked at from afar on TV or whatever, they weren't supermen. They weren't as fit as us.

'When I, say, chased Charlie George down, I was fitter than him. Charlie George might have scored the winning goal in the FA Cup final the year before, but I was fitter than him. And he was going to have to chase me.

'We never gave any team a minute and for a certain length of time we frightened the life out of people.'

Come Christmas, however, and the Canaries were fast running out of steam. For not only were the years of sheer, unrelenting graft under Saunders starting to take their toll, but Norwich's eyes were also straying elsewhere – in particular to a first-ever Wembley appearance courtesy of a storming run in that year's League Cup competition. Arsenal were brushed aside 3–0 in the fifth round before a two-legged semi-final against Chelsea loomed out of the mists – literally in the case of that infamous, abandoned home tie at Carrow Road.

First up was the away leg at Stamford Bridge. Once again it was the Cross and Bone show as City raced into a 2–0 advantage with Norwich's strike pair sharing the goals.

'Jimmy and I destroyed them that night,' said David. 'We killed them. Absolutely killed them. They were a typical, experienced First Division back four who assumed because they were good players that they would cope, but they hadn't really come up against what we had, the movement that Jimmy and I had.

'We scored one each and beat them 2–0 there which was a fantastic result in the first leg of a semi-final – to go away and win 2–0. And we just knew that all we had to do really was just to come back and I think we were 3–2 up, 5–2 on aggregate, when the fog came in. And we just couldn't believe it.'

The match was duly abandoned little more than six minutes from the end and Norwich knew they'd have to do it all again in the replayed second leg.

'We weren't happy with the decision – six minutes from time. The fog had been drifting around, off the river. You could see it. But that quite often happened at that time. But when it came down, I think we all thought that we should have played on.

'We thought that they'd let Chelsea out of jail. We couldn't believe it – it was like someone had stolen the Christmas presents on Boxing Day.

'We're 5–2 up; six minutes away from going to Wembley and you could see, Sod's Law, that come the replay we'd bloody lose. Chelsea were a quality side. But again we just got on with it, Steve Govier scored the one goal and they never really threatened us in the second game. But that first home leg was an amazing game. There was real, real upset in the dressing room.'

Part of the problem, it seems, lay in the fact that between that semi-final epic and the Club's first-ever trip to Wembley on 3 March 1973, lay two, nail-biting months in which – by comment consent – neither the players nor the city of Norwich could really concentrate on the league. In fact, Norwich lost all six of their league games between semi-final and final.

David also lost his No.1 sidekick as Jimmy Bone was sold to Sheffield United that February and, with the money, Trevor Hockey arrived. Saunders, ever the pragmatist, was doing what it took to survive that season, as Bone's attacking flamboyance was deemed a luxury Norwich could ill afford as they plummeted down the table. Hockey's arrival added steel – first and foremost in the toe caps of his over-sized boots.

'Trevor Hockey came in, just at that back end of our first season in Division One when we were struggling and he gave us a bit of a competitive edge. He was a wild man. He had the big rugby boots and he just kicked the ball as far as he could.

'But Ron knew we were struggling. We couldn't get a result for love nor money. The League Cup final killed us in some respects – it took us all over that much. It did me. It became all encompassing. And then, after it, everything was so flat.'

All in all, it was not the greatest preparation for Norwich's great Wembley day out and Tottenham – complete with a certain Martin Peters – won 1–0.

'My memories of the final are not good,' said David. 'We just froze, I think. I certainly did. There was too much going on in the build-up. I think Ron sort of fell out with me because I was quoted in the paper as saying that I thought he got our build-up wrong.

'As I remember we went down on the Thursday to the hotel in Croydon and I think we went a day too early. We'd nothing to do in the hotel so we went out and were training all the time. And when the boredom came, we'd go out and have a jog and I think we left it all on the training ground.

David Cross

'I remember feeling drained as *"God Save The Queen!"* was coming on. And I looked at some of the other lads, I looked along the line and wondered if everyone feels like I do. And it was a slog, a big, big slog. I thought we did well to only lose 1–0. We never threatened Tottenham.'

In the end, Norwich would just scramble to safety in their first season back, but the magic was fading. Perhaps Saunders' voice was becoming too familiar; perhaps some of his bark had lost its bite. Either way a parting of the ways was heaving into view as the 1973–74 season ground into gear.

Two of Saunders' star turns – David and Graham Paddon – were first out of the door as the City boss cleared a bit of the deck ahead of his own exit to Manchester City not long afterwards.

'When I left I didn't want to leave. I didn't want to go to Coventry particularly,' said David, whose last game in a Canary shirt was a 2–0 defeat at Stoke City in the second week in November.

'I went and then Graham went about a week or so after Ron. In fact, West Ham wanted to take the two of us but Ron wouldn't sell us both to one club. And at the time that I left I wasn't playing all that well. That was one of the reasons that Ron let me go. And I remember saying to him: "You've given me everything – I want to stay here!"

'And he said: "Well, I won't be here very much longer and if that's your only reason for staying, if I were you I'd take your chance now."

'I had gone off the boil. And I really needed a move in that respect. Looking back at my career it was the right thing to do. Maybe I'd done what I could have done with Norwich. I would have loved to have stayed, but I couldn't have afforded not to financially – to go to Coventry for much better money.

'Deep down I would have wanted to have stayed – if Ron was staying. But once he'd said: "I'm going!" I thought that the whole thing could fall apart. They'd been two fantastic years, but I didn't want to be a part of it if it was all going to fall apart.'

The legacy of Ron Saunders would, however, stay with David for the rest of his career.

'I had the common sense to know that if you worked hard you got your rewards, but it was Ron that taught me the value of that; he taught me that that was absolutely right – that if you did work hard, you did get rewards. Not just the physical rewards, but there's also a kind of mental thing – you feel more confident.

'He was everything really. He was what had got the Club together. We wouldn't have been the same without what he had. He was no fool. He knew what was required.

'Iain Dowie's very similar now. Iain will settle for nothing from his players other than absolutely everything – 99 per cent is not enough. You've got to give everything and a little bit more. Ron was like that.

'People say to me: "Who is the best manager you ever had?" and I can't split them up. I've had some that I wouldn't mention, that I didn't like. But I've always said Ron Saunders, Johnny Giles and John Lyall in their own way all gave me something.

'But, if I hadn't had two years with Ron I wouldn't have been able to take advantage of what Johnny Giles gave me and then subsequently John Lyall. John kind of put the finishing touches to me and he always said – he signed me on my 27th birthday – that if he'd have got me when I was 21 he would have got me to play for England. And I think he would.'

'I'd have to confess that my spell at West Ham – I was there five seasons, got 100 goals for them, won the FA Cup and got the Golden Boot – that was probably the most satisfying period of my career, but without any shadow of a doubt, my two years at Norwich were a magical period. Absolutely magical.

'Because of Dougie Livermore, Graham Paddon, Duncan Forbes, Clive Payne – that group of players. We had something that you couldn't buy.'

Two years ago, amidst the Club's Centenary celebrations, the '71–72 promotion team was reunited on the 30th anniversary of that famous triumph. Ron Saunders wasn't there – a family wedding intervened. He did, however, send the Club a warm and affectionate letter that was later read out at that evening's gala dinner. The man charged with reading Saunders' letter was the MC for the evening, Keith Skipper – one of the rare occasions that he ever gave the famed Canary reporter some decent copy.

'It was strange when I went back for the reunion, the 30-year thing. Because all of a sudden you saw people you hadn't seen for 30 years who were young men then. One woman said to me – and I remember her being a supporter back then – "You've aged better than most of these fellas!" but I'm 53 now, I still play football, still play cricket and I still feel 21.

'And then I look at Alan Black and Blacky's got completely grey hair. And Graham. At that time, Graham would have been the David Beckham of East Anglia. Good-looking young lad, the hair, everything right, bang up to fashion with everything. And last time I saw Graham, he wasn't that young man any more. It really was strange.

'My wife – and she really doesn't enjoy the big football thing, all of that – she really enjoyed it. And she said: "It must have been good here – the people were so good on the night…They've been so good to you here, you must have enjoyed it then?"

'And I said: "Yes, it was. It was fantastic."

'When we walked round the ground before the match that day would have brought a tear to a glass eye, the reception we were given. And you looked at the crowd and there were people there that were 25, 35, even 45 who were only ten, 15 or whatever then – who probably didn't know you at all. But the reception they gave us – I was very emotional. And I don't get emotional.

'But walking around that pitch. I could have walked around it forever.'

David Cross

One final postscript to the David Cross story. You would have thought that for a player of whom so much was expected, on whose 20-year-old shoulders so many hopes and, indeed, careers lay, that Ron Saunders might just have watched that final piece in his promotion jigsaw play before splashing the Canary cash on a young man from Rochdale.

'I found out a staggering thing talking to Terry Allcock at the reunion – that Ron Saunders had never seen me play when he signed me. And I found that absolutely mind-blowing. I couldn't believe it. I had this thing firmly in my mind for 30 years that he'd watched me play and knew what I was about when he took me.

'Terry had watched me a couple of times and he'd said: "Sign him! Sign him!" And I've no reason to doubt what Terry said was true – that he watched me a couple of times, they looked into my character and in the end they said: "Look you need to sign him or else someone else will move in! If you want him, get him!" but Ron had never seen me play.'

6 Martin Peters

Regarded by many City fans as "the best player to ever pull on a Norwich shirt" – Martin Peters' time at Carrow Road is always fondly recalled by the Canary faithful.

A World Cup winner in 1966, Martin enjoyed great spells at West Ham United and Tottenham Hotspur before joining City in March 1975. His arrival at Carrow Road helped inspire the Canaries to promotion back to Division One just ten games later.

Martin's five-year stint at Norwich coincided with the Canaries playing some of the most attractive football Carrow Road has ever seen. He scored 50 goals during his 232 appearances and did much to help nurture the emerging skills of Kevin Reeves and Justin Fashanu. Such was his influence at Carrow Road he was handed a testimonial match during the 1978–79 season and 19,000 turned out to pay tribute to his efforts in the Canary cause.

An inaugural member of the Club's Hall of Fame, Martin was back at Carrow Road for the official opening of the Jarrold Stand in February 2004 when City took on West Ham United.

Martin Stanford Peters

Born: Plaistow, 8 November 1943
City Debut: 15 March 1975, Manchester United (a) 1–1 Division Two
Final Game: 3 May 1980, Derby County (h) 4–2 Division One
League appearances: 207
League goals: 44
FA Cup appearances: 12
FA Cup goals: 3
League Cup appearances: 13
League Cup goals: 3
Total appearances: 232
Total goals: 50

For someone who has won virtually every gong in the game going – and that, of course, includes the biggest one of the lot, one balmy summer's day in 1966 – the affection that England World Cup legend Martin Peters still holds for his back-to-back Player of the Season awards at Carrow Road should warm the cockle of any City heart.

Martin Peters

'I loved it,' he said simply. 'It's a small thing, but a big thing to me – to twice be voted Player of the Year.'

To this day, the respect between player and supporters is mutual. Here, after all, was that rarest of football breeds – a World Cup winner – who swapped the bright lights of London town for the "Fine City" of Norwich and, for more than five years, produced the kind of football that would inspire a generation of Canary supporters.

It was also the kind of football that would keep John Bond's Norwich in the old First Division at a time when both the odds and the finances looked stacked against them. Likewise, he also proved exactly the right kind of footballer to usher in the next young crop of Canary heroes as, one by one, the older guard bade their farewells to Carrow Road.

Little wonder, therefore, that the name of Martin Peters commands such affection and respect.

Martin's own, quiet love affair with Norfolk actually started long before the one-time Essex youngster took his first steps on the path to lasting sporting glory when he signed for West Ham United as a 17-year-old in November 1960.

'I used to go to Norfolk for my holidays,' said Martin. 'As a kid I was taken to Seacroft and Hemsby with my mum and dad and so I had a warm feeling for Norfolk anyway.'

His switch up to the far end of the A11 in March 1975 was also helped by the presence of two, very familiar faces from his Upton Park days – City boss John Bond and his then assistant, Ken Brown.

Steeped in the ways of Ron Greenwood and the famed West Ham Academy, Bond and Brown were tailor-made for Martin's needs, as his glittering career hit something of a crossroads that spring following the arrival of Terry Neill at White Hart Lane. Still only 31, Martin's achievements in the game up to that point could comfortably fill a book by itself – a point not lost on the man himself as he begins to put pen to paper ahead of the 40th anniversary in 2006 of that Wembley triumph.

Given the time and space that a single chapter allows, to try and sum up Martin's achievements pre-Norwich in little more than a paragraph or two is a task and a half.

Put briefly, his 11-year association with the Hammers would not only straddle events of 1966, when his second strike in England's 4–2 triumph over West Germany put Sir Alf Ramsey's side within touching distance of history, but also include a European Cup Winners' Cup medal in 1965 in the course of 302 appearances for the East End side, bagging 81 goals in the process.

Come March 1970, and the switch to White Hart Lane saw Peters' name once again splashed across the nation's back pages as the legendary Jimmy Greaves and the small matter of a then record £220,000 headed in one direction, Martin in the other.

Still the honours flowed as League Cup and UEFA Cup glory followed. Only a championship medal and an FA Cup final appearance eluded him. At White Hart Lane, his 189 Spurs appearances would yield 46 goals before Tottenham and Peters parted.

Precisely why Peters felt compelled to leave the old First Division for a new life in Norfolk in the old Second may well have to await the publication of Martin's book. Suffice to say, one or two of the older guard were beginning to bristle under Neill's rule, as the one-time Arsenal centre-half succeeded a genuine North London legend, Bill Nicholson, in September 1974. Neill was just 32 at the time of his appointment.

'I wasn't getting on too well with Terry Neill – I think mainly because he wasn't very much older than me. I was 31. There was Mike England who was 32, Martin Chivers, 30, all around that 30 age and if you look at what happened to Spurs in those days most of those players left for one reason.

'I understood that Norwich were interested and, of course, John Bond was the manager and Ken Brown was the assistant manager, both of whom I'd known and played with in my career with West Ham. So it was just a matter of speaking to John and seeing which way we were going to go.

'I wasn't looking to get away. I was just unhappy at the way I was being treated – by the manager in particular – and I obviously wasn't part of the long-term future there. John came in very close to the transfer deadline, we had a meeting and it was done and dusted.'

For the less than princely sum of £50,000, the Canaries had bagged a piece of World Cup royalty. The fact that Martin's move involved a drop into the old Second Division appeared to matter little. There were still plenty of big names to rub shoulders with and, besides, City were themselves upwardly mobile that spring as they gunned for the third and final promotion spot behind Manchester United and Aston Villa.

'At that time it was Manchester United, Villa, Sunderland and Norwich who were the top four teams and three went up automatically,' said Martin, who would make his Canary debut away at Old Trafford in a 1–1 draw on Saturday, 15 March 1975.

'Obviously knowing of Norwich and knowing the players, having played against them in the League Cup final of 1973, I was obviously interested enough to be part and parcel of trying to get them out of Division Two and into Division One.

'The fact that John and Ken were there was a massive influence. If it had been, with no disrespects, Ron Saunders for instance, who I didn't know at all, then most probably I wouldn't have gone.

'But because it was John and Ken, who I'd known since, well, I was 15 when I first went to West Ham – they were most probably in the first team then – it was obviously a major influence in me going to Norwich.'

It was not simply a matter of the right personalities. Bond and Brown had something else in common with their star signing – a shared philosophy on the right way to play football, born out of the Greenwood influence at Upton Park. It was that same "West Ham way" that Bond had put into motion at Bournemouth and was now busily injecting into Norwich's way of thinking.

'I knew the way John wanted to play,' said Martin, never a likely candidate for the Ron Saunders approach which, with an element of pass, pass, pass to it, owed far more to the run, run, run school of thought.

'I'm not saying that that's the right or wrong way to play because Ron Saunders was successful in his own way – he got promotion, he went to Wembley – we played against him at Wembley.

'And he had people like Graham Paddon, who was a skilful player, in the side. So it wasn't just the kick-and-rush kind of thing.

'But John was educated in the West Ham way. He loves the West Ham way; he talks about the West Ham way, because he got it from Ron Greenwood. At the end of the day he fell out with Ron Greenwood, I fell out with Ron Greenwood. You do. But he still kept that so-called West Ham Academy in his mind, used it at Bournemouth and everywhere he's been.

'I'd actually played against Bournemouth in a pre-season friendly with Spurs. So I knew his ways – and Ken is a great man – so it wasn't that hard really. The biggest problem was moving the family up from Essex to Norfolk.'

What he discovered on his arrival in the Canary dressing room was a bit of Saunders steel mixed with a spot of Bond-style panache. Be it luck or design, Norwich were about to nick that third promotion spot off Sunderland's toes with a marriage of styles made in footballing heaven.

'Was it the West Ham way of playing? It was and it wasn't really,' said Martin, as he looked back 30 years later at Bond's 1974–75 promotion side. At its heart, of course, lay the towering defensive presence of Duncan Forbes – not someone you'd immediately suggest was a graduate of the Upton Park Academy. More the school of hard knocks.

'Maybe John had instilled a bit of strength to the back – or not, as it was already there with big Duncan and Dave Stringer which West Ham, you could say, most probably lacked.

'Maybe if they had a bit more strength at the back they would have done better than they did when I was there, but obviously Dunc and Dave were a pretty strong central defence and from there the team went forward and played with more of a West Ham style of football.'

With the steel supplied by Messrs Forbes and Stringer – not to mention a certain Kevin Keelan in goal – the style, as Martin suggests, came from those further forward.

'They'd taken on Ted MacDougall and Phil Boyer from Bournemouth so they had a great goal-scoring forward line plus I'd played against Suggy (Colin Suggett) on numerous occasions. So the main players of the team I'd either known or played against over the years.'

If slipping into the dressing room proved to be an easy transition – Martin's first goals would arrive in the back-to-back 3–0 wins over Nottingham Forest and Portsmouth that April – winning over the locals would take a little while longer.

Naturally wary of big names up from the Smoke, the natural suspicion was that Mr Peters was here to take their money and never really run. He was putting himself out to grass in Norfolk; taking the early retirement offered by his two old Hammers pals.

'I tended to believe that the fans thought I was only going to be there for a short period of time. This Londoner coming up to Norfolk. You know "You've got to watch him because he's a Londoner!" type of attitude.

'I think that was in the air to start with because obviously Norfolk people are different. They are different to where I come from,' said Martin, the family's cause not helped by the fact that the season would end with a tour to Kenya.

'At the time the children were four and eight and it was quite difficult for my wife – more difficult to overcome than playing with the players.

'She's an East Londoner so the difficult thing was to take the girl out of East London, plonk her in the middle of Norfolk and say you've got to get on with it because I'm going to Kenya. With the family it takes time and that was a slight problem. And obviously what affects my wife, affects me.'

The fact that within ten games of Martin's arrival, Norwich were heading back into the big time helped all concerned.

'Going up was a big boost for me,' he said. 'I was back playing in Division One, and also for the county, the Club and all involved with Norwich City.'

Bond had also laid down the blueprint for future success – a formula that, in many ways, would underpin the best Norwich sides for generations to come. A great goalkeeper, a solid, unyielding defence and – ideally – two players up front who could score you goals. The whole package was then knitted together by willingness – and an ability – to pass the ball.

'The qualities in that team were the defensive structure with a goalkeeper who had been there for years and the two strikers who would always score goals,' said Martin, with Boyer and MacDougall between them adding 33 goals to Norwich's promotion cause that season. A year later, as Norwich made a mid-table place their own in the top flight, the pair would hit 34. Martin, for the record, grabbed ten in his first full season at Carrow Road.

'You have to have a mixture in a side to be successful and we had a good mixture in the team,' said Martin, with the Canaries offering a strong backbone on their return to the top flight – in every sense of the word in Big Dunc's case.

'The nucleus was the centre, the structure down the middle. You had the goalkeeper, the centre-half and the centre-forwards so you had the players to work around. It ended up right that season and for the five seasons I was there, it continued.'

Martin Peters

Characters were never in short supply. Take Mr Keelan, for example.

'I was very lucky to play with Pat Jennings, Gordon Banks and Kevin Keelan and I think Kevin was one of the great goalkeepers of his time, really,' said Martin.

'Not only was he a great goalkeeper, he went on to play for a long time, mainly for one club, and earned two testimonials – that can't be bad, can it?

'He was very outward going, colourful, and he was a good person to have in the dressing room.

'I've met him a couple of times since and he doesn't look much different, to be honest with you. He still dyes his hair!'

Look back now at Martin's playing record and – aside from the many tales of the total quality at work – the one thing that stands out is the sheer quantity of games he played.

Even in his final season before a switch to Sheffield United beckoned, Martin missed just two league games in the course of the 1979–80 season. No mean feat for a player who celebrated his 36th birthday that season. It also made a mockery of those early suggestions that he was simply on the lookout for an easy life.

'I didn't have too many injuries over my career really. Mainly cuts, ankle cuts. I guess I had two bad injuries. I had a knee problem when I was at Spurs and then I was out for about six weeks at Norwich with an Achilles problem which happened in pre-season.

'In fact I ended up playing, taking pain-killers before the game and at half-time to get me through. I didn't train during the week.'

For all his many and glittering achievements, a simple and straightforward appetite for the game underpinned Martin's professional life. Age never wearied that one, enduring love.

'I was always willing to play and I loved training. Training wasn't a problem for me even when you had to run. I was never quick, but I had good lungs in that I could run distances. I hated missing games. I hated being out for six weeks.'

Particularly when it entailed missing out on a trip to Upton Park at the start of the 1977–78 season.

'I watched the team go to West Ham in the first game of the season and win 3–1,' said Martin, as two goals from David Jones burst the Hammers' bubbles. 'I was sat next to John in the stands. I wanted to get out there – it was a great result.'

The myth of the man seeking a comfortable retirement – a Cockney chancer out to pull the wool over sleepy Norfolk's eyes – was long, long buried.

'I was never like that. I'm not perfect in many ways, but football was my life from when I was a little 'un, to when I got into a team at schoolboy level right through to when I finished.

'And moving to Norwich at 31 wasn't that old to me. I knew I could still run up and down the pitch. I didn't think I was going out to grass. I think other people may have thought that, but I didn't.'

Ask Martin which of today's generation of players he most resembles and we're swiftly off into fascinating territory. For one thing, few players offer his degree of versatility, even less his instinctive ability to ghost into penalty areas unseen and rack up goal after trademark goal from his nominal midfield berth.

'I think there have been people similar to me, but I can't think of anyone the same. If you look around and try to look for someone, then maybe there's Paul Scholes – he scores goals from midfield. David Platt scores goals from midfield. Or Bryan Robson. But not being funny or anything, I don't think there is anyone quite like myself really, in that I was adept in quite a few positions.

'In fact I played for West Ham in every position – in goal even. So I could end up at right-back and do OK, left-back, centre-half. I played sweeper a couple of times for John,' remembered Martin, one experiment that didn't quite go to plan.

'We played Forest at home, we were 3–1 down at half-time, I was playing sweeper. He put me back into midfield and we drew 3–3.'

As for playing up front, Martin was never a Darren Huckerby. For all the many strings to his bow, out-and-out pace was not one of his strengths. Dedication was. The man loved his football. Did then, does now.

'I was never quick but I could run – run distances. And I wanted to do it; I wanted to train. I wanted to go out on a November morning when it was a bit chilly and train and do things like volley balls – even do the things that I was good at.

'And then you have to do things you're not good at like sprinting. I hated sprinting because I knew I would normally come last.

'It all started at West Ham where we'd do sprints. I knew that at long-distance running I would come first, second or third, but you can't be good at everything. And besides, if you can read the game you don't have to be quick.

'The enthusiasm was there. I've had the enthusiasm all my life to do well in sport, any sport really. But I was never quick enough to play up front. I was a pretty good target man being fairly tall, but I just wasn't quick. John asked me to play up front, not much, when other players were injured, so I did play in most positions. I don't think you could say that the other players that I've mentioned could do that.'

But then what Martin might have lacked in terms of simple speed, he more than catered for by way of swiftness of thought. Like Terry Allcock before him, the first couple of yards were always run in his head – a trick developed and honed at the Hammers' Academy.

'Bobby Moore wasn't very quick, but he always read the ball before he got there. And I had a bit of that in me as well.'

Martin Peters

six

Once again the conversation turns to Ron Greenwood and the lasting influence the future England boss would have on that generation of West Ham players – three of whom would figure so large at Wembley (Peters, Hurst and Moore) and two of whom – Brown and Bond – would come to figure so large in Norwich's post-war history.

'Ron was introducing ideas and coaching methods way ahead of his time,' said Martin. 'It was based on his association with European football. He used to go and watch coaches in Europe. He was very enamoured with Germany, in particular.

'Certainly the training we did wasn't all running. We did the odd run, but you'd do just as much running with the ball as without it.'

There was another Greenwood trait that would pass directly into Norwich's way of thinking – particularly when City had Martin Peters on one end of the pass, Ted MacDougall on the other.

'Ron also introduced the near-post ball which was something that never kind of occurred before,' said Martin, as the penny dropped with Greenwood that, when it came to scoring goals, there was more than one way to skin a rabbit. Banging the ball long to a hulking, old-fashioned centre-forward in the hope that something would drop wasn't exactly the appliance of science. It was trench warfare – launching the big battalions over the top in the hope that the use of sheer weight down the middle of the park would break the enemy's lines. Why not try and work the flanks – apply a spot of brain to the problem, not brawn, and look for the enemy's weak spot. At his near post.

'Ron worked on going down the right or left-hand side and then knocking the ball into the near post. The centre-forwards who were in there would make runs to the near post all the time.

'Each would know when the other one was going to deliver the ball. And if you can just get that half a yard in front of the defender and get a touch to the ball, then you've got a good chance of scoring.'

With Peters, Hurst and Moore in the England team – not to mention such a perfect poacher as Jimmy Greaves – it was almost inevitable that Sir Alf Ramsey would give this near-post nonsense a whirl.

At Norwich it was MacDougall gunning for the knock into the near post and Heaven help the winger that didn't deliver the ball on cue. Boyer was there to do the leg-work outside the box, to keep the wheels in motion.

'Ted was our goalscorer and Phil was the worker,' said Martin, as MacDougall stuck rigidly to his task. His job was to get goals inside the box. End of story.

'I guess sometimes we didn't think he worked too hard outside the box, but then when he scores goals on a regular basis you have to take that on board. You can't be perfect at everything. Jimmy Greaves was very similar and was England's greatest goalscorer. He worked in the box.

'Phil was a great foil to him. Phil was a real, hard-working front man.

He'd chase everything down – sometimes to his detriment. Sometimes you've got to leave it, know that I'm not going to catch that. But he had a wonderful, fantastic attitude and he got his goals. They were great to play with and I enjoyed playing with them.'

Given Martin's ability to deliver a ball on cue, he escaped the odd MacDougall barb. Others, it seems, were less fortunate.

'Ted moaned a lot,' said Martin, with Johnny Miller and Steve Grapes bearing the brunt. 'I think he could destroy wingers who didn't supply him with the ball in the right place. If he got in front of somebody and the ball didn't come in right then there was hell to pay for that winger.

'But Ted knew that if I was wide, either left or right, I would knock it in early. Other players would be the same. I knocked one in for Suggy, and he scored, because again he knew I'd get wide and knock it in. It's a habit I got into throughout my career – a habit introduced by Ron Greenwood. That if I got wide, I would knock them in early.'

Nor was the manager always all sweetness and light.

'John was quite aggressive at times – he didn't care for people who didn't give 100 per cent,' said Martin, as Bond's infectious enthusiasm occasionally bubbled over. 'He loved being involved, he loved being involved with five-a-sides, he loved training sessions.

'You could see the excitement and enthusiasm in him on the training pitch and when you get that you get a good feeling within the team – especially if the team are doing quite well as well. John loved his football. He lived and died for his football, really.'

As indeed did the then chairman, Sir Arthur South. It all made for one, big happy camp come the glorious summer of 1976 as the Peters family – now happily settled in their Sprowston home – hosted pool parties for all concerned.

'We lived in Sprowston – just outside the city. We had a swimming pool, a nice house, a lovely garden. It was 1976 when the summer was fantastic and I had a couple of pool parties which the lads came along to and we had some great times. And Sir Arthur came.

'He was a great character and I don't know what in terms of money he put into the Club, but he certainly put his time and consideration into it. I liked him very much.'

There was another reason why it was all smiles. 'It was a happy club because the team were successful,' said Martin. That success was, he admits, based on very limited horizons. Norwich looked no further than simply surviving in the top flight. Anything else was a complete bonus.

'I think we always thought let's survive and, hopefully, get a cup run,' said Martin, a hope that proved somewhat distant as Norwich's cup fortunes deserted them.

Opportunity at least knocked in 1976 when the prospect of an FA Cup quarter-final home clash with Southampton loomed – provided City could dispose of Fourth Division Bradford City at home in the fifth round. They couldn't. The Bantams staged a memorable cup shock, won the tie 2–1 and another Wembley dream died.

'I think we did as well as we could have done for the time I was there,' said Martin, now about to captain a side that would contain the blossoming young talents of Justin Fashanu and Kevin Reeves, as the Big Man himself, Duncan Forbes, slowly headed for the sunset.

'I'd been captain at Spurs and at West Ham. And England, of course. Not that many times – about six times,' said Martin, 'but I enjoyed being captain and I had carte blanche to change things on the field if I wanted to – if I thought that things weren't happening.

'It wouldn't be every game, but on the odd occasion if I thought I could change it. It mainly revolved around where I was playing. I could push myself up behind the front two or something.'

Drifting into the centre inevitably put Martin nearer the thick of the action. And if the opposition fancied a bit of that action, the Dagenham lad was quite happy to mix it with football's finest. He was no show pony – one reason why he could command such respect in the City dressing room.

'I had the experience of playing at a higher level, so I could talk to people and shout at people if I wanted to,' said Martin. 'And if I did, I would get response – maybe because of what I'd achieved and was still achieving at the Club.

'Maybe some of the players thought I'd come from London, played for England, was a World Cup winner and all that rubbish and perhaps thought: "What's he going to do? Is he going to play us?"

'But I think once I got there and showed them that I was still up for it at 31, with a lot to play for as far as I was concerned, then I got a lot more respect from the players. And if you get respect from the players, they tend to listen to what you say.'

A perfect role model wasn't exactly hard to find. This was a man who, after all, had played over 300 games with Bobby Moore. He'd followed him up the steps at Wembley.

'Bobby was a bit quiet really – not that I was animated – but Bobby was quieter than me,' said Martin, looking back on the qualities of one of the all-time great sporting captains.

'But it was the way he played. If you look at West Ham and England, 70 per cent of the play came from Bobby at the back.

'Watch the World Cup final and see how many times Bobby's on the ball at the back, and playing it from the back. It's amazing. And that's the way he played.

'And he'd never shout. I don't remember Bobby Moore ever raising his voice, ever, apart from: "Another lager!"'

The captaincy also coincided with a positional switch, as Bond realised that Martin's undimmed talents needed to be centre stage. His lead violin became the orchestra's conductor.

'I started on the left side of midfield – that's where John first played me and for two years I played that side.

'Then John and I had a chat, instigated by him, and he moved me into the centre of midfield which is where I played for the rest of my career there.

'I guess it suited me because by then I was about 33 and when you're put on the left or right side of midfield you've got to get up and down, in the box. And I didn't have to do that, so it suited me in terms of the age I was. I was still getting in the box, but maybe not as many times as I was supposed to from the left or the right. It was easier and I was on the ball more.'

After all, Martin had never been an out-and-out winger. Like all the finest footballers, he let the ball do the hard work.

'I didn't go past full-backs – you just let the ball do that,' said Martin. 'I wasn't quick enough to go past them. David Beckham is the same. He's not quick enough, so he makes space and bends it in. It's easier for him because he's got the right foot – and I was right-footed as well. If I had the space, I would just take one step, kick and curl it in.'

So much for when he had the ball. When he didn't, it was time for the appliance of a spot of West Ham science – that and good, old-fashioned sweat – to ensure that if the ball was played in from the right, City's left-sided midfielder was there at the far post to meet it.

'People say to me this thing about being "the Ghost" – about appearing from nowhere to score goals, and things like that,' said Martin, revealing one or two tricks of his goal-scoring trade. Lesson No.1 is the virtue of simple, hard graft.

'They would see the goal I scored, but they wouldn't see the other nine times I made a run but didn't get the ball.'

You have to speculate to accumulate, it seems.

'You take a chance – that's what it is. Taking a chance. You see the ball, see spaces in the box and you find that space. It may not come. But when it comes, you're there and you put it away.' It was a concept that not everyone wholly appreciated – of the untold number of runs that ended with little more than the move breaking down and Martin being forced to about-turn and chase his marker back towards his own half.

'I used to get a bit sick – especially at Spurs – of people saying: "Martin Peters is not in the game". And then suddenly it's: "Oh, he's scored! Where did he come from?" That attitude. But they didn't see the other nine times I was going in there.

'Some players sit there and think: "Oh, I won't go in there, there's nothing!" Take a chance. Run in there, go in there, put yourself in there, you could score. Be there!'

And once you get there, get something on it.

Martin Peters

'I was a good header of the ball; I was tall; I could get in front of people. I think you always get more goals with your feet, but I got quite a few with my head. That's only natural – you've only got one head, but you've got two feet!'

Feet that also served him well in other areas – as in "putting the foot in".

'I had a history with certain players and it was a bit of a battle at times,' admitted Martin. 'But you can't be a pansy in football. You've got to hold your own – you've got to put your foot in.'

It was a lesson he learned the hard way – as a tender teenager at West Ham United.

'I remember the first time. I was 18 or 19 playing at Everton, at Goodison Park. At that time I didn't know what "over the top of the ball" meant. Until it happened to me. Suddenly this guy comes in and whack! Didn't go anywhere near the ball, over the top and I had a whacking, great big cut on my ankle. And I learnt from that.

'It puts a bit more steel into you because you know now it's not all West Ham Academy. It's a bit more than that at times. That's why you have to have a mixture of players in a side – as we did at Norwich and as we had at Spurs. But not so much at West Ham, though.'

It all helped when it came to that fiercest of local fixtures – the great East Anglian derby.

'The games I really looked forward to on the fixture list were obviously West Ham and Spurs – they were always the fixtures. And Ipswich, of course, that was the big one wasn't it, for the Norfolk people? That was the one we always wanted to win.'

It did, it seem, pale in comparison with the bitterness and fury that erupted between the two, great North London rivals, Spurs and Arsenal. Sheer volume of numbers fuelled that little row between the neighbours to even bigger heights.

'I don't think the passion of the Norwich–Ipswich game surprised me because Arsenal v Tottenham is a massive, massive game every year.

'And although the Norwich–Ipswich derby is a massive game, because it's played in smaller stadiums I don't think it can be quite the same. Certainly not in volume compared to Arsenal v Tottenham. Remember, when I was at Tottenham there used to be 60,000 there. It just seemed that there was more noise, more aggression from the supporters when Tottenham played Arsenal than when Norwich played Ipswich.'

Off down the East End, West Ham were a far more friendly crowd. More good, old-fashioned knees-up as opposed to the punch-up down the Seven Sisters Road. Or rather that's the way it used to be.

'At West Ham there wasn't one big derby game, really. Just every London club really,' said Martin. 'But I think over the years it's developed into West Ham v Spurs – and not very nicely either. They have a real hatred and I don't know why. I don't like to see it.

'When West Ham went down the other year, I was working at Spurs and it came up on the screen, and all the Spurs supporters were cheering. I don't like that. Not just because I was at both clubs, but it never used to be like that.'

Put the whole package together – the World Cup and derby warrior, the goal-scoring, midfield maestro and the City skipper who learned much of his leadership trade at the feet of Bobby Moore – and it is little wonder that Martin swiftly found himself acting as such a major mentor to two of Bond's younger jewels, Kevin Reeves and Justin Fashanu.

Such a wealth of knowledge had to be passed on and in the young City pair – one fresh from Bournemouth, the other beginning to find his feet in the world after a childhood with foster parents in Norfolk – he found two willing and able pupils. Alas, the career of one would be cut short by injury, the life of the other by tragedy.

'Kevin, in particular, was the shining light, wasn't he? It's just a shame that, at the end of the day, he had those injury problems at Manchester City and got out of the game at a young age.

'And we all know what happened to Justin. It's a shame because he was a good boy. He really was a good boy and it's a real shame – even more so than Kevin.

'They started well; they did well; they worked hard. I was like the old man to them. I cajoled them, I helped them, obviously as John and Ken did, and they really did well for themselves.'

There was, it seems, much of Martin Peters in Kevin Reeves. Both were naturally at ease with the ball; both enjoyed an instinctive eye for goal; both had a quiet, steely determination to make the most of their many footballing gifts.

'Kevin was a thinking footballer. But unfortunately at the end of the day, I don't think Kevin had an opportunity – his career ended too early,' said Martin, noting the way that he himself matured as a player in his late 20s – a chance denied the luckless Reeves.

'He wasn't very old, was he – when he had to give up? 26 maybe. I was 26 when I went to Spurs and I really changed as a person – and to some degree in the way I played. I was very naïve as a kid and as a player. But when you're older then, with learning, you can take yourself on to another, higher plane.

'And Kevin never had the chance to do that; never had the chance to take it on. He still had that nice boy image that he always had. And he was a very nice lad. A real class act.'

Throw in the return of Graham Paddon and the emergence of Kevin Bond from beneath his father's imposing shadow to the Peters, Fashanu and Reeves show and come Martin's final season in a Canary shirt, Norwich were still finishing in comfortable mid-table. Mission accomplished as far as the player himself was concerned. The fact that he was making 48 league and cup appearances that season merely added to the Peters legend. His final game was at home to Derby County, on 3 May 1980. City won 4–2 and finished the campaign in 12th position.

'The job I was taken there to do I achieved – by getting them up, albeit ten games,' said Martin, whose greater achievements were still to come. 'That and keeping them in the old First Division.'

Precisely – that was Martin Peters' lasting claim to Canary fame. In fact, Norwich never really came close to the drop with their very own World Cup winner in their midst.

'We didn't have that many close calls. It was always reasonably comfortable mid-table or just below. Certainly in my last season there I think we were quite comfortable. We ended up beating Derby 4–2 at home.

'Personally, I think that was a success. Whether John did I don't know – I think he was happy to keep the Club in the old First Division.'

When it came to moving on, his body had little or nothing to do with it. Time was far from catching up with the seemingly ageless City star. To Martin's lasting regret, it was the money that did the talking when he left for a player-coach role at Sheffield United in the summer of 1980.

'It was the '80–81 pre-season and John spoke to me about the interest. I think I had one year left on my Norwich contract,' said Martin.

'I made a mistake – I shouldn't have gone. Should have stayed at Norwich. It was an offer I couldn't turn down – but I should have done. There were not too many mistakes in my career, but that was one of them.

'I rue the day that I did it, really. I guess it was the money. Which was the wrong reason. And the opportunity to get into coaching because I did want to do that. There was an opportunity and it was a big club. But it didn't turn out right for me. I shouldn't have gone.'

Not that he severed all his Norfolk ties. The family stayed put as Martin commuted to Sheffield and within little more than a year, Dad was back on a full-time basis – helping out Yarmouth Pleasure Beach owner Jimmy Jones with a spot of PR and playing for Gorleston to boot.

It was all further evidence of an Essex boy that had long been won over by both club and county. The passing years serve only to soften the heart even further.

'I see it as a very enjoyable time. I loved playing for the Club and we lived in the area for eight and a half years,' said Martin, well aware of the pivotal role he played in the Club's history – keeping the Club afloat in the First Division as John Bond and his No.2, Ken Brown, slowly dismantled the legacy of Ron Saunders and, bit by bit, began to fashion a side and a playing ethos of their own. In simply buying the Club that kind of time – and, above all, the chance to rebuild and regroup in the middle of the First Division as opposed to the midst of either a fraught relegation fight or a tight promotion battle – Martin's lasting place in City's history is assured. The London boy done good.

'I think before they thought I was this "London boy"; they were not so sure about London people. But once I managed to get them on my side, it was good,' said Martin. 'Working with the past as Dunc and Dave became and the future – as Justin and Kevin became.

'And, hopefully, I gave the older supporters who saw me playing there a few more good memories. And I understand, and I am very proud, that I was voted the best player to have played for Norwich City a few years ago. That means a lot to me.'

A testimonial game in the midst of the 1978–79 season saw player and supporters cement their bond as 19,000 City fans saluted not just Martin, but seven of his fellow 1966 World Cup heroes.

'It was a fantastic night,' he said simply. 'I think eight out of the eleven played and it was great for the supporters to see the likes of Bobby Charlton, Jimmy Greaves, Bobby Moore, Geoff Hurst, Roger Hunt come to play at Carrow Road – even if it was a testimonial.'

As a one-off night it marked a very special moment in Martin's career. 'Everything else I achieved was with a team, but that night – that was just for me and my family, I guess. Sir Alf Ramsey was there. It was really good. Very special.'

It created a warmth and a respect that lasts to this day. 'I like to think there's still a lot of affection for my time at the Club in the city, in Norfolk. People still recognise me when I go there. People come up to me and say: "Hello, Martin!" and things like that and I'm very happy.

'But then I'm very lucky that out of the four clubs that I played for, I get good responses from three of them – West Ham, Spurs and Norwich. Not Sheffield and I don't expect it, to be honest. It was a cock-up. I should have stayed at Norwich longer.'

7 Kevin Reeves

Kevin Reeves took the popular path from Bournemouth's Dean Court to Carrow Road. After progressing through the ranks at his local club, a chance to try his luck in the top flight was offered by the Canaries. After an initial trial spell, John Bond had no hesitation in spending £50,000 on bringing the teenager to Carrow Road on a permanent basis in February 1977.

Kevin wasted little time in making his mark at Norwich and soon became a firm favourite with the Carrow Road faithful. Goals flowed and international recognition followed, firstly with the England under-21s and 'B' team before he earned two full caps while plying his trade in Norfolk.

A £1 million move to Manchester City followed, as Kevin became the first in a long list of players to leave Carrow Road for that magic seven-figure-plus fee. The move angered fans who felt the sale was to finance the new River End Stand at Carrow Road. Indeed to this day the stand is still referred to as the 'Kevin Reeves Stand' by a small section of fans.

Always popular at Carrow Road, Kevin received a great reception when he returned to Carrow Road for the Club's Centenary celebrations in 2002.

Kevin Philip Reeves

Born: Burley, 20 October 1957
City Debut: 15 January 1977, Arsenal (a) 0–1 Division One
Final Game: 8 March 1980, Brighton & Hove Albion (h) 2–2 Division One
League appearances: 119
League goals: 37
FA Cup appearances: 5
FA Cup goals: Nil
League Cup appearances: 9
League Cup goals: 5
Total appearances: 133
Total goals: 42

It was, I'm sure, not the first time it had been suggested. Likewise, I'm sure it wasn't the first time that he'd admitted as much.

But the story of Kevin Reeves' three years at Carrow Road is inextricably linked with the John Bond tale. The former City boss did, after all, pluck the South Coast teenager out of relative obscurity in January 1977 and, if after something of a false start on his Canary debut against Arsenal, put his young charge on the road to a £1 million transfer as his England international career began to take off.

The two men would, of course, be reunited at Manchester City and again at Burnley where Kevin's playing career would come to an all-too-early end. Little surprise, therefore, that many have chosen to see the Reeves-Bond show as being kindled from something approaching a father-son relationship – a suggestion that Kevin himself doesn't deny after losing his own father within weeks of his arrival in Norfolk.

Coming on the eve of his first derby appearance away at Ipswich Town on 15 February 1977, it was a moment that appeared to deepen further the pair's respect for each other – as well as persuading Kevin's grieving mother that her boy had joined a decent club; a family club that always looked after its own.

'My mother still talks about it now – that when she went to my dad's funeral there was a massive bouquet of yellow flowers with Norwich City Football Club on it,' said Kevin.

'That recollection has stuck with my mother ever since. She's never forgotten it. Did Bondy become this father figure to me when my dad died? I think he did, yes.

'My dad had had a stroke and was paralysed down one side for about ten years but he passed away on the Sunday and we were playing Ipswich on the Tuesday. So obviously it was a big decision whether I should play in the derby or not. And I remember the respect he gave me when my father died, in terms of the Ipswich game, and whether I played. He sort of left it with me completely.

'To be honest from my point of view it was a nice way to relieve it for me, so I played. We lost 5–0. Shocking day.'

Shocking day it may have been, but out of such tragedy lasting bonds were formed – be it between player and manager, mother and football club, the Reeves family's affection for Norwich City Football Club was firmly up and running.

The Kevin Reeves story actually begins in the leafy surroundings of Dean Court, Bournemouth – or rather amongst the wild ponies of the New Forest where Kevin was actually raised.

As he followed in his cousin's footsteps and began to show real footballing promise, so the first big career decision of his life swiftly loomed – whether to stick with family tradition and opt for The Dell, the old home of Southampton Football Club, or go for a footballing apprenticeship at Bournemouth.

'Southampton or Bournemouth, I had a choice of the two,' said Kevin, about to buck the recent Reeves trend. 'My cousin had played for Southampton, my brother had been an apprentice there. In fact, my cousin

1 Bernard Robinson

ABOVE LEFT On the run, Bernard in action during an early match at Carrow Road.

ABOVE RIGHT A youthful Bernard at the start of his Canary career.

RIGHT September 2002 and Bernard (right) is joined by the late Ron Ashman at Carrow Road for the Centenary celebrations.

2 Johnny Gavin

A man with an eye for goal – record goalscorer Johnny Gavin.

3 Terry Allcock

ABOVE LEFT Terry in action during the famous 1958–59 cup run.

ABOVE RIGHT Putting pen to paper – flanked by Chairman Geoffrey Watling (left) and Manager Archie Macaulay, Terry signs for City in 1958.

BOTTOM With 223 Canary goals between them – Terry Allcock and Iwan Roberts.

Plate II

4 Dave Stringer

LEFT Dave looks on from the bench as City boss in the early 1990s.

ABOVE In his playing days ahead of the 1971–72 promotion-winning season.

5 David Cross

BELOW Friends reunited – David meets up with Duncan Forbes during the celebrations that marked the 30th anniversary of the 1971–72 promotion-winning campaign.

RIGHT During his playing days.

6 Martin Peters

World Cup winner Martin Peters enjoyed five great seasons with the Canaries.

7 Kevin Reeves

RIGHT Kevin swings in another tantalising cross from the right during City's 1979–80 campaign.

BELOW Kevin heads for goal during a 3–0 victory over Leeds United at Carrow Road in 1978.

8 Dave Watson

ABOVE Dave with the 1985–86 Second Division championship-winning team.

LEFT Captain Dave shows the City faithful the trophy during a lap of honour of Carrow Road after winning the 1985-86 Second Division title.

BELOW His finest hour with Norwich – Dave holds aloft the Milk Cup at Wembley in 1985.

Plate V

9 Jerry Goss

ABOVE Gossy smashes home the equaliser against Bayern Munich during City's 1993–94 UEFA Cup campaign.

LEFT Man of the Match against Ipswich Town in 1993 after scoring the only goal of the game.

BELOW Happy days – Gossy celebrates the win in Munich with Chris Sutton (left) and Rob Newman (right).

Plate VI

10 Bryan Gunn

LEFT All smiles – Bryan in action during the 1989–90 season.

BELOW Top-stopper – Gunny prepares to smother the ball during a goalless draw at Villa Park in 1994.

11 Iwan Roberts

RIGHT Something to shout about – Iwan puts City in front in Cardiff.

ABOVE Iwan and son Ben with the First Division championship trophy.

12 Nigel Worthington

BELOW Training time – Nigel gets down to business at the Club's Colney training centre.

RIGHT Reaping the rewards – Nigel with the First Division championship trophy at City Hall during the 2004 civic reception.

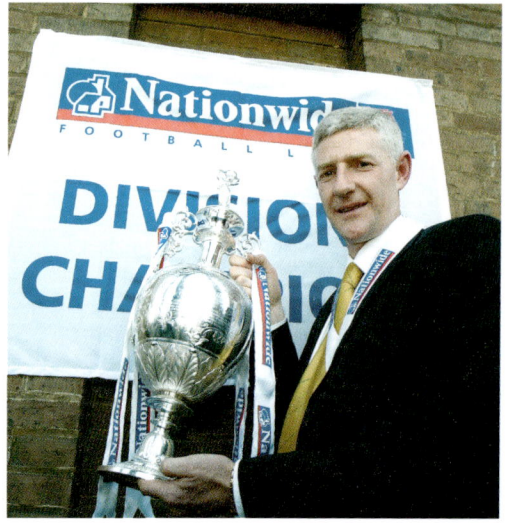

Plate viii

– Derek Reeves – still holds the record there for most goals in a season. So there was a lot of family influence to go there, but I'd been to school in Christchurch which was midway between Southampton and Bournemouth; I'd played for Bournemouth Schools; it was the next, logical progression for me to go to Bournemouth. I was more comfortable with the place, really.'

It was a decision that would have lasting implications, given the man in charge of the Cherries as 14-year-old Kevin signed his schoolboy forms – John Bond.

This time, however, the two didn't exactly have much time to gel as Bond packed his bags for Norfolk and promptly took half the club with him. He'd just return for Kevin a few years later – once his long-time pal 'Benno' gave him the wink.

'There was a bit of bad feeling at the time between Bournemouth and Norwich with John Bond taking all those players with him – Dave Jones, Tony Powell, Mel Machin all went,' said Kevin, now a 16-year-old apprentice under Bond's successor Trevor Hartley.

Kevin Bond, Phil Boyer and, if in a rather more roundabout way, Ted MacDougall, would all tread an increasingly familiar path between Bournemouth and Norwich as Bond began to fashion his own side out of Ron Saunders' legacy.

Not that it was all one-way traffic. John Benson would head back to the South Coast to take over the reins at Dean Court – just in time to hand the club's blossoming young striker his first-team debut.

'It was John Benson who gave me my debut and a year and half later he'd sold me to Norwich,' said Kevin, as the Bond-Benson link ensured that the Cherries became something of a nursery club for the Carrow Road side.

That said, Kevin's move still came as something of a bolt from the blue as the 19-year-old – with 20 goals from his 63 Bournemouth appearances – suddenly found himself on a bus bound for Highbury, having planned his weekend around a rather more humble trip to Hartlepool.

'I was completely unaware of anything happening until a Thursday training session at Bournemouth,' recalled Kevin. 'We were due to be playing Hartlepool away on the Saturday and Benno called me out of training and said: "Look, Norwich have come in for you and want to take you on loan..."

'I think they had a few injury problems at the time, so I ended up playing at Highbury on the Saturday instead of Hartlepool, which was a bit of a culture shock.

'To be honest on the day it was a bit much for me and I got dragged off after about 70-odd minutes.'

Kevin's cause was probably not helped by Bond's typically understated reaction to the young man's arrival in City's midst. Had there been a

'Match of the Week' ahead of that Arsenal game, 'This boy is going to be shenshational, Gerry!' may well have crossed his lips.

'I think it certainly had an impact on the way I played on that Saturday,' said Kevin, as Bond sung his praises to whoever would listen.

'I remember going down to the hotel in north London on the Friday night and we had a lot of media attention – that was all new to me. It was a fantastic occasion to make your debut, but it did get to me on the day, I think. I can't remember too much about the night before – only that the whole thing was surreal in a way.

'From thinking you were going away to Hartlepool and ending up at Highbury was very strange. And the actual game was probably the first time I'd been in a football match when my legs didn't respond to the rest of my body.'

At least the highlights on *Match Of The Day* that night spared many of the young man's blushes. It would also serve a second, greater purpose in that it enabled Kevin's father to see his son make his first appearance in the top flight of English football before he died little more than a month later.

'The highlights weren't too bad, really. They were fairly flattering, but I knew myself that I'd had a nightmare that day. But my dad was alive at the time, and it was great for him to have seen me play in the First Division,' said Kevin, now fearing that his loan spell at Norwich would be just that – a brief loan and a "Thanks, but no thanks!" at the end of it.

'I feared the worse, to be honest, when I came off,' said Kevin, eager to be up and on his way from Dean Court after serving his lower league apprenticeship in a manner very similar to David Cross's 60-game education at Rochdale.

'I think from my career point of view I probably needed to go somewhere, to do something. I'd had a great first season at Bournemouth; goal scoring was OK in the second season, but I was not playing quite so well.

'I think Bondy thought I had the potential to play at that level and perhaps I just needed to get away from the area to fulfil that.'

Playing at a higher level would, in any case, prove that much easier for a young man whose game was not based around such lower league virtues as strength, power and the possession of two, sharp elbows. Kevin Reeves was always a player and in the First Division – as they still do in the Premiership today – players got the chance to play.

'I don't think it's changed – even nowadays,' said Kevin. 'I think if you have ability it's easier to play at a higher level. You certainly do pick things up from the lower leagues, but I would have to say in the First Division at that time there were still many tough lads at centre-halves.'

One, of course, awaited him at Trowse as Kevin began to settle in to his new surroundings.

'Forbesy was unbelievable. He was as tough as they come at any level – and sometimes in the First Division they're a bit cuter as well. So it was a hard league.

'But Duncan (Forbes) was a lesson in himself in training. I was always a very determined lad. I could take the knocks and it didn't bother me.

'But Forbesy was unbelievable. I remember controlling a few balls and then the next thing I know I'm up in the air. And I'd say to him: "What are you doing?" and his classic line was: "I'm going for the ball!" when the ball was about three yards in front of him with a pair of legs in between. It didn't bother him.

'He would also give everyone a nickname within five minutes of them being in the football club. He reckoned that I looked like Sylvester Stallone off *Rocky* so he started calling me "Rocky" after about 20 minutes.'

It was all part of a warm welcome for the Norwich new boy as he swiftly settled into a dressing room that not only boasted such a Norfolk institution as Duncan Forbes, but a World Cup winner in Martin Peters.

'Martin was a very quiet, but lovely man and I think he would try and welcome anybody to any football club and try and settle them in. Kevin Keelan was a character; real laugh-a-minute; always immaculately dressed. But then I don't think there was anybody at the Club who you could look at and say: "I'm not too sure about him…" or "I'm not particularly keen on him…" or whatever. It was a great bunch of lads.'

But, above them all, presided John Bond. Schooled in the West Ham way under Ron Greenwood at Upton Park, the City manager had little time for the Ron Saunders way. Yes, he liked his players to be fit; yes, he liked his players to work. But just as all work and no play made Jack a very dull boy, so work, work, work was not the Bondy way. He wanted to play. He wanted to entertain.

And in the likes of first Martin Peters and then Kevin Reeves he brought players to the Club that were just that – players.

'Bondy was a very, very forward-thinking coach. He knitted it all together and I think the players, particularly the likes of Martin, had a lot of respect for Bondy as well.

'Plus he would always be receptive to people having an opinion as well. Particularly people like Martin, Kevin Keelan and people like that. He would listen to them – and then do his own thing anyway.

'He was very gregarious, very enthusiastic, with a real outgoing nature – which all rubbed off on the players. At times he was infectious. In training sessions he would get involved and if you didn't pass the ball within a yard of his feet, he would stamp his feet, look at you and criticise you. He was notorious for it, but it was all part of a joke within the Club. The lads would just laugh.

'And if you were playing well and doing well then he was fantastic. He would put his arm round you; give you plenty of confidence and a lot of accolades. Not only privately; but in front of the team and in the press as well. I thought he was superb in that respect. The spirit was superb.'

There was, as always, a flip side to the heaps of praise that the manager would liberally sprinkle around that dressing room. There was a spot of rough to go with all that smooth.

'You certainly had to be able to take a rocketing from Bondy because that was something else. I got used to it over the years and I think as long as you picked out something relevant from it, learned from it and got on with it you were OK. But you had to be able to take those because there was a few floating about – and it tended to be the centre-forwards and full-backs that got it the most.'

Part of that was undoubtedly inspired by nothing more malicious than a real passion for the game. Call it enthusiasm bubbling over.

'The only thing I would say with John was sometimes that if you couldn't handle the criticism then you very often fell by the wayside. But that was just his nature. He was so passionate about the game that it would definitely spill over – particularly into his half-time talks and end-of-match talks.'

It was a rare chink in Bond's armour. Like his No.2 Ken Brown, it was part of his success as a manager that he could blend such a rich array of characters together and still command their respect and attention. The manner in which someone of Peters' ilk played for him over the course of his five years at the Club is another testament to Bond's ability to manage.

'One of the joint strengths that both he and Ken had was, despite all those characters, he let them live. He let them breathe, but he still managed them.

'I think any manager worth his salt has to be like that – I think any manager in any business has to be like that.

'Bondy had an eye for a player; he knew the way he wanted the game played. And you can't have people like Martin Peters, a World Cup winner, play superbly for five and a half years for Norwich if you've not got something as a manager.'

Playing with Martin Peters was, it seems, a revelation for a young man just finding his feet in the game. 'I think Martin was the best player I played with,' said Kevin, as he began to play the wizard's apprentice.

'Sometimes people would say he never really stood out in games, but he is unbelievably simple. You look at him sometimes and he's passed the ball five yards and you think: "Why's he done that?" But it was the right ball to play at the right time. Plus he obviously had this other ability of finding space in the box and scoring goals.'

After the false start at Highbury, fortune now rode to the on-loan youngster's rescue. Dropped for the home game against Liverpool the following week in favour of his new pal and fellow teenager Roger Gibbons, an injury to Viv Busby that day forced Bond to reshuffle his strike pack again for the home clash with Stoke City a week later. Two minutes into his first appearance at Carrow Road and Kevin was banishing those Highbury blues with his first goal for the Club. That first fortnight had also bought Kevin just the time he needed to win over early doubters around the training ground.

'I'm from a small village in the New Forest and while I'd played for Bournemouth it was a big step up from that to a First Division club – particularly being amongst players that you knew about.

'But I have to say that, after that initial game against Arsenal, I settled in fairly quickly. I was able to train for a couple of weeks with the players and I think, without blowing my own trumpet, once you've shown them you've got ability and you can train with the best of them, then you get that respect. You're welcomed into the fold a little bit better.'

Come the Stoke game, however, and Kevin knew the clock was ticking on his one-month loan spell. 'There was only about a week to go before I was due to go back to Bournemouth. Because Bondy was sending me back – there was no two ways about that.'

Cue one of those life-changing moments. 'As I say I had improved with training through those two weeks and I think that caught the eye a little. But to score after two minutes, so early on in the game, it gave me an enormous confidence boost just to score at that time and it all went on from there.

'It's amazing how it snowballs, really. I scored against Stoke and then towards the end of that season I was scoring pretty freely really,' said Kevin, the ink long dry on his £50,000 permanent switch from Dean Court.

Indeed, come the end of the 1976–77 season and Kevin would finish as the Club's second top scorer with eight goals from his 21 league appearances – three behind Busby.

'The one against Manchester United was particularly pleasing – it ended up being the winner as well and we had a good finish to the season,' said Kevin, his style of play long since evident. For that he had one of his Dean Court mentors to thank – Phil Boyer.

'I was never an out-and-out goalscorer. When I actually went to watch Bournemouth as a kid, Ted (MacDougall) was the goalscorer, Phil Boyer was one that worked off him and I always tried to be something like Phil.'

For anyone requiring an up-to-date point of reference think more Alan Smith than Craig Bellamy, and with a little less of the pair's attitude.

'I worked off a front man, off a big man; I'd work the channels; back to goal mainly. I think Craig likes it over the top – he's got pace to get away from people. I was more a twister and turner, into feet. But I think my anticipation was good. If it was going up to Justin or whoever, then I read the flick-ons pretty well. More Alan Smith, I would say.

'Plus I think my awareness was good; probably I wasn't as greedy as I should have been, but that's the way I was. I think my temperament was good as well. I didn't miss many games. And though unfortunately I retired through injury at 26, I didn't miss many games up until then. I was always getting in 40-odd games a season.'

And the more he worked with Messrs Bond and Brown, the more his appreciation of time and space – that West Ham way of doing things – grew.

'I think a lot of the ability is natural, but what Bondy gave me was he opened up my eyes to the timing of runs. Where to run – things like that. He made me more aware of the game itself. And that was the key for me because I was bright enough to take it on board and to learn from that.'

Come the following season and Kevin was proving to be a model pupil as he hit 12 goals from his 37 First Division appearances that season. As for a strike partner, a succession of names came and went before, finally, in January 1979, he found his ideal match – a former British Schools heavyweight boxing finalist and Dr Barnardo's boy, Justinus Soni Fashanu. Raised in the Norfolk countryside with his younger brother John by loving foster parents, Fashanu was just 17 years old when he made his debut alongside Kevin in a 1–1 draw at home to West Bromwich Albion on 13 January 1979.

Over the next 14 months, together the pair would score 34 goals between them in 104 league and cup appearances. On paper perhaps not the most prolific partnership of all time, but one that still resonates real class down the passing years. After all, both were still young men when each left with £1 million cheques attached.

'I remember Justin as a kid coming through; seeing this fantastically confident lad being interviewed on TV and radio a couple of times as I was walking out of Trowse…He had a great way about him with the press and I would say that, out of all the players that I played there with, Justin was the most enjoyable for me to play alongside

'He was a tough lad; a hard lad; took all the knocks; created goals as well as scored them…For me he never got the credit he deserved for simply the ability he had as a footballer. Justin was equal to John, if not better.

'You know it's a funny thing when you're at a football club and you've got four or five strikers there – all you're concerned about, first and foremost, is keeping your position…So at that time I was thinking Justin's got a great talent there – I hope it's not my position he's going to take. But fortunately I managed to keep my place and when he got in the side I think we worked off each other really well. He was a great foil for me and I was for him as well.

'He had a decent touch. He was a powerful lad; wasn't frightened of anybody; he had this real cockiness that obviously helped with his game. Sometimes he looked a bit gangly and then he'd strike the ball out of nowhere.'

As he did to memorable effect in an extraordinary 5–3 home defeat by Liverpool on 9 February 1980. It was the goal that, in many ways, proved to be Justin's lasting legacy as player. Everyone remembers that goal, that Goal of the Season.

'I remember the goal he scored in the Liverpool game. He wasn't really particularly strong with his left foot, but that was what he was capable of. He could go from looking gangly to produce a bit of quality like that.

'And as I say Justin was a lovely lad, a great character, and I think everybody liked him in the side. He had this little bit of a nasty streak that caught him out a couple of times with Bondy. I remember him elbowing Steve Foster against Brighton once and it was a real nasty one. He'd gone up for a header and just whacked him in the face and got sent off. And Bondy slaughtered him.

'I'm sure Justin would argue, as well as most centre-forwards, that he was using his elbows to climb, but he did have that little bit about him. It would now and again flare up out of nowhere; he could look after himself. But I think that also helped him with his reputation. I think there were a few centre-halves that were frightened of Justin.'

And whilst they were getting embroiled with the former schoolboy boxer, Kevin was left to play his stuff.

'It definitely helped me. It was a case of: "Off you go Justin! You take care of the centre-half. Let me play all the stuff, you take the knocks…"

'The only thing with that was that Justin always used to get the big, bruising centre-half – and I used to prefer the big, bruising centre-half because I was good with my feet. I could twist and turn and they were sometimes a bit cumbersome. So I very often ended up with the more cultured centre-half playing against me.

'A prime example was Roy McFarland who looked after Justin and Colin Todd, who was the best centre-half I played against in terms of reading the game. I always found it difficult playing against him.'

Kevin was long gone by the time Justin made his ill-fated move to Nottingham Forest. Both in terms of his professional and his personal life, Justin would never quite seem to enjoy the same sure foothold on this world that he had at Norwich. He was at home in Norfolk. He was safe. Secure. It's where Kevin remembers him best – as the confident, cocky kid giving his radio interviews on the steps of the old training ground at Trowse.

'It was just a bad move for Justin. And then all the other things cropped up as well. When he was a young lad at Norwich – just coming through – those are probably my happiest thoughts of him.'

Out of Norfolk, the world somehow seemed a far more brutal, unforgiving place as Justin's personal and professional life began to unravel with, ultimately, tragic consequences.

'I had a mate of mine who lived in Nottingham, my best mate actually, and he was always filling me in with what was happening at Nottingham Forest with Justin and the stuff that came out about his private life,' said

Kevin, like so many of his ex-Canary colleagues wholly unaware of the complex character in their midst.

'When it all came out about him being gay I was surprised in many ways because I remember him having this gorgeous-looking girlfriend at Norwich,' said Kevin.

'He was very much an individual. I wouldn't say he was a loner because he was a real sociable lad. At functions and things he was a very funny lad as well, had a good sense of humour and a cheeky way about him.

'Remember we're talking about a young lad who has come in and held his own in a fairly strong dressing room. And Norwich hadn't had too many coloured lads at that time. So the two of them – Justin and John – needed to be strong characters from day one.

'I think Justin still holds a special place in the supporters' hearts and I'm pleased about that because all he ever did for Norwich were good things. And you speak as you find. Over the years I've been asked questions many times about Justin and all I can say is he was a lovely lad. He was a great character and a great footballer. That's as much as I can say about him.'

It was that strength of character that Kevin thought would stand Justin in such good stead – particularly given the character that awaited him at the City Ground, Forest boss Brian Clough.

'When he first went there, I thought it was a good move for him. And although Cloughie was a very strong character, I knew Justin well as well and I thought he would be strong enough to be able – not so much as have a go back – but be his own man and take in whatever Cloughie had to offer. At the end of the day, just get on with the job and do his stuff. I thought he was more than strong enough to take it at that time.'

Back at Carrow Road, safe on his home turf, Kevin and Justin had undoubtedly clicked on the pitch – not hard when they were given all the help in the world from the likes of Paddon and Peters. Having a manager like Bond also helped – it was part and parcel of the West Ham way to provide telling and intelligent service to the front two.

'The majority of my goals would have come from crosses really. Bondy used to work so much on that – when to get the ball wide, the timing of the run to the box; all that.

'I more often than not would go near post and Justin would speed down to the far post and then if it did go far, it was a case of looking back for the flick-ons from Justin. I think I scored a lot of headers. I like to think I was fairly decent in the air as well and brave – you had to put your head where you might get hurt.

'I didn't think of it as bravery as such. If there was a chance of a goal I'd do it. There's nothing quite like scoring.'

It was all part of the reason why the Canary faithful took the quiet young man from the New Forest so much to their hearts. Sure, he was a player. But he always tried and every crowd loves somebody like that.

Kevin Reeves

'I was fortunate – the fans took to me. And there's nothing better than having your name sung out before every game, let alone afterwards if you've done well.

'What you always have to bear in mind is the fact that the adoration you get from the fans is there – but it can go. They'll accept it maybe if you're not playing too well, but they will not accept a lack of effort. And I can hold my hand on my heart and say I never gave less than 100 per cent and I think the fans could see that as well.

'There were certain times when maybe things were a little bit low, but they were always with me – all the time I was there. You sensed that even if I went through a barren patch and didn't score for six games or whatever, that it was actually a relief for those fans when I did score. They were fantastic. Through the years the Norwich fans – like Ian Crook subsequently – they like a player don't they? And they like good football as well.

'And the one thing I will say about Norwich fans, and that's only through my experience of being at other clubs and being around other grounds, is that they're not so quick to jump on your back there either.'

Not that they had much reason. After all, it wasn't every day that the City supporters had a fully-fledged England international in their midst. For having first come to the attention of the national selectors as an England Youth international at Bournemouth, Kevin continued to rise up through the ranks while at Norwich.

'It was a steady progression. I played for England Youth when I was at Bournemouth so I was known within the England set-up which is the crucial thing,' said Kevin, well aware that – even today – asking anyone from the upper echelons of the England Establishment to get their butt up the A11 once in a while is next-to-nigh impossible. Once again Bondy's friends in high places would help. For by now a certain Mr R Greenwood was England manager.

'When I went to Norwich, of course, Ron Greenwood was the England manager and Bondy had a great relationship with him. I think he was instrumental in people coming to watch me – and, to be fair, the press. They, I would say, more than anybody, helped to get me into the England squad. They were raving about my performances.'

First off, however, were several tours of duty with the England under-21s – trips away that would not only introduce the Carrow Road favourite to some of his future senior international colleagues, but, in the case of his England under-21 room-mate and pal Gary Owen, would also put one early plank in place when it came to pondering a move to Manchester City.

'I remember I made my England under-21 debut in the Olympic Stadium in Rome in the quarter-finals of the European under-21 Championships. Glenn Hoddle was there, Peter Reid, Peter Barnes, Gary (Owen), Graham Rix, Chris Woods in goal.'

His senior debut would finally arrive against Bulgaria in 1980. For all the people back in little old Norwich it was quite a day – or rather quite a night – when one of their own stepped out in an England jersey.

'It was a massive thing for them – the support, the telegrams and the coverage I got for that was unbelievable. I think people were very proud. With Norwich being a bit of a backwater and out on a limb a bit, that somebody from the Club had got into the England squad was a big, big thing.'

It almost never happened. A spot of fog ruined Kevin Keegan's week, but – 24 hours later when it had finally cleared – made Kevin Reeves' night.

'Glenn (Hoddle) was always going to make his debut that night, but on the Wednesday the game was due to be played, the fog came to my rescue. Keegan was in Hamburg at the time and once the game was put back 24 hours to the Thursday night, Hamburg refused to let Keegan play. So I took his place and ended up making my debut.'

By now a big-money move was firmly in the wind. After all, full England internationals don't tend to stay too long at Norwich – even if they are more than happy to stay put. However bitter a pill it is to swallow at the time, some moves simply develop a momentum and a logic all of their own. For Kevin Reeves read Chris Sutton and Craig Bellamy. There was a similar air of inevitability hanging around Carrow Road that season – even if Bond managed to parry Manchester City's first advance.

'I'm not even sure if the fans were aware of the first bid earlier on in the season, probably not,' said Kevin. Trevor Francis was setting the tone by becoming the first £1-million player in English football when he switched from Birmingham City to Nottingham Forest – just as Malcolm Allison was setting his sights on prising Kevin out of Carrow Road.

'Trevor had gone – the first million-pound player – and it was just after that,' said Kevin. 'Bondy called me and said: "Look, City have come in for you!"

'We were going well at the time and I said: "I'm not sure – I'm enjoying it here, scoring goals. I think I'll stay put for a bit."

'I didn't want to go at that time, I was happy at Norwich and Bondy was great. He said: "If you don't want to go, don't go!" So there was no: "Look, we need the money!" There was no pressure on me at all which was great as far as I was concerned. Then it sort of crept up.'

By now million-pound moves were all the rage, as Allison's wild spending spree saw Steve Daley arrive at their then home of Maine Road for the magic seven-figure mark, while Sky TV pundit Andy Gray also went for the million.

'I ended up being the fourth,' said Kevin, whose last City appearance came at home to Brighton & Hove Albion on Saturday, 8 March 1980.

'I think circumstances had changed. The first approach came fairly early in the season and when it came up again, the Club had drifted off a little bit. And it was a big offer. They had increased it again so I went.

'In the end, the move to City turned out to be a great one. But my football suffered when I first went there – I think to the detriment of me staying in the England side.

'Because when I got my second cap I wasn't playing well for Man City – and in a team that was struggling. Maybe if I had stayed at Norwich then maybe I'd have got a few more England caps because my form was really good with them. And Norwich is one of those clubs that you can quite happily stay at for a long time.'

The move – almost inevitably – roused fierce emotions amongst the supporters as they feared the Canaries were simply settling for life as a mid-table First Division side. Where was the ambition to make the next step up? To follow Ipswich's example and become a top three side – as they were that season – and gain a regular ticket to Europe into the bargain.

"No Reeves, no fans, no future!" ran the banner, as a bitter round of soul-searching began. The fact that the coveted Carrow Road star in question wouldn't be 23 until the following autumn hardly helped their dark mood. In age terms alone, Kevin had the best years of his footballing life before him. He was to be someone else's future, not Norwich's.

'For me it was flattering, the fact that the fans thought that much of me,' said Kevin, equally aware that a £1 million cheque was nigh-on impossible for either Bond or then chairman Sir Arthur South to ignore.

'Basically it came down to economics as well. Breaking that £1-million barrier for a player was massive at the time. I've been coaching for the last 20-odd years now, and it's probably worth about £20 million in today's market.

'Did I want to stay at Norwich? Yes I did – the first time definitely. The second time, I think the Club were happy with the £1 million, as you would be really.

'Without it being like "You've got to go!" there was a bit more pressure. "It would be great for the Club, it would be great for you…" And I thought about it as well. I thought: "It's a big city club, we're in mid-table again, maybe I could go and win some trophies." So I think all round, second time round, it was great for everybody really.'

But the fans didn't see it that way.

Sir Arthur, it seems, was happy to stand back and let events take their course.

'Sir Arthur never influenced me in any way. I think he just let John get on with the job – whatever he thought. I'm sure in the background he was probably having a word with John, he must have been, but he never put any influence on me at all.

'He was a lovely fella'. The relationship between the players, directors and the chairman at Norwich was fantastic and you don't often get that. We used to get hampers at Christmas time. Not just with turkeys, but there'd be a couple of bottles of wine and goods. And we used to have a Christmas do every year with a big cabaret, in Norwich, at The Talk, and all those sort of things helped to make it a really friendly club.'

And just as legend maintains that Maurice Norman's exit to Spurs in 1955 paid for the first set of floodlights at Carrow Road, so Kevin Reeves' lasting legacy to the football club was the new River End Stand – the Norwich & Peterborough as it is now.

'That's right – yeah, that's my stand,' laughed Kevin, well aware of the link people make between his departure and the first, major re-development at Carrow Road since its opening 45 years earlier.

'It's amazing when I go back the people that remember that and speak to me about it. When I went to Man City people would send me clippings and things like that saying that it should be named after me. "The Kevin Reeves Stand".

'For me, it was just so flattering – the thought that something like that should be named after you and the fans wanted it named after you. And that fact has stuck.'

The time for the fond farewells came with that 2–2 draw against Brighton. 'I remember that last game against Brighton and coming off the pitch. I was nervous about the move and the fans knew as well, I think. A lot of them came on the pitch. I have a photograph at home of two lads with their arms around me walking off the pitch. I'd gone off in a nice way. I'd scored and set up the other one.

'I definitely wanted to go out with a bang. The fact that Man City want to pay £1 million for you means you're on cloud nine anyway, but it was a very sad day in a lot of respects. A lot of apprehension, and a lot of excitement about what was going to happen in the next stage of my career.'

Awaiting at Maine Road was, of course, one of football's more colourful characters, Malcolm Allison. Never one to do anything by halves, Allison flashed City's cash this way and that with little or no regard for either the club's bank balance or, just occasionally, to plump for a spot of experience ahead of the rich promise of youth.

'There was so much hype over the move – Steve Daley had come in just before me so there were City with two £1-million players,' said Kevin, finding in Allison a similar, camera-loving showman to Bond. Away from the bright lights and the microphone, however, Allison was a far quieter man than his lasting image would have you believe.

'Malcolm was larger-than-life outside the football club, but in it he was fairly quiet. He was a very astute coach, though his ideas at the time were really viewed as quite eccentric. Things like sports science, which have now come into the game. Looking back now, I think he was just well ahead of the game.

'But the major thing with Malcolm was that we were all just so young and inexperienced. I'd come in as a big £1-million player but I was still only 22. Steve Daley wasn't that much older. It was a difficult time. And the crowd at City were a demanding bunch if things weren't going well.'

With the likes of Kevin's England under-21 pal Gary Owen gone to West Bromwich Albion and such traditional Maine Road stalwarts as Dave Watson, Mick Channon and Dennis Tueart all departing, Allison's young guns were still struggling to fire on all cylinders come the start of the 1980–81 season. It was time for yet another change on Moss Side. And guess who is heading up the M6.

'I think we only had four points after 12 games. Though I got my second England cap, I wasn't playing well. But then Bondy comes and the whole thing turns round,' said Kevin, with John Bond succeeding Allison as Manchester City manager in October 1980 – little more than six months after Kevin had made exactly the same move north.

'Again it was great for me because I knew all about him. All the lads were asking me what he was like and I have to say he came in and turned the club around in that season. He knew the side needed a bit of experience, a bit of leadership, which it did. And he brought in big characters – people like Tommy Hutchison and Gerry Gow.

'He took over after 12 games and from there until the end of the season we had the best league record of any team in the league. We got to the FA Cup final that year; we got to the semi-final of the League Cup; we had that great league form. He just brought this massive confidence to the club and I think he was made for a big city club. He relished it.'

Manchester City being Manchester City, such glory, glory days inevitably ended in self-inflicted disaster as with Bond gone, Billy McNeill presided over relegation to the old Second Division.

Having barely missed a City first-team game and having scored 34 goals from his 130 senior appearances, for the first time in his playing life Kevin picked up an injury as the club crashed out of the First Division in the summer of 1983. With the Maine Road board and then chairman Peter Swales keen to cut their cloth accordingly, it was left to McNeill to make the phone call.

'The season Man City were relegated I picked up an injury and I got a phone call from Billy McNeill saying: "Well, we've obviously been relegated and wages need to be cut back. We might have to unload you." And I said: "Well it's up to you."'

McNeill was not the only familiar voice on the end of the phone that summer. One, in particular, had a trademark Cockney twang. 'I actually had a phone call from Terry Venables, he was at QPR. I knew Terry because he was my England under-21 coach and I loved him. I thought he was a fantastic coach and I was very taken with going to QPR.'

The other person on the phone needed no introduction. Bondy was back at Burnley. 'At the same time I got a call from Bondy. He said: "I've been given some money. Tommy Hutchison's coming to play, Gerry Gow, Willie Donachie. Come and be a part of what we're doing at Burnley."

'So I did. I was playing very well, scoring a lot of goals and then I had a hip injury. It was my groin first of all. I got my groin strapped up, but it was steadily getting worse. It was my hip, it wouldn't respond to treatment and that was the end of it really.' He was just 26 years old.

'I actually had a hip replacement about 12 years ago and the hip I've got has been absolutely fantastic. I play charity games and things. I don't know if it would have stood up to the rigours of First Division football, but the way it feels and the way it's been over the last ten years it hasn't hindered me at all in any of the coaching that I've done or the matches that I've played.'

Even Bondy couldn't prise a smile out of Mother Nature this time. He could sprinkle all the magical managerial dust he liked, but Kevin's reluctant hip refused to play ball. It was such a shame. After all, the two men made such a great team.

'Bondy was fantastic with players at that time,' said Kevin, citing one perfect example of how he looked after his boy.

'I remember when I joined the England under-21 squad he called me into the office,' said Kevin. 'Money was never the thing for me – it was playing football. And he knew that I wasn't any good at things like that and I didn't have an agent.

'So he called me in and said: "Look you're in the Under-21 squad now, I'm going to see the board about a pay rise – that's your reward for getting into the Under-21 squad."

'And in the end I had three wage rises in one year at Norwich – I got in the B squad and then, of course, the full squad. I think that's where the likes of myself and other people that have played for him have got so much respect for Bondy because he could have easily let it slide.

'But he'd call me in again and say: "Look you're an England B international now, you should be on this amount of money!" And he'd rip up my contract. And, as I say, I ended up signing three contracts in one year at Norwich. So you're always going to play for somebody like that. He looks after you.'

At which point we return to where the Kevin Reeves story first started – with a family-orientated football club that went out of its way to look after its own.

Do the Canaries still have that reputation for being a family club? 'They do,' said Kevin. 'It had it at the time I was there – that's for sure. And I think, talking to players that have been there down the years, they've experienced the same thing.

'Maybe it's because it is out on a limb and because of that people concentrate on looking after people a bit more. I think there are other clubs like that – I don't think it's exclusive to Norwich – but geographically they don't become much more remote, for a big club, than Norwich.

'I mean those are the things that stick in my mind – the hampers at

Christmas, the general friendliness, the fact that there were no barriers between the board and the players.'

Nor, it seems, were there many barriers between the players and the supporters, the players and the city. 'Within a week of signing at Manchester City we went on a penny-pushing charity thing and, on that occasion, we went with two Manchester United players.

'I couldn't believe it when you went into a pub. By about 9pm we were in this pub in Salford and the landlord was getting threatened for bringing in City players. You go out in Norwich and they're all Norwich fans. You might get the odd Ipswich fan that lives in Norwich, but in general everywhere you went in Norwich it was lovely. They were all friends.

'Everyone wanted to buy you a drink. It was a lovely city, a lovely place.'

8 Dave Watson

Surely one of the finest defenders to pull on a Norwich City shirt, Dave joined Norwich City as an unknown 19-year-old who'd played only a handful of matches for Liverpool reserves prior to arriving at Carrow Road in November 1980.

He enjoyed a rapid rise to fame with the Canaries under the watchful eyes of Ken Brown and Mel Machin. A tower of strength in the City defence for five years, Dave went on to captain the side and lift the Milk Cup at Wembley in March 1985.

His impressive displays for Norwich soon earned him deserved international recognition and he still remains the Canaries' most capped Englishman. A £1 million switch back to Merseyside came in the summer of 1986 as Dave joined Everton. He went on to enjoy further success at Goodison Park and in 1995, ten years after captaining the Canaries to Wembley glory, he lifted the FA Cup as Toffees' captain.

Always well respected and well thought of by the Carrow Road faithful Dave always enjoys a warm reception whenever he returns to Carrow Road.

David Watson

Born: Liverpool, 20 November 1961
City Debut: 26 December 1980, Ipswich Town (a) 0–2 Division One
Final Game: 6 May 1986, Liverpool (a) 1–3 Screen Sport Super Cup
League appearances: 212
League goals: 11
FA Cup appearances: 18
FA Cup goals: 1
League Cup appearances: 21
League Cup goals: 3
Other appearances: 5
Other goals: Nil
Total appearances: 256
Total goals: 15

These days 'Scottie Road' is a wide dual carriageway carrying the A59 swiftly north out of Liverpool city centre.

Long gone are the days when Scotland Road boasted a pub on every street corner, though the stories and the legends live on.

eight

Dave Watson

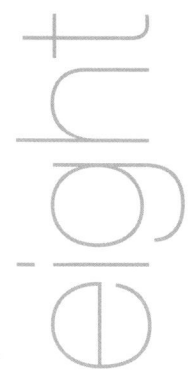

A tough, staunchly working-class area with a fierce sense of community, Scotland Road produced more than its fair share of characters, both good and bad. It wasn't, one suspects, an area of Liverpool that gave birth to shrinking violets and florists. Liverpool L3 forged rather tougher individuals – steely 16-year-olds whose first, natural instinct was to head for the docks in the search of a half-honest living and a regular weekly wage. Little surprise, that for one Liverpool Schoolboys star, vague promises of a football apprenticeship at Anfield didn't initially hold much appeal. Words didn't put food on the table. An apprenticeship as a sheet metal worker, now that did.

'It was a hard slog,' said Dave Watson, whose qualities as both a man and a footballer were swiftly being forged on a factory floor following a childhood on Scotland Road.

'There was all this banging machinery; it was a noisy factory; all heavy work with sheets of metal.

'But at the time it was a good job – don't get me wrong. I started off on £16.71 a week and by the time I left it was up to £65. But to carry on doing that for the rest of your life, well, it wouldn't have been as good as football, let's say.'

As it proved, football was very good to David Watson. But then he was a very good footballer. One, crucially, who knew exactly what it was like on the other side of the street. And he wasn't going back.

'As it turned out I was offered an apprenticeship at Liverpool,' said Dave. 'So I had this decision to make – do I want to become a footballer? Or stay in my job as a sheet metal worker?

'But if I made the decision to go and be a footballer, I'd have to go on to be a good one. Or else I'd just fall out and I wouldn't be able to walk back into a job.

'So once I opted to be a footballer, I thought I've got to do it properly. I've got to work as hard as I can. And that's what I did.'

Though not before turning down the chance to be an Anfield apprentice – opting, instead, for three years as a semi-pro, as the Liverpool teenager left his boyhood firmly behind and got himself a trade. That way, he reckoned, he was never going to be beholden to football's fickle fortunes. He'd find a way to stand on his own two feet and walk tall out of Scotland Road – with or without football's help.

'I decided to go to work and try and get a trade behind me because the chances of people making it in football were very slim, so I did sheet metal work for three years and got qualified.

'You hear stories of how some managers would take their teams down the mines to see how the miners used to work and things like that and it really does open your eyes – being at work for eight hours a day and then, after work, you've got to go and fit your training in.

'To go and be a footballer and knock all that work on the head, it really is a nice, comfortable job. You do need to experience the work side to appreciate the football more. I definitely did.'

It was, one senses, a hugely formative experience that made a man of the boy long before his teenage contemporaries at Anfield ever got out of their youth-team nappies. Scotland Road was, he admitted years later, 'quite a rough area.' A rough area that, in Norwich's case, yielded an absolute diamond.

'I got the call to go in and see Bob Paisley, the then Liverpool manager, and he just said that there's a club in the same division as ourselves that are interested in you – and it was Norwich.

'And he asked would I like to go down and have talks, which I did. So I came down and had a chat with Ken Brown and the two clubs agreed on a fee of £50,000 down, £50,000 after 20-odd appearances and if I was lucky enough to get an England cap – which Norwich and Liverpool tongue-in-cheek must have thought, he's got no chance of an England cap because I'd only played 12 reserve games – then they'll give him another £100,000.'

As transfer moves go, it was a master stroke. At that price, an act of nigh-on genius by Brown and Co. Dave had, after all, never got near to making a first-team appearance as the likes of Mark Lawrenson and Alan Hansen held sway. Indeed, the part-time centre-half had barely a dozen Central League games to his name, but someone, somewhere, had seen more than enough – even if the Canaries would have to "cough the full whack" once the boy from Scottie Road met the boys from Brazil on his England debut in the Maracana Stadium, Rio de Janiero, on 10 June 1984.

'I'm not sure whether it was Forbesy or it might have been Dave Stringer or Dougie (Livermore) saw me play at Villa Park in a Central League game – and they made a decision on that there and then. So all credit to them for spotting a bit of talent and making a decision that early on,' said Dave, ready for the move as opportunity suddenly knocked.

'I was quite realistic really because at Liverpool at the time in the first team they had players like Phil Thompson and Alan Hansen. Mark Lawrenson was about then.

'Whether if I'd have stayed there I'd have got in the first team only time would have told, but I wasn't really prepared to wait for two or three years to try and get a first-team chance because I thought you needed to be playing when you were 19, 20.'

Norwich, he admitted, might not have been his first choice. It wasn't exactly on the doorstep.

'When he said it was Norwich, I never actually jumped for joy. My instant reaction was that I'm moving away from home.

'But, on the other side of it, I thought I'd possibly get a chance of getting in the first team a little bit quicker than I would at Liverpool. So it had like a double-headed feel to it – a bit wary at first because of the sheer distance of the place, but optimistic of getting into the first team.'

Dave Watson

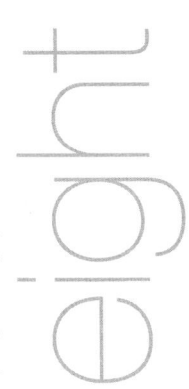

eight

It was, he would admit, a journey into the unknown, as budding star and his old man boarded the train for Norfolk in November 1980.

'I didn't really know an awful lot about it to be honest, apart from it always used to have one or two of the older players – I'd certainly never been there,' said Dave.

'I remember I got the train down with my dad and Norwich told us to travel first class so they must have had a few bob in those days. So me and my dad had a nice meal on the train going down, I think my dad must have drunk a bottle of brandy by the time we got there – and Ken met us at the station. It all happened from there, really.'

What follows is the bit that probably matters; the first hint of "the X-factor" that bound that particular dressing room together; that within five years would find Dave lifting the Milk Cup trophy at Wembley; within six, storming away with the old Division Two title in a memorable championship season.

For, as he himself would readily admit, Dave walked into a dressing room bursting with larger than life characters.

The fact that within a relatively short space of time he would be skippering a side that included such vocal, strong-willed individuals as Mick Channon, Martin O'Neill, Steve Bruce and Joe Royle says much about the natural leader they suddenly found in their midst; equally, it says much about Ken Brown's abilities as a man manager, that he could mix the young and the old, the shy and the retiring, the bold and the brash together with such apparent ease.

Certainly you can sense how the Watson-Brown show might work – the former demanding almost instant respect on the pitch through the sheer, steely strength of his personality, the latter working wonders off it through the natural warmth of his own, welcoming character. The two men clicked.

'It felt right,' said Dave, as he met his new manager for the first time at Thorpe Station.

'First impressions of Ken Brown – and last impressions, by the way – were "What a lovely fella!" and that was a big pull straight away to have someone greet you with a nice smile and a face like Ken.

'Them meeting us. Dougie Livermore, at the time, Mel Machin – it just had the right feel about it.'

Four weeks later and the new boy would really get a feel of his new home as he made his league debut for the Canaries – away at Ipswich Town, on Boxing Day 1980.

'We lost 2–0,' said Dave, like many non-natives taken aback by the ferocity of the occasion as the two, age-old rivals indulged their often overlooked passion for tribal warfare.

'I was surprised at the atmosphere, to be honest. I'd only ever really experienced the Liverpool derbies and they were always full-blooded affairs with great atmospheres and I was thinking it would take something to match that.

'But as soon as you turn up, the sheer dislike between the supporters hits you and the passion rubs off on you.

'I'm sure that if there was a bigger stadium in Norwich, you'd fill it. If you had your 50,000-seat stadium, you'd fill it for Norwich-Ipswich,' he said, delighted to make his debut in such a low-key, understated affair as an East Anglian derby.

'If you're going to make your debut, especially in the league, it needs to be a good game to play in, where everyone's up for it – they're the easier games to play in. And they don't come much bigger than that one, so it was a great game for me to play in. I think at the time they had the likes of Mariner, Brazil, Gates, so I was really put to the test.'

John McDowell's absence that day gave Dave his first taste of first-team action. McDowell would return for the home clash against Spurs a day later, but come the FA Cup trip to Cambridge United on 3 January 1981, Watson's name was back on the team-sheet. There it would remain for the next five years – an unyielding force at the very heart of the City defence. 'Our jewel in the crown,' was Brown's simple verdict.

The new boy took little time to settle in. Even if life in the top flight was proving something of a struggle in that opening season, there was a certain buzz about the place.

'As soon as I walked into the dressing room, there was a great feeling to it straight away. Most football clubs are the same; the sense of humour is the same wherever you go and I was made welcome straight away,' said Dave, still very much the hard-working Scottie Road boy with a living to earn.

'Looking back, I'd say I was a shy, determined lad. I wasn't one of the sorts of outgoing lads, but I had a good determination about me.'

He was also fast working out who was who in that 1980–81 dressing room as he settled into his Devonshire Road digs. One of his predecessors at centre-half swiftly made a big impression, Duncan Forbes.

'Big Duncan was still in the reserves, so I played a few games in the reserves with big Duncan and he used to frighten the life out of you – just by saying: "Good morning!"

'He couldn't just say "Good morning!" It would have to be "Good morning, Watson!" He was a good character.'

There were, of course, other quieter, more complex characters in the dressing rooms of Carrow Road and Trowse, then the Club's basic training HQ. Dave would, for example, watch Justin Fashanu go to work that season, before his ill-fated switch to Nottingham Forest that first summer where Brian Clough and, years on, tragedy awaited.

'My lasting memories of Justin? A lad who worked hard to get where he got; a big handful of a centre-forward.

'He really did work hard. He got his move to Forest because he was such a handful through his sheer size and strength. He was a hell of a strong lad.

'And he did have a good touch. Looking back now I didn't really ever analyse his game that much, but he did have a lot about him – particularly for a young lad. That was why he was attracting all the attention.'

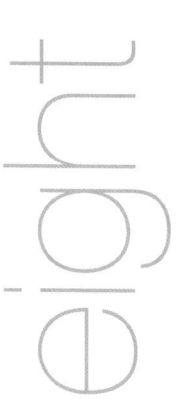

Attention for all the right, footballing reasons. Ask anyone who played alongside Justin at that, somehow innocent, stage of his career and they will all echo Dave's verdict. 'Justin was a decent lad; he came over really well. He'd do anything to help anyone. He came over as one of the nice sort of characters in that dressing room.'

Those rogues that were there, it seems, fell firmly into the loveable category. Crucially, the team that Brown built and Machin coached had another, all-important trait – genuine quality. Many of the arrivals over those years might not have been in the first flush of youth, but they knew their way around a football pitch – just as much as they knew how to make a dressing room laugh.

'I came in and just felt it was right. And that dressing room was fantastic – it really was. It was a joy to walk in of a morning because there were so many characters there; there was always banter going on…If you look at any successful team you need a good team spirit and we certainly had that – we had great characters.

'John Deehan, Keith Bertschin as well. Stevie Bruce would come a little bit later on. We had a team of characters.

'If you had that team together now, all of a decent age, you'd be competing near the top of the Premiership. The ability was always there.'

An ability that ensured that City's return to the Second Division in 1981–82 was mercifully short-lived, as 40 points from an available 48 that spring saw the Canaries nick the final promotion spot off Leicester City's toes.

City's final game of the season was actually at Hillsborough – a 2–1 defeat that lingers long in the memory.

'I always remember we got beat on the day, but a fan ran onto the pitch – into the penalty box when they scored their goal.

'And we thought the goal was going to get cancelled, but it never did. So we came off the pitch a bit despondent, not knowing the results about us. It wasn't until we got into the dressing room that we found out that we'd been promoted. We actually came back out onto the pitch to wave to the fans but I think most of them had gone home!'

The long treks back to Norfolk were one of the few downsides to Dave's foray to the far east of England.

'Every day was a three-day camel ride, wasn't it? I remember Keith Bertschin when he first came to the Club, just sitting, looking out of the window on the bus on the way back to Norwich and him saying: "If I see another cabbage I'm going to crack!" because that's all you could see for miles and miles – all these bleeding cabbages.

'We had the card schools; the characters – there was always something going on. Plus quite a few were into the racing in a big way.'

Cue another one of those curious X-factors that binds a team and a dressing room together; something out of the ordinary that underpins the extraordinary. For as much as City's success at that time owed much to events at Carrow Road, the sporting distractions to be had at Yarmouth, Fakenham and, above all, Newmarket also played their part.

'Thinking back to it, how they used to attract the old players, I'm sure Newmarket races had something to do with it because after training most days Mick Channon and the lads would be in the car off to the racing.

'Martin O'Neill likes the horses, Big Joe (Royle) likes the horses and, yeah, I went racing with them on a number of occasions. Micky taught me one or two tricks of the trade!'

Channon's influence is fascinating, as the former England striker began his slow transition from one sport to the other. Today, of course, he is one of the country's leading Flat trainers. Back then, the former Southampton frontman with his trademark windmill goal celebration was an enthusiastic, if not obsessive, amateur with one eye always roving for the latest race results. Suddenly, keeping track of the 2.40 at Kempton and the 2.45 at Haydock on a newly-installed television in the corner of the dressing room would become part and parcel of matchday life – irrespective of the fact that kick-off might be no more than ten minutes distant.

'Before Micky came, it wasn't known to have a TV in the dressing room. These days you do have them in dressing rooms – to put videos on and show things. But it was unheard of in those days.

'He'd been at the Club for about a week before he got this telly put in to catch the 2.30 and the 2.45 or whatever. And Mick's warm-up used to be to just stand there, just watching the telly.

'But that was great. The lads used to have a little bet on them races and depending on how the races went, if they'd won, then the lads would be going out to the game in good spirits. And if they didn't win, then we'd have to win the game to get our money back, to make up for it.

'But for me, that was good management. You need a happy dressing room. If something is going to help to make a dressing room happy, like the TV, then do it. Some lads can worry too much about a game beforehand – it was a nice little refreshing thing to get the lads together and take their minds off the game.'

As for the 3.45 at Ascot, some things had to give.

'It wasn't straight on with the telly at half-time, the football did kind of come first,' said Dave. 'But after the team talk and all that, Micky would have a little flick around to see how the results had gone.'

If anyone is getting the impression that good times were being had by the young Dave Watson, you'd be spot on. He was, it seems, having an absolute ball – on and off the park. And if it wasn't off to the races, then it was down the river to fish.

'I was with the fishing crew as well – we used to go fishing all the time and have a really good laugh. But that's team spirit.

'You talk about the lads who'd go racing, the lads who'd go fishing and then there'd be the night out in the city. There's only seven nights in the week and there's three of them. And we'd have to fit a bit of training in as well!'

'They were great times,' he admitted simply.

'I'd known nothing like it. I hadn't been in football really – I'd only played a dozen reserve-team games so I'm coming into a dressing room and there's Joe Royle, he's a big Evertonian. I used to watch these boys on the telly...Martin O'Neill's a European Cup winner and I'm in the same team, the same dressing room. Micky Channon playing for England. I couldn't believe it, really. It was like being in a dream.'

The "shy, determined lad" was no more. Determined, certainly. Shy? In that kind of company? No chance.

'You couldn't be a shy and retiring type in that dressing room – you'd die in there. You did have to be a character to live with them.

'But it was good, character-building stuff for the younger players. Just to sit and listen to the senior pros was an experience in itself.

'And it didn't take me too long to come out of my shell,' admitted Dave. 'I did have the other side to me where I could come out, but going to a new club I'm not one to go in and be the party-goer straight away. I just wanted to get a feel for the place and once I got the feel for it, then, yes, I'd come out my shell, no problem.'

If any further encouragement were needed, Messrs Brown and Machin provided it in the shape of the captain's armband.

'Mel and Ken showed a lot of faith in me when I got into the team. They gave me a good run in it and that's the only experience you get – by playing in the team.

'I held my own and they made me captain not long after that so they must have thought an awful lot of me.'

As did the players. After all, it was no mean feat to command a dressing room that boasted such lively characters as Royle and O'Neill in what was still only your first full season earning a full-time living as a professional footballer. By one account, if the management had any doubts as to the wisdom of giving the young man the nod, it was Royle's recommendation that swiftly sealed it. Raw as he was, when it came to the art of leadership the lad from Liverpool L3 had it. In buckets. The respect was mutual.

'You didn't order them people about – your Joes, your Martins,' said Dave. 'You had too much respect for them and they knew far more than I did. But all credit to them, whenever I did say something they listened in. What they would have thought of me, I don't know. But if you asked them, I think they'd say one or two good things.'

O'Neill the player was just the same as O'Neill the manager. 'Martin was fantastic,' said Dave. 'He was a great motivator. You see that when he's on the touchline now, but he had that in the dressing room as well. He used to get so frustrated if things weren't going right and, as I say, when you see him throw a wobbler on the touchline he used to do that in the dressing room.'

Royle was the joker in the pack – as a goodwill visit to Kenya revealed. 'We went to Kenya one time and I don't remember who the president was at the time, but it was a big political trip to get the English over there. We're all the best of friends and all that.

'And I remember as captain introducing him to the whole team and as I came down to Joe, I said: 'Mr President this is Joe Royle and Joe just tapped him on the shoulder and said: "You can call me Joe!"

'And there was all these cameras and press around the place, but Joe just had that grin on his face. "You can call me Joe!"

'It's just little things like that that stand out. But they were going on all the time.

'You had to have humour. If you haven't got humour in football you've got no chance – particularly with them lads. As I say, there was always something going on.'

The other point, of course, is that in amidst all the wisecracks, the likes of both O'Neill and Royle had the wisdom to match. There was brain and brawn in the team that Ken built and led out of the Second Division in the summer of 1982. Above all else, however, there was character.

'There were bigger characters in that Norwich dressing room than there were in the dressing room when I moved to Everton – without doubt,' said Dave. 'At Norwich there were more senior pros with more experience. You can't buy it, can you? The experience. The likes of Micky and Joe – they tell good stories.

'And you could see that the likes of Joe and Martin that they were going to go on and be good managers. To be a good manager you need to get on with players and they need to respect you for what you've done in football and they've got all the credentials.'

Promotion was one thing, staying up was another and it would call upon every last ounce of nous and nerve to keep the Canaries bobbing about above the relegation zone for the next two seasons before the trap-door loomed open wide again in Wembley year.

'It was always going to be backs to the wall in the top division. We were a team that was too good for the old Second Division, but not really quite good enough for the First. We were a yo-yo club and that's what we proved to be. It was a constant battle.'

That the Canaries defied the odds owed much to both Watson's inspiring leadership on the pitch and Brown's efforts off it as he kept the older guard on song and on form, while introducing the odd pair of younger legs to do all the running – Peter Mendham, Mark Barham, Paul Haylock, Louie Donowa to name four.

Throw in Chris Woods in goal and City had the kind of spine every manager yearns for – particularly when in the summer of 1984, Brown

Dave Watson

disappeared down the old A2 and raided Gillingham for the services of Steve Bruce. All of a sudden the sheet metal worker from the docks of Liverpool had a one-time plumber's apprentice from the shipyards of the Tyne for company. Thereafter steel was never in short supply at the heart of the City defence.

'When Brucie came in we did gel straight away,' said Dave, as one of the great defensive partnerships in City's history was born.

'He moved in a few doors away. He came round, knocked on my door and he had this big bulldog with him that wrecked my garden.

'He was a typical Geordie; a good, outgoing lad, and we did hit it off straight away. Again when it came to playing with him, it did click straight away.

'He was a top-class player. He'd been top man for Gillingham for quite a while and he was just waiting for that move and as soon as he came in at Norwich straight away he used to score vital goals for us…He was a good footballer and I was quite surprised that he didn't go on to get capped by England.'

For all the shared resolve and massive hearts, the pair's individual styles complemented each other perfectly.

'I think I was more of a defensive type of player, where Stevie could pull the ball down on his chest and could pass a 30-yard ball. Stevie liked to gallop forward now and again whereas, again, I'd be the more defensive one.

'As far as commitment going into the tackle and winning your headers, I think we were very similar. If anything I think I could possibly get a bit more out of Stevie. I was more the determined one…I could give a rollocking and he'd react to it. In fact, I think I used to frighten Stevie in a few ways in the tackles I used to go in for.

'He used to just look at me and shake his head and I think he went on to say that I was the hardest player in football he's ever seen or something.

'I don't know whether that was because I was bit daft in them days, putting my head in where I possibly shouldn't have. But I got away with it.'

The biggest battles were reserved for down the road at Ipswich and back in Merseyside – particularly once Everton paired Andy Gray and Graeme Sharp together.

'Everton were flying at the time and they were a handful. They could play football and if you wanted a fight they could fight you as well. They had everything,' said Dave, not exactly one to duck a challenge – particularly from the blue half of Merseyside.

'I like competing and you've got to accept that if you give a bit, you're going to take a bit,' said Dave. 'I'm a Liverpool lad, rather than Everton, and in them days I was up for it. I got my cheekbone broken one game up at Everton – accidentally, of course – but they were always good, competitive games. But if you look at Stevie's face now, he's taken a little more stick than I have!'

As for the blue half of East Anglia, City's progress to Wembley for the 1985 Milk Cup final produced a two-leg epic. For after a relatively low-key run to the last four, as goals from John Deehan in particular helped brush Preston North End, Aldershot Town, Notts County and Grimsby Town aside, who should await in the semi-finals but Ipswich Town.

'An Ipswich-Norwich derby semi-final is absolutely fantastic because someone is going to end up gutted,' said Dave. 'Obviously if you're on the wrong boat and you get beat in the semis then it's got to be the worst feeling in the world – more so with it being a derby match.

'Our fans made the most of that and rightly so because I'm sure that if the boot was on the other foot they'd have done the same.'

It wasn't exactly plain sailing.

'Looking back now we got absolutely annihilated down there and could have lost 3–0 and it would have been game, set and match. But we hung on and came back having just got beat 1–0.

'We got off to a great start in the second game – Dixie (John Deehan) scored the first goal in the first few minutes. The atmosphere was absolutely electric.

'And then late on in the game Brucie went up, scored the goal and then it was "Here we go!" with the fans, the celebrations. I can still feel it now.

'I remember they threw big Terry Butcher up front late on and he was smashing us all over the place. But it's amazing how high you can jump when you have to because we were beating Terry Butcher in the air – and that takes some doing.

'And that was sheer determination that was getting us through that. It was a great performance and come the final whistle it was like a dream come true – you're at Wembley.'

Before that, however, Dave was in the city. It was party time. 'At the time, the city was just on fire; an absolute tremendous atmosphere about the place.

'I remember we went out into the city that night after the semi-final, into Tudor Hall. And I was break-dancing long before it had come out!

'We used to always go out, but certainly after that game we did. We used to go to the Murderers, The Hole in the Wall, they were the haunts,' said Dave, who would actually meet his wife on one such trip to The Murderers.

Needless to say, Norwich being the big village it is, it was rarely a quiet night out. 'You get to know everyone in the city. You know all the lads on the market stalls. Wherever you go, you're known. It has its advantages and its disadvantages. You can't just go for a quiet bite to eat, certainly not when you've just been promoted, but it is nice to have that sort of feeling that everyone knows you.'

By now both the city and the county were in the grip of cup fever as the Canaries prepared to meet Sunderland in the final.

Dave Watson

'The city was on fire in the weeks leading up to the final. Everywhere you went – it was the talk, the papers, the radio, everything was geared to the cup final.

'To actually have got to Wembley and lose would have been unthinkable because of all the passion that everyone had shown in the city and in Norfolk – it would have been such a let-down to have gone and lost it. Everyone was really up for it. There was yellow and green everywhere.

'So there was a confidence, yes. We certainly didn't fear Sunderland. We knew we had a good side so it was case of "We can win this!"'

Come cup final eve and it was time for everyone to steel themselves in their own, individual way. Again Brown's management came to the fore as his ever-ready smile calmed any fraying nerve.

'On the night before the final, it's all individual stuff isn't it? Different players react differently. I think my own build-up was quite a tense one. I was still quite youngish and I'd be quite tense, whereas Micky Channon would most probably have a glass of red wine or something!' Cue Brown to the rescue.

'As soon as you look at Ken, you're relaxed anyway aren't you? He's just got that smiling face; never shows any sort of tension.

'And there's an art to that as well because there must have been times when he was being driven up the wall, but he used to keep his cool about him and looking back that certainly rubbed off. Well, it rubbed off on me anyway…When you thought it was a crisis and you'd look at Ken and you'd realise things weren't quite as bad as you thought.'

For all that Dave Watson would go on to achieve with Everton, there is no doubt that City's 1985 Milk Cup final triumph – courtesy of that 1–0 win over Sunderland – still figures very, very large. It was one proud man talking when he recalled the day itself – Sunday, 24 March 1985.

'My lasting memory of the day is actually lifting the cup. And thinking: "This is it!" You've had your dreams to play at Wembley and you're actually walking up to pick the cup up and thinking: "This is it!"

'It was a proud moment – particularly to be captain of the Club. And I looked behind me, there were some characters there. Deehans, Hartfords, Keith Bertschin, Bruce, Chrissy Woods, Channons, all top players.

'That's what was good about it. You had your lads who used to do the races and have the nights out, but when you came in to train – and Mel Machin was a great coach – if you weren't training right he'd let you know straight away.

'He had the discipline. And that's where the good management comes into it because when we trained, we trained hard. But when we had a night out, we played hard as well.

'For all the banter, the laughs, there used to be fights in training if you got beat in the five-a-side. There was a real, competitive atmosphere about the place. People hated losing and I think that came from the senior pros.

If they got beat, they'd really be up for it and it rubbed off.'

Character, there it is again. In Chris Woods. 'Chrissy Woods done great – he was a top 'keeper. We've talked about the backbone of the team before and Chris was good – a good, single-minded character which you've got to be as a goalkeeper. On numerous occasions he won us games, kept us in games and he had a good presence about the squad,' said Dave, as another of Brown's little forays into the transfer market turned up trumps.

'But then Chris was really sort of proven anyway, being understudy to Peter Shilton at Nottingham Forest. He had a good pedigree so I don't think it was a gamble on Chris Woods; it was just a case of he needs to be playing regular football and as soon as he got the chance he proved what he can do.'

The Hartfords. 'There's another one – Asa Hartford. A character? He was a great lad. He really was.

'He's one of them he used to travel up and down the motorways or go home on the train, things like that. He'd seen it all. He'd done World Cups and that and all the banter about the hole in the heart and that, it just used to bounce off his back.'

Dave missed out on the party back in Norwich that night. For by now England had – finally – come a-calling and the seeds of his eventual departure were being sown.

'Me and Chris Woods went off to England duty straight after the game so we missed out on the celebrations. I regret it in a way, but if you're going to join up with the England squad rather then going back to maybe just watch it on the telly then that's a bit different. But I'd liked to have been there, obviously.'

Dave's England call-up had taken a while to arrive. Norwich has never been the easiest of places to get to if you're an England scout and it probably helped that Bobby Robson, now the England boss, had a spot of local knowledge to call on ahead of a certain trip to South America.

'I know they do have scouts all round the country but Norwich is a little bit out of the way like that. I was a little bit fortunate with Bobby Robson being at Ipswich because he saw Norwich quite a bit. But it is a difficult one. Not many people travel to Norwich in one day, do they?'

A debut in the Maracana Stadium made up for the wait. 'I suppose if you could pick somewhere to make your England debut then Rio is where you'd make it.

'We were fortunate that day to win 2–0, John Barnes scored that memorable goal and you look back at your career, that's in the top four or five highlights. Tremendous debut.'

Milk Cup triumphs notwithstanding, Norwich's yo-yo status found Ken Brown's side yo-yoing back into the Second Division that summer as Everton romped away with the First Division title.

Dave Watson

And while Watson, Bruce, Woods, Drinkell and Co would fire the Canaries back into the top flight the next season, with the minimum of fuss and a lot of performance, the desire to strut a bigger stage was beginning to niggle away at the City skipper. Missing out on the last ticket to the 1986 World Cup finals hardly helped.

'Come the 1986 World Cup it was between me and Gary Stevens at Tottenham. The squad got narrowed down to 25 and I think they took 22 and I was the 23rd player.

'The reason I got left behind and he took Gary Stevens was that he could cover right-back as well as centre-back. I was pleading with Bobby Robson; I was saying: "I can play in anywhere, get me in there!" But that's it. I missed out on that.

'Before that I wasn't really getting frustrated because you had people like Terry Butcher, Mark Wright, who were doing good jobs for England. And by moving to a bigger club there was no guarantees that I was going to be an England regular because you still had those players in front of you.

'But when it came to leaving, that England thing was part of my thinking. I wanted to push myself to the limits.

'I look back on when I was in the Liverpool reserves and I wanted to get into first-team football. I still had that drive; I wanted to get higher up; I wanted to win the FA Cup; the league championship. I wanted to go on winning things and, no disrespect to Norwich, we weren't going to win the championship.

'We'd possibly have a good run in the FA Cup, but I think it was quite limited what we could have done.

'It was the right time. Five years at a football club – he says after just doing 13 at Everton – five years is a long time and I think you do need a break, you need a move to freshen things up.'

Some 20 years on, there seems a large degree of inevitability to all that followed – particularly when Watson's move had a cheque for £1.2 million attached.

'It started off with rumours in the paper. Obviously Everton wanted to talk to me and the clubs just sat down and agreed a fee. My family's all Liverpool, but they're not that strong Liverpool supporters, so it was just a case of doing what was best for me.

'I'd be coming back home, closer to the family, and I'd be moving to the top club in the country – as they were at the time.'

On 22 August 1986, Dave Watson headed home to finish his playing career at Goodison Park not far from where it all began – in the back-streets and narrow alleys that once ran the length of the A59.

For all his talk of the great characters in the Carrow Road dressing room of that time, there is little doubt that he was one of the greatest – more forceful than funny, perhaps, but a formidable presence nonetheless.

And yet for all his obvious leadership qualities on the pitch in taking City to their first – and still only major cup triumph – it is to Brown's managerial abilities that Dave often returns. For man management is an art. And Brown had it. Add to that a Harry Redknapp-like ability to wheel, deal and spot a player and a few of the secrets of that Milk Cup team begin to emerge.

'Ken's management had a lot to do with it. He knew how to look after the big name players and he also had a good eye for youngsters – Peter Mendham, Mark Barham, Paul Haylock,' said Dave.

'If you want to look for a similar manager now take Harry Redknapp. He's got an eye for a player that can do a job for him. Doesn't matter how old he is, how young he is. That's his job. I'm sure you don't see Harry out on the field coaching. He'll be doing his work behind the scenes and Ken had that.

'Good vision for a player and how to treat a good senior pro. There is an art to keeping all these huge characters together; you've got to keep all these strong characters happy and Ken had it off to a "T".'

It did wonders for Watson, but then he did wonders for Norwich. Handed his big chance to leave a Liverpool factory floor far behind, the boy from Scottie Road never looked back. He also made sure he repaid Norwich's investment ten, a hundred times over.

'I do a bit of after-dinner speaking now and my memories of my football career start off with the Milk Cup win because that was my first big trophy and that's the one that you always remember.

'It was fantastic. It was the place where I got my start and I'm always going to be grateful to Ken Brown and Mel Machin for giving me the chance,' said Dave, his Norfolk heart still beating strong.

'My wife's from Norwich so I still go back there a lot. And I often go into that pub on Thorpe Road, the Mustard Pot, on a Sunday afternoon and watch the football.

'For a place to live, when you're 15 minutes from a lovely coastline, people would give anything for that. It's a lovely city; a lovely coastline; a great place to live. Yeah, it was great. A good time.'

9 Jerry Goss

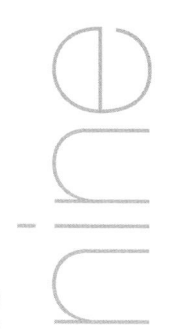

In 1993 the Canaries were flying high both at home and in Europe and the man at the hub of it all was Jerry Goss. He may well have spent 12 years as a Carrow Road professional but he will always be remembered for his achievements in '93.

After progressing through the youth and reserve-team ranks Jerry made his Canary debut at Coventry's Highfield Road during the penultimate fixture of the 1983–84 season. Despite plying his trade at Carrow Road for the next 12 years he made under 250 first-team appearances for the Club and admits himself that he should have clocked up far more.

Jerry made up for lost time once Mike Walker took charge of first-team affairs at Carrow Road and matched some outstanding performances with wonderfully struck goals. For the king of Europe who silenced the Kop – international football soon followed with Wales as Jerry Goss became one of Carrow Road's favourite sons.

Like team-mate Bryan Gunn, Jerry is now working back at Carrow Road in the Club's sponsorship sales department and has worked wonders to assist with the financing of the Canaries' Youth Academy.

Jeremy Goss

Born: Dekalia, Cyprus, 11 May 1965
City Debut: 12 May 1984, Coventry City (a) 1–2 Division One
Final Game: 6 April 1996, Tranmere Rovers (a) 1–1 Division One
League appearances: 188
League goals: 14
FA Cup appearances: 18
FA Cup goals: Nil
League Cup appearances: 17
League Cup goals: 3
Other appearances: 15
Other goals: 6
Total appearances: 238
Total goals: 23

There are certain individuals within this book that made the writer's job very, very easy. Wittingly or not, they gave great quote. Jeremy Goss is one.

So ask City's UEFA Cup hero to explain what sort of player he was – for the growing generation of Canary fans that are already too young to remember that magical autumn in 1993 – and the undoubted Master of Munich pauses briefly, reaches up to the appropriate mental shelf and dusts off the perfect story to illustrate his point.

'When I came in I wanted to be a player like Peter Mendham – a workaholic that doesn't cheat; gets about. And Alan Ball, I thought the same,' said Jeremy, as he happily started to sketch away at a picture of himself as a City player.

'One day I went to listen to Alan Ball speak and it was a fantastic talk. He talked about what his job was in that team – the England team that won the World Cup in 1966.

'And he said: "My day on the World Cup final was this: I woke up in the morning, we did a bit of training and then the big faces – Geoff Hurst, Bobby Charlton – came over to me after training and they said: "Look, you're the young lad in the team, have you got a dog?"

'And he thought: "Have I got a dog? What a stupid question to ask me on the morning of the World Cup final!" Anyway he said:

"Yeah, I've got a dog. Why?"

"Well what would you do when you walk your dog?"

"Well, I throw a stick, the dog goes and gets it and brings it back to me."

"Brilliant, son. That's what you are in this team – the dog. That's your job. The stick is the football and you're our dog. You go and chase that stick and bring it back to me, OK? And let us do the rest of it."

'And I thought in a small story that's basically explained my game throughout my career. I supported the ball all over the pitch; I tried to get tackles in; I tried to give the ball to the people who could play.'

And that's it. Jeremy Goss – in a perfect nutshell.

Stand back from the finished sketch, however, and another point swiftly emerges. That for all the small stories that Jeremy has at his easy command, it is the big story of his life and times at Carrow Road that is the real epic.

How, after years of struggle, one man – largely via the influence of one manager – finally reached the mountain top and for six, amazing months stood astride the football summit in a blaze of glory. The route down thereafter was, in many ways, more dramatic than the long haul up. The ground started to slip from beneath Jeremy's feet the day Mike Walker quit for Everton. And where the player went, so the Club itself followed. A decade on and the individual fortunes of Jeremy Goss and the broader fate of Norwich City Football Club in those roller-coaster years seem ever more intertwined.

'When he walked out of the door at Trowse – I knew that was it.' The runaway train that was the Munich express was coming off the tracks.

How the Canaries got to board the train to Bavaria that year can, for now, wait. The Jeremy Goss story actually starts ten years earlier as the Kent youngster – typically – bust the proverbial gut to find a football club. Nothing ever came easy for the Army colour-sergeant's son and, to borrow a cheesy phrase from TV, if fame costs, the young Goss started paying at a very early age.

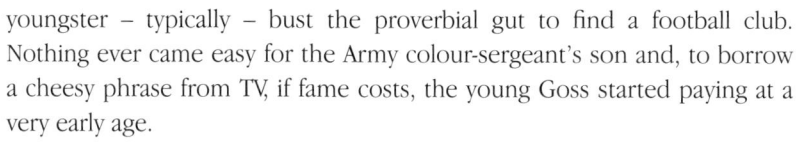

'It was Ronnie Brooks that first brought me in after watching me play for the England schoolboys – the Under-18s I think it was,' said Jeremy, having already been on the end of two, "No thanks!" routines before Ronnie rode to the rescue of a young man's dreams.

'Before that I'd been rejected at Aston Villa, having spent five days training with them; rejected at Southampton, same scenario,' said Jeremy. 'Going home on the train, both times, from Villa and then Southampton, it was a real kick in the nuts. I'd always wanted to be a footballer.

'But you've got to lift yourself up and I was lucky I had a really, really strong family who'd always pick me up and get me going again.

'So Ronnie Brooks came along; another session in Norwich and it was a case of: "Right, let's go for it!" And they put me on the very first government youth training scheme – I was on the YTS. And that gave me six months' leeway.

'The Government paid my wages for the first six months – £25 a week – and the Club paid my digs, £25, at the Stracey Hotel. Eventually I moved into digs with a great couple, Wally and Shirley Tolliday, it was a home from home.

'So that was me settled for a six-month spell and I could prove myself over a course of time as opposed to two sessions, no thanks, on you go.'

In many ways, it was just the start of a nine-year struggle to pin down a place in someone's first-team thinking; to prove yourself the best of a midfield bunch – no easy task given the quality of players in the queue ahead.

Winning the FA Youth Cup did help to put "young Gossy" on the map. Shrugging off the "young Gossy" tag – now that was a different matter.

'We won the FA Youth Cup in 1983 and I think that's what secured it for me,' said Jeremy, as the YTS boy finally got his name on a professional contract. He was also one of the first names on Dave Stringer's team-sheet as the future Canary boss made his first big mark in management with the Youth Cup silverware.

'We'd been on a great run, we were unbeaten in the South East Counties League and players like Jon Rigby, Paul Clayton, Tony Spearing were a great bunch to be with, a talented bunch to be with.

'I managed to get myself a goal in the first leg of the final when I scored against Everton at Carrow Road – we won 3–2 on the night – and if I remember we got the South East Counties League Cup presented to us that night as well. So it was kind of a heroic night for the youngsters of Norwich, which was brilliant.

'Then back we went to Everton, lost 3–2. And having lost the toss of coin, it was back to Everton for the "third" leg of the final and we won 1–0.

'That particular season, going unbeaten and those three games against Everton kind of made it for me.'

What else was the making of the young Jeremy Goss was the training regime Dave and Ronnie pressed upon their young charges. It was, literally almost, the survival of the fittest as the teenage midfield star lapped up all that his coaches could throw at him. It laid the foundations for what, in later years, Jeremy would admit was an 'obsessive' addiction to his fitness.

'It was incredibly hard – fitness-wise,' said Jeremy. 'As I said, I'd been to Aston Villa, Southampton and we never trained like we did at Norwich. The training at Norwich under Dave and Ronnie Brooks was magnificent. Very, very hard.

'I can remember Ronnie Brooks giving us double-legged jackknives as sit-ups and none of us could do them. He'd done a lot of boxing training. He knew how to do them, he thought they were good and there we all were learning how to do these double-legged jackknives.

'Today we know that they are just hip flexes and because they put pressure on your lower back are ruled out of the game altogether now. But Ronnie was there with a whip above us: "Come on, 50, 51, 52…" and that was a nightmare learning these different sit-up routines from Ronnie Brooks. But he was a great man and had a big influence on us all.'

In March 1983, those early days of sweat and tears reaped their due reward in the shape of a professional football contract with Norwich City Football Club.

'The moment I signed my first pro forms was the best moment of my life because I then went home and there I was, a professional footballer, walking back into my mum and dad's house.

'All the time, effort, finance, commitment and sacrifice that they'd made to get me where I was – it was just so emotional at the end because it was thanks to them really for getting me there.'

Famously, the family would be there in force for the home clash against Bayern Munich at Carrow Road ten years later, as Mother Goss became front page news after being pictured hitting the party button with her hero son.

It was the fact that they were there ten years earlier – pitch-side at Trowse some squally, Saturday morning in November – that, Jeremy insists, made all the difference. Particularly given the fact that the family home was still back in Kent.

'It took a long old while to get up here, but they were here. Supported me every home game, every away game.

'And it's because of them that I've had the career that I've had. No doubt about that. My two brothers, Mike and Tim, and Jenny and Jane, my sisters, we were and still are a very, very close-knit family going round in the Army together and I put them up on the pedestal as the ones that got me here. Definitely.'

Jerry Goss

The next step on the ladder came away at Coventry City on 12 May 1984, as "young Gossy" came under the wing of then boss Ken Brown and the first-team coach, Mel Machin.

'John Deehan actually got a smack in the eye at Coventry away, off of Tony Spearing by the way! And that got me a sort of ten minutes "Welcome to the game!"'

'I remember getting my first touch and doing something with it and not giving it away and I was happy with that – that's all I wanted to do. I was just delighted that I was wearing that Norwich shirt, representing my family, representing Mel and Ken Brown who put faith in me.

'Even though it was just for ten minutes, for me it was the ultimate. "That's it – I've made my first team debut! Is it on *Match Of The Day*?"'

And that was, in a way, that. For the next four, five, six years, Jeremy sat there, on the launch pad, waiting for his professional career to blast into orbit. It didn't happen. All that did was an entry into the Club's record books for the most consecutive appearances on a substitutes' bench.

'Looking back I think I wasn't horrible enough. My dad has always told me "sometimes you've got to be a nasty sod" and he was right – I should have rattled my cage harder about the fact that I wasn't getting first-team football,' said Jeremy, with typical honesty.

'I was always "Young Gossy!" Everyone on the streets, around the Club, called me "Young Gossy!" and "My time will come!"

"Don't worry, son, your time will come!" But my time was slipping away without me knowing about it and for all the years that I've been here, I've only made 230, 240 appearances which over the course of 15 years is terrible, really.'

In fairness, there was a bit of traffic up ahead; names, faces and talents that, with the best will in the world, would take some shifting.

'When I first came to the Club it was Peter Mendham, Martin O'Neill, Mick McGuire; Micky Phelan that came along; then it was Ian Crook, Andy Townsend.

'Those players alone were bloody impossible to move out because they were senior professionals brought into the Club, players that the Club had paid money for who were out there doing it. And I think I had to be someone very spectacular to push them out and make them sub – although as I've said I should have been a bit harsher, a bit more aggressive.

'I did mention to Ken many times that I was disappointed not to be in the side. Especially to Dave Stringer when he was manager. I was knocking on his door all the time: "Get me in the team! Get me in the team!" but when you look at those players they were tremendous assets to the football club and being bought players, they had to play.

'I didn't cost a penny; I'd come through the ranks; you can't have your two, three hundred grands' worth of midfield player sat on the bench – I should have moved on.'

Opportunities, now and again, did knock elsewhere.

'Through my career I did come close to leaving several times. One in particular I remember was Man City, where I was on the motorway with my dad going up there to sign with Mel Machin and I got a call from Ken Brown saying: "It's all off, you're coming back!"

'I didn't know the real reasons. I certainly learned a little more about what you'd call the politics of football. Because I think it was above me, the decision-makers, the two chairmen – Robert Chase and Peter Swales – who fell out, had a row, whatever, and it wasn't going to go through. Simple as that.'

Enter the man who would light the blue touchpaper. Mike Walker – recently axed as Colchester United manager having, bizarrely, just won October's Fourth Division Manager of the Month award – arrived at Trowse in the late autumn of 1987 as City's new reserve-team boss. Together the two men, player and manager, would embark on a remarkable journey together as "Young Gossy" finally came of age on the playing fields of Europe.

'I think I broke out of my shell a bit more when Mike came in. He was that type – he gave me the confidence to believe more in myself,' said Jeremy.

'I think I just never broke out of my shell early enough or young enough. I say to my dad now: "I should have been that horrible bastard in the game!"

'If I was a nasty bit of work, a horrible person, I may have got on and done more, who knows? Got to a higher level – if there was a higher level – but that's over and done with and I'm happy with who I am.

'Mike gave me the confidence – most definitely. He basically just told me to get out there and do what I wanted, when I wanted and if I didn't shoot when a chance came around, he'd fine me. That he'd give me a row because that's how much he wanted me to get on.'

In fairness, everyone had done their bit to fire him into life – be it Ken Brown, Mel Machin, Dave Stringer. Somehow, it seems that he and Mike just clicked. He pushed one last button, the one the others had missed, the one marked: "Go!".

'I don't know, somehow I found an extra gear in the game and I think it was confidence,' said Jeremy, typically quick to share the credit around.

'But playing around the players that we had at the time you could only have become more confident – Ian Crook, Mark Bowen, Gunny and all the boys in the team then, Chris Sutton, Ruel Fox, whoever you were you could only be inspired by the type of football that we were playing.'

Walker's name is, however, never far from his lips – particularly once his reserve-team mentor stepped into Dave Stringer's shoes as first-team manager in the summer of 1992.

Jerry Goss

'Mike knew what sort of player I was – he'd seen it many times in the reserves – and he said: "Just do exactly the same for the first team and you're in my team…"

'And I think it was then, when Mike took over, at the end of that season, that I actually thought I'd finally cracked this first-team nut.

'As soon as Mike turned up I had a brilliant pre-season. I was in the pre-season games. Starting the pre-season games and I thought: "Blimey, I've done well here!" Little things were making all the difference.

'The best feeling in the world is when your time's finished in a session and you've played the game yesterday, then it's: "Right those of you that played, that's enough, rest! Go and get yourself a cup of tea. Those that didn't play, over here!"

'And I'd been "Over here!" for the last ten, flipping years. Nearly. From '83, '84 to almost all the way through. It's embarrassing. No, it's not embarrassing because it's great to be a professional. But I was sub 18 times on the spin; that's the "nearly man" tag there, right on my forehead.

'I got ten minutes, 20 minutes, five minutes, whatever it may have been in every game – sometimes I didn't get on – but I must have run up and down the side of that pitch at Carrow Road so many times that I got to know the individual fans.

"OK, Gossy, how you doing?"

"Yeah, brilliant."

"Been fishing?"

"Yeah, went the other day…Oh, hang on mate, I think I might be on…"

One other key relationship was also on the point of bearing fruit. For alongside Jeremy in the heart of that Canary midfield was the man who pulled all City's strings – Ian Crook. In Jeremy Goss he found the perfect partner. Someone, a bit like Alan Ball, who would run and fetch that stick all day long. The contrast between the two fitness-wise could hardly have been more marked.

'I was obsessive about my fitness. Yeah, I was,' admitted Jeremy, fit as the proverbial butcher's dog… 'I was the fruitcake who did all the training through the summer to stay fit for pre-season. But Crooky summed it up great. He said: "Pre-season? I use pre-season to get fit – I don't get fit for pre-season!"

'And that's a quote I'll never forget him saying, but in the end that was my game – my strength was my fitness.'

Crook's game, by contrast, was to stand still and ping the ball this way and that with all the vision and precision of a genuine maestro. The fact that his daily diet would include a bottle of flat Coke, a Big Mac, large fries and the odd puff from a pack of Marlboro' mattered little. That's what Gossy was there for – to do the running.

'I think I only shared a room with him once or twice – that was a nightmare. He was smoking all over the place. "Chippy, what are you doing? Put that fag out! For God's sake!"'

There lies a rare regret. That Jeremy didn't take a little leaf out of the Crook book and stand still for a moment.

'I realised too late that I could play myself if need be – I should have got on the ball more; I should have stood still more; I should have trained less and read the game better than what I did.

'Gary Megson said to me when he took over: "Gossy, Gossy – just stand still!" And I couldn't – I found it impossible. I felt as if I was cheating the team because I knew that in relation to the ball I should be here, here or here. And if I wasn't then I was cheating everybody. But he was right. Stand still and the ball will come to you.'

Megson the manager would await on the other side of the mountain top. For now, Jeremy was flying up towards the summit – now little more than four months away.

For having figured large in Walker's first full season in charge, come the summer of 1993 the Goss-Crook partnership was ready to blow the opposition apart – be it at home or abroad.

'I think I set my stall out from the very, very first pre-season game,' said Jeremy, as Walker began to put his pieces into place and prepared for European battle.

'I remember we had a trial game down here at Carrow Road – the amount of running I did in that game, I felt a million dollars. I felt so strong, so good in my running – we'd just come back from Denver, Colorado – and I was getting beyond the forwards all the time.

'So when, say, Ian Culverhouse had the ball, not only did he have an option into midfield, into Chippy, or into Chris Sutton's feet, they had me going beyond, into the channels. And in that practice game down here I think I sort of stamped my authority on the team – "Look, this is what I can do!"

'The gaffer pulled me afterwards and he said: "You were fantastic! This is a training game, no one's here watching and you were brilliant. Absolutely outstanding. In every department."'

And as much as Walker-Goss clicked, so too did his principal midfield pair.

'I think in the end me and Chippy did know each other's game inside out. He knew where I was and where I should be; he knew that if the centre-half came forward and he pressed, I'd be right behind him. There was that understanding. And I think the biggest word is respect – I had so much respect for him and I think he did for me as well. We certainly didn't want to let each other down.

'He's probably the greatest midfield player I've ever played with here at Norwich – no doubt about that. I was inspired by him. Every time he got it and did something special – in the end I was trying to copy him. That's where the confidence grew in my own ability to play and pass.'

As good as the two were, they were not the only show in town that autumn.

Jerry Goss

From Bryan Gunn the Scottish international 'keeper, to Welsh international full-back Mark Bowen, to the fast-emerging talents of Ruel Fox and Chris Sutton, City were where they were for a reason – they had some very, very good players playing some very, very good football.

'These were footballers at their very, very best – at their peak. And although we did get the recognition at the time, I don't think people really realised how great a side we were – or what great individuals were in the side.

'It was a solid team. One of those rare occasions where we all gelled incredibly well coupled with two things – really hard work and a lot of talent in the side. And those two things are always the pointers to a side that will do really well.'

A year earlier, in October 1992, that particular Canary side was bound even tighter together by events far removed from Saturday afternoons on a football field. The death of Francesca Gunn gave that side an emotional cement which was still holding fast as they boarded the bus to Leeds United and boarded the plane to Bayern Munich.

'The 7–1 thrashing we had at Blackburn didn't matter on the coach home because Bryan was there saying to the lads: "My daughter's taken a turn for the worse…"

'And I think we all grew up very quickly with tragedy right on our doorstep, amongst our mates. One of our best mates; one of the team; one of the lads has had this happen. I don't think we could comprehend it at the time exactly how bad it was for him. We just wanted to be there to support him.

'Perhaps it was just growing up – football doesn't matter, does it? We wanted to be there for Gunny at every given opportunity. The character of the man shone through. He was there, training again the next day. He was in goal, having balls smacked at him and I thought: "Bloody hell! What a guy, what a bloke…" And I still think that now because he is one in a million. He's a rarity in terms of his character. And, for me, he was the dad of the team.

'I was the last one to sort of break into that particular side. Not so much in age, but in appearances I was the inexperienced one and he was the one that you'd always go to. He had the right answers; he was the father-like figure. And when Francesca died I think it did bring us together as a whole unit; as a whole squad.'

For this particular writer, the power and the beauty of that Norwich side hit its domestic heights at Elland Road on 21 August 1993. They blew Leeds United apart with a truly fabulous display of attacking football crowned by a stunning, 20-yard strike from their flying midfielder as the ball was whipped from one end of the pitch to the other before being blasted beyond a stunned home 'keeper. Leeds lost 4–0 that day. Jeremy's goal was August's Goal of the Month on *Match Of The Day*.

'As I said, in that pre-season I've never felt anything like it in my life – doing running sessions I was absolutely bombing by people. I couldn't do anything wrong – even in the sprints I was only a little bit behind Foxy. I was on fire.

'It was like a bandwagon – a group of lads who were at their peak, they couldn't be touched, no one from the outside could hurt us, or break us up.

'We had this brilliant Premier League to go into, the very first games are coming along and it was a case of: "Here we jolly well go – let's just steam into them!"'

Music, too, was part of their inspiration. 'Anything from rock 'n roll to Buddy Holly to the latest, crazy disco stuff that Foxy liked. It was all sorts.

'Certainly for myself and Rob Newman who were room-mates at the time it was all rock 'n roll.'

The Munich express had left the station.

'It was like going on this train and this train couldn't be stopped. We all felt untouchable at the time. And I think that was proved in the way that we played – we had no fear.

'Maybe seasons ago we would have gone out, panicked and been jelly-legged on the ball on big occasions – i.e. the flippin' semi-final against Sunderland. And the goal that I scored against Leeds was a "No fear!" shot – exactly.

'Even in the changing rooms before that particular game we knew we were going to win. We were going to places knowing that we were going to win. Even if we got battered for 89 minutes we knew we were going to score and nick it in the last minute.

'Certainly that particular game. When we said it, we actually believed we were going to go out and flipping hammer Leeds at Elland Road in front of a full house. And we did.'

And hammer a goal home, too. Confidence can be a truly wonderful thing. 'Two seasons before, I would have taken a touch. I'd have tried to bring that one down and hit it. But that wasn't the way the mood was and the feel. My confidence was at its highest.'

Gone was "Young Gossy"; gone was the "nearly man" tag once stitched to his forehead.

'For me, personally, it was a huge obstacle to get over; to get that "nearly man" tag off me, to get the "Young Gossy" thing off me. I wanted to be "established first-team Gossy".

'Not being funny, but I wanted to score every goal; I wanted to make every tackle; I wanted to make every pass; be an influential player in the first team; do my bit and not let anyone down. That '93–94 season I seemed to accomplish all of those things.

'It was huge relief and a massive weight off my shoulders. I walked round with a bit of a spring in my heels because I was an established first-team player. I wanted Mike to build his team around me and, at least for a season, it happened.'

On 15 September, Norwich made their UEFA Cup debut at home to Vitesse Arnhem. It was a new experience for all concerned – to boldly go where no Canary team had gone before.

'After the first half hour, I think that's when we found the same "No fear!" that we had in the league,' said Jeremy, who would bag the first of his three European strikes in the 3-0 win that night.

'Because we didn't know how they were going to play. Whether they were going to play with a sweeper, 4–4–2, 4–3–3. Didn't know what they were going to do.

'In the end we trained and did practice games on the strength of all three happening. So we went out there thinking they're going to play with a sweeper; no, they're 4–4–2; no, they have got a sweeper in, we'll stick as we are. So there was that: "If this happens, you come in, you fill in and we're solid. If that happens, you go out, you go there instead…"

'And I think for the first half-hour we expected them to be European footballers, i.e. Ian Crooks all over the pitch, and we stood off them a little bit and we were a little bit fearful of what they had.

'Once we had that first attack and got our first goal, it was plain sailing. And we thought: "These guys are nothing. We're better than these guys…" You just go on from there and believe in yourself even more.'

A comfortable passage through to the next round completed with a 0–0 draw in the return leg in Holland, City were ready for whoever they drew next. Even Bayern Munich – unbeaten by any English team in their Olympic Stadium fortress.

'Bayern Munich comes out of the hat and even then – people laugh at us – but I certainly, and I'm sure the other guys would agree with me, felt that we'd definitely be able to beat this team. We'll take the game to them.

'Let's get solid. We're fitter than them, that's for sure. No one's fitter than us the way we train. We were training very, very hard. Let's go to their backyard, in front of their fans, and first of all let's not let any player sit and settle on the ball. No matter what player's on the ball, let's have two players shut him down. And that's how we set our stall out.'

Above all, play with no fear. And if this looping, defensive header is falling perfectly into your stride, simply smash it home.

'As an 18-year-old kid who's just signed first-year pro with Mel Machin and Ken Brown, I would probably have taken it on, miscontrolled it and that would have been that. But all those years later I just had one thing on my mind – I knew I was going to score. I didn't have any fear at that time.

'In training prior to it I used to whack balls at Mark Walton down at Trowse. I used to bounce them on the edge of the box and literally volley them at him. And I'm not missing the target and I'm thinking: "Christ, I'm on fire!" Every training session, I'm just pinging balls. Some would go Row flippin' Z, obviously!

'But as that ball came out to me I had one thing on my mind – I knew I was going to hit the target. It fell perfectly well and all I had to do was get the technique right and follow through.'

Away pitch-side somewhere a camera clicked and caught the moment on film – one image of an in-flight Jeremy Goss that, more than any other, has come to symbolise Norwich's mini-conquest of Europe that autumn. Well, Bavaria and a bit of lowland Holland.

'I was just so pleased for myself and the lads, at 1–0 up and we can now get the bit between our teeth and carry on.

'But on the way running back, I thought: "I wonder what that looked like on the box..."And I thought about home; I thought about my wife Margaret watching it at home; I thought about my mum and dad. "I wonder if they saw that...I wonder what that looked like..." And as I'm stood there, waiting for the kick-off, I am thinking: "That must have looked pretty good..."'

Quite how good it looked, Jeremy would soon discover.

'We landed the next morning and the papers were all laid out for us as we were getting our bags off and every single picture was of me, all the "Gozza" headlines and stuff and the boys caned me a bit "Oh, here we go..."

'But I honestly believe that they were thrilled for me as well, they knew that I wasn't any big-time Charlie, they knew it had been hard work getting into the team.

'So there I was, along with Mark Bowen – the men who scored at Bayern Munich. Although I was slightly embarrassed by the fact that I was getting all the headlines, another part of me was saying: "I flipping deserve that!"'

It was a goal that launched a thousand "Gozzamania!" headlines and, more importantly, laid the foundation for a truly memorable night in Munich as the Canaries came and conquered.

'When I got my goal it lifted everybody; it gave everybody that extra energy – suddenly we were refreshed and we were closing down even tighter, even madder. And then Taff came up with what was another brilliant goal.

'If you look at it, that is a hard header to score. He definitely didn't get the credit he deserves for that header because of my goal – most definitely.'

Come the final whistle, emotions were running riot as the Norfolk club created a little slice of history in the Germans' backyard.

'Those five, ten minutes at the end, after the final whistle had gone, were very special,' said Jeremy.

"Bayern 1, Norwich 2" was up on the scoreboard and the guys were going bonkers in that corner. I jumped over the advertising boards and then all the photographers gathered round and I spotted my mate Roger Harris.

'And they're all clicking away. You don't know what you're doing at the time; you're just hugging each other; you've got your arms round each other and you're punching the sky. You can't explain it. No words can describe the feelings.'

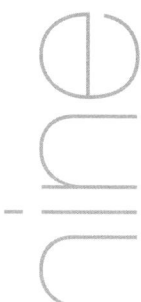

There was, of course, the small matter of the home leg still to come.

'I had two weeks building up to the return leg, training and playing, and I felt great. I felt just as good. The phone was always ringing; people were wanting to take pictures; do interviews. It was my testimonial year – we were going through that as well – and I remember saying: "I've been the hero, if that's what you want to call it, for the one game; the game coming up tomorrow night or whenever, someone else has got the chance to be that hero. It'll be someone else's turn."

'I honestly thought that – I thought we'd definitely hang on to the win and that someone else would score and be that hero for the next night. Little did I know it was going to be me.'

The date for your diary is 3 November1993. German international legend Lothar Matthaus is in Norwich; defeat by the little English club is not on his agenda.

'We conceded an early goal and that knocked the stuffing out of us, I think,' said Jeremy. 'I don't think we folded as such. In fact I think we rode that goal well because it was so early on.

'But I can picture it now, what people were saying around the country when they were watching it on TV: "It was a fluke away performance. They're going to get battered tonight. Look they're 1–0 down already…"

'It was just sheer determination not to let that happen. And a determination not to lose an incredible advantage, basically. What's the point in winning in Bayern Munich if they come here, beat us and we get knocked out? And I think that rattled us on. We got going again.'

With extra time and penalties beginning to loom, Norwich were holding out for a hero. He arrived in familiar fashion – bursting into the box perfectly on cue.

'It's the second half, Foxy's checked to cross the ball with his right peg and I literally saw Chris Sutton make this run and I thought: "He's going to nod this on – because he can't score, not from the position he's in…"

'And that's exactly what happened. The ball came over and he flicked it on. And I judged my run for that flick-on. What was it? Four, five yards out?

'Side-foot volley; house comes down; the noise feels like there's 40,000 people in the stadium. And I just put my arms in the air and just screamed basically – with this huge, gigantic smile on my face,' said Jeremy, about to have one of those impromptu family reunions which would again make for a fantastic front page picture.

'And at that moment I was running on adrenaline – I ran and ran – it just happened that I ended up in front of the mums and dads, the families and friends of the players, where they all sat at the time. I didn't know what I was doing. I was just running and I've ended up smack, bang there.

'I've seen my mate, Mark Walton, right in front of me with his arms up in the air with a big smile. And then my mum is there in front of me and she'd run down the steps. Suddenly I'm hugging my mum and I can't believe what I'm doing – I'm hugging my mum and the crowd are going bonkers.

'Everyone thought it was planned, but it wasn't at all. It was a sheer fluke. Incredible memories. The sheer frustration for ten years of not getting in the team and then all this – every dog has his day and here I was, having mine.

'For though all the emphasis was on me, I was a little bit modest with all the quotes I was giving. I was trying to put all my attention on the other lads and the team who'd won this game, not just me. But deep down I thought: "Flippin' well played son, well played!" I deserved that. I'd worked my nuts off to get in the team and get myself into the position where I could run round Carrow Road as a bit of a hero and that was the night. That was the night.

'I could talk to you about 50, 60 occasions when they'd been terrible nights; stuck in the reserves.

'But that was my night. It seemed to be my particular season. Everything went in, the Liverpool goal; it all happened for me and will never be forgotten.

And nor will my team-mates. They were my inspiration because they were such good players.'

The hat that year had another surprise – Inter Milan. Only this time the likes of Ian Crook, Ian Culverhouse and Ian Butterworth would be suspended, John Polston injured. Norwich would head to the San Siro with one hand tied behind their back team-wise, a goal down score-wise.

'Mike never raised an eyebrow: "That's that!" he said. "If they're suspended, they're suspended. Can't worry about it. We've got good players to take their place."

'That was his attitude and it had to be really. We were all devastated for them as individuals that they'd missed out on one of the biggest occasions in the Club's history, in one of the biggest stadiums in the world.'

Gozzamania was still in full swing. He just needed one opportunity to knock. 'I remember the training session the night before and the shooting sessions that we had, I was pinging them. I just needed one chance, one effort, one little go.

'When we got them here, I did get that chance – 20 yards out, a dipping volley, and I've flippin' hit the thing too high and it's hit the bar. From there we concede a penalty and that's it, that's the end of it.

'We'd lost 1–0 and we're going to the San Siro and we've got to score. Gary Megson had a great game that day; Rob Newman had a great game, but the clear-cut chances never really happened for us. I always felt: "We've got to score, we've got to score…" But the time was ticking away, the ball was going out of play, they were wasting time. At free-kicks, corners, set-pieces they were taking their time. In the end we never created enough to get the equaliser and that was it. It was the end.'

Or rather the beginning of the end. For within four weeks Walker would walk as that runaway train came off the tracks in truly spectacular fashion.

'I remember the day Mike left,' said Jeremy. 'He came out of Trowse training ground and said: "I'm off – that's it!" I was the first one to see him, coincidentally. I was just walking out.

'And he said: "That's it, I've finished!"

'And I said: "What do you mean?"

'"We'll get the lads together, but that's it. I've left the Club. I've signed for Everton."

'I think I said something like: "Oh, Jesus Christ!" I said something like that. To choose your words at that instant is quite hard. Nothing like "Take me with you!" came into my head; nothing like that. Perhaps it should have done!

'I think I said something like: "Well, it'll never be the same, Mike, you know that don't you?" Something like that. I was trying to get home to him that we may have come to an end now – now that you've gone. Chris Sutton went, Foxy went, everyone maybe got a little bit single-minded about things, I don't know.

'But I was devastated that he left – in my mind, the Club had one way to go or the other way to go at that particular time. We could have stayed in the Premiership and been a force to be reckoned with. No doubt about that in my mind – had we have kept Mike.

'I think I did resent him walking out when he did. I felt that the way the mood of the camp was, the whole club was moving forward in such a big, emotional way – getting results and the whole Europe business, I thought we'd be at that level for ever and a day.

'That was my frame of mind and I think that was the mood of everybody, but as soon as he went it was like the leader of the pack's gone. The big, numero uno is out of the way; he's moved on.

'And then I had the question: "What makes Everton a bigger club than us?" It's like "Why have you gone there, Mike? Why can't you sort yourself out here with the chairman?" These things occur to you sometime after, but at that moment in time when he left, I just felt: "Boom! It had burst anyway…"

'And that's what I said to him: "That it'll never be the same; that we can't keep this going without you…" That type of affair. And then I thanked him for everything that he'd done for me. And that was it.

'I can't even remember him coming back and saying to the whole club that he's going. Saying goodbye. In fact, I don't think he did.

'Later, I was angry about it. You get very personal in football; very blinkered about you, you, you, me, me, me and self, self, self. This is what

I'm doing; I want that successful trainer this minute; we're going 100 miles an hour down this track and nothing's stopping us and that's how we were.

'But suddenly the flippin' train's come off the track. Most definitely. And we're coming to a shuddering halt here – whether we like it or not.'

Something had gone – blown away in the wind. Or rather had driven up the M6 to Merseyside as John Deehan bravely stepped into the breach.

'Because the manager moves on doesn't mean to say that we become bad players, but I just felt everybody became a little more individual.

'Sutty did go, Foxy did move and, no disrespect to John Deehan, but Dixie was one of the boys. He was a bloody good coach. No doubt about that. He made it enjoyable; he knew when the boys were tired; when to give us more, when to give us less. He knew when to give us days off – he was a great coach – one of the boys who had total respect from us all.'

'After the times we'd had, on trips away, pre-season, end of season, we were like really close brothers – all of us. The whole team; the whole squad. Including Dixie; including Mike. We'd all have a little drink; we'd all have a little laugh. We'd all do silly things.

'And they're the best memories for me; not the memories around bars and clubs, but the memories of things like pre-season tours when we were such a close-knit unit. Enjoying life as professional footballers and coaches and managers.

'Up to that stage – before I'd married Margaret and had my two twin boys, Jacob and Joseph – they were the best moments of my life. And as soon as Mike walked out of that door, that kind of ended it for me.

'Dixie immediately went out and bought loads of players that he thought were going to do well for the Club. I think Dixie wanted to bring them in quickly to establish himself and I knew that; I knew that would happen. And I knew it was the end of Mike, of Mike's team, an end of an era.

'I don't know – the whole thing had just gone. It had just disappeared. And that was it for me. When he walked out of the door at Trowse – I knew that was it.

'I knew we'd ended. This magnificent train ride that we were on – with the rock 'n roll music and all sorts – boom! Gone out of the window as soon as he'd gone.

'And that's a terrible thing to say bearing in mind that Dixie's just taken over. He's one of your best mates and one of your best coaches, but unfortunately I think that was the feeling.'

There was one, final footnote to that season of "Gozzamania!" as Jeremy grabbed the final ever goal in front of the Anfield Kop with the Canaries ruining Liverpool's farewell party with a 1–0 victory. It was a good goal, too – an instinctive, 20-yard thump into the top corner that somehow befitted the occasion.

'I see that Liverpool goal every now and then,' said Jeremy, still a hugely popular figure at Carrow Road as he works alongside Bryan Gunn in the sponsorship sales and marketing department of the Club.

'And I thought we played well there that day. It was a brilliant game to be involved in, but I stole the limelight. And though it was great – and deep down I again felt I've worked friggin' hard for this, that I deserve this little bit of limelight – there's a small part of me that's thinking: "Ian Rush should have scored that goal, not me! Not Jeremy Goss of Norwich – what's that all about?"'

By the time Martin O'Neill succeeded caretaker boss Gary Megson as full-time manager a year later, the Canaries had tumbled out of the top flight. With barely a bean to their name, everything and everyone was on the slide as the debt-ridden Norfolk club slipped off that mountain top with frightening speed.

It was, after all, only two years ago that Jeremy Goss and friends had put Elland Road to flight with a glorious display of counter-attacking football. And there they were, back in Yorkshire, meekly saying their farewells to the Premier League on the back of a long-disputed penalty.

O'Neill's arrival did little to help Jeremy's situation – nor did an ankle ligament injury. The two never saw eye-to-eye. Martin wasn't Mike.

'I remember I had a 45-minute meeting with Martin in his office, face-to-face, and I had to tell him exactly how I felt. He stressed that he wanted to win three points; he didn't want to win friends. So be it. Ten years down the line I fully respect what he said; his style and his manner is obviously very, very successful. And well played to him.

'But I take nothing away from what I said. I haven't changed my thoughts and my emotions from that day, although I do realise what he said does make a little bit more sense now.'

At least he had that Bayern Munich goal to call his own – a game, a shot, a picture that will, for ever one suspects, come to symbolise Norwich's moment of European glory. A club – and a player – at the peak of their respective powers.

So what follows might come as bit of a surprise.

'I still haven't watched the Bayern Munich game. That was then, this is now. You can't live off your memories can you? I don't want to do that. When my little boys get a little bit older and they want to watch it, I'll stick it on.

'Meeting Margaret changed my life – it's no coincidence that my footballing fortunes changed for the better the day I met her. She, along with my own family have been the rock on which I've stood. My ultimate aim was to never let them down.

'I've got a future to look forward to with Margaret and my family. Joseph and Jacob are the most important things in the world to us; I'm not a footballer any more and you've got to meet the challenges ahead. They were great times, but I just want to move forward in my own way.'

10 Bryan Gunn

One of the most popular players to play for the Canaries in modern times, Bryan joined the Canaries in November 1986 and over the last 18 years has become one of the most recognisable and well-respected members of the Norfolk community. Upholding the Club's long and proud tradition of fielding great goalkeepers, Bryan's form at Carrow Road saw him twice lift the Barry Butler Memorial trophy as the Canaries' Player of the Year.

Despite the tragic loss of daughter Francesca in 1992, Bryan went on to make an outstanding contribution to Mike Walker's City side that finished third in the inaugural season of the Premier League and set the Club up for its UEFA Cup adventure the following season.

A real Canary great, Bryan is currently the Club's Sponsorship Sales Manager and after spending 2002 as the Sheriff of Norwich the former 'keeper is viewed by some as Mr Norwich City.

Bryan James Gunn

Born: Thurso, 22 December 1963
City Debut: 4 November 1986, Coventry City (h) 2–1 Full Members Cup
Final Game: 31 January 1998, Crewe Alexandra (a) 0–1 Division One
League appearances: 390
League goals: Nil
FA Cup appearances: 27
FA Cup goals: Nil
League Cup appearances: 38
League Cup goals: Nil
Other appearances: 22
Other goals: Nil
Total appearances: 477
Total goals: Nil

I'm not sure at what point the thought first occurred to me. One night when the burning midnight oil was just starting to flicker, I suspect.

But as each of the dozen Norwich City characters chosen for this book began to emerge from each successive page, so one common theme began to thread their many and varied stories together. For as much as each interview was designed to illuminate the Canary hero concerned, so it also served to shed new and revealing light on the City teams involved.

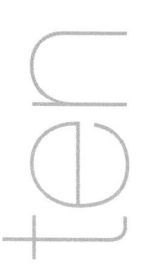

In the case of Bernard Robinson, the passage of time ensured that his memories of life at The Nest merely enabled the passing author to snatch the briefest of glimpses of Tom Parker's 1933–34 championship side.

In the case of Bryan Gunn, the memories are, of course, more vivid. Many people will still have a clear picture of the near-certain goals the Big Man saved; a few might even claim to know full well what makes the Gunner tick. He has, after all, been very much part of Norfolk's close-knit footballing community for the better part of 20 years in which time, if part-prompted by the cruellest of fates, he became pretty much public property following the death of his daughter Francesca in the autumn of 1992.

Inevitably, such an event will do much to shape the man. It also, it seems, did much to shape a team.

Who and what shaped the young Bryan Gunn prior to his arrival in Norfolk in November 1986 has – like so much of the 40-year-old's life – already been well-documented.

One figure above all others has always tended to loom large – Manchester United manager Sir Alex Ferguson. At that stage the future master of Old Trafford was busily making a name for himself across Europe as he swept Aberdeen Football Club to extraordinary heights, culminating in their 1983 European Cup-Winners' Cup triumph against Real Madrid.

It is a feat of arms – much like Norwich's own European adventure ten years later – that has probably never got the lasting credit it deserved. The team that May night in Gothenburg is worth repeating, if only to highlight the fact that there were one or two other famous faces shaping young Gunn's early development after the 16-year-old Invergordon schoolboy had swapped the gentle shores of the Cromarty Firth for the boom city of Aberdeen two and a half hours drive to the south, its famed granite walls suddenly awash with black gold as the riches of the North Sea started to flow forth.

Leighton, Rougvie, McLeish, Miller, McMaster, Cooper, Strachan, Simpson, McGhee, Black and Weir wrote themselves into Dons legend that night as a small, provincial city side managed by a fiercely-driven 41-year-old from the wrong end of Glasgow beat Real 2–1 after extra time. Add Ferguson's No.2, Archie Knox, and an old-school trainer by the name of Teddy Scott to the Pittodrie mix and it is easy to understand how the promising young Highland goalkeeper swiftly came on leaps and bounds – be it as a man or a footballer.

'It was a great place to learn how to play football,' said Bryan, as Jim Leighton's understudy blossomed in such formidable and demanding company.

'In terms of growing up and learning the game, not only was there Jim Leighton, but also defenders like Ally McLeish, Willie Miller, professionals like Gordon Strachan and Mark McGhee, all guys who have gone on to be managers in their own right…They were guys who demanded the best out of youngsters as well, so I think, all in all, just being part of the Aberdeen squad at that time certainly gave me the right education.'

Nor, it seems, was it all "Yes, boss! No, boss!" – despite Ferguson's readiness to reach for the famed hairdryer. Having courage in your own convictions, being of an independent and forceful mind – if the subsequent, high-profile managerial careers of Messrs McLeish, Strachan and McGhee form any sort of guide, such qualities can only have been encouraged within the Fergie camp.

'They'd not always agree with Fergie; they've obviously got their own opinions on how to play football,' said Bryan. 'But mixing it all in with Fergie's man-management skills and his coaching skills, they've developed their own careers and taken it on.'

Ferguson, however, was always centre stage.

'I was very close to him,' said Bryan, as the Ferguson family found a willing babysitter in their midst. Years later and Bryan's hours on the family sofa keeping the junior Fergusons company would be richly rewarded in the shape of Manchester United providing the opposition for his sell-out testimonial game at Carrow Road.

Looking back now, the warmth and humour evident in the press conference with Sir Alex held in the run-up to that game would provide compelling evidence of a deep and enduring respect between the two men.

No surprise, therefore, to find Ferguson at the heart of Bryan's move to Norfolk as the 22-year-old's growing desire to escape Leighton's shadow prompted the pair to search for pastures new.

'We'd talked about it – Alex Ferguson and I, the year before,' said Bryan, with Ferguson's own, impending move south about to add an intriguing twist to his transfer tale.

'It had got to the situation where Jim Leighton was Scotland number one and I was Scotland under-21 goalkeeper and I was only appearing in the first team when either Jim was injured, which was very seldom, or when he just wanted to give him a gentle kick up the backside – just to remind him that someone else was waiting in the wings.'

A freak gardening accident in which Leighton lost the end of a finger, when his young daughter accidentally switched on the lawn-mower, finally gave Bryan his chance to shine. 'I played in the Scottish Cup semi-final that year. 1986. Ironically against Hibs. We beat them 3–0 at Dens Park and Fergie acclaimed the victory to me having pulled off two blinding saves in the first ten minutes,' said Bryan, as the Dons boss found himself with a big decision to make – stick with his flourishing rookie or, with the Mexico World Cup looming, recall the Scottish No.1 for the final at Hampden.

'Jim played the reserve game on the Wednesday before the final;

played and was fit, and then on the Friday before the Cup Final, he told me he was playing Jim. He was his No.1 goalkeeper. He was also Scotland's No.1 and as Fergie was also Scotland manager at the time, he was obviously under pressure to play him before going to Mexico.

'I knew then that was more or less my final nail in the coffin. It was great experience to be at Aberdeen, but I knew I had to move on and stand on my own two feet and be a first-team goalkeeper somewhere.'

And so to the twist. For Bryan was far from alone in being at a crossroads in his career. Ferguson, too, had big decisions to make as he outgrew Pittodrie – a fact not lost on his willing pupil.

'I could see that Fergie was destined for bigger and better things; whenever a top English job came up, there was always a couple of snippets in the papers. But having been there for so long you didn't expect him to move on. But when the Manchester United job comes up that's going to turn anyone's head.

'I'm sure a lot of hard thought went into it. And I don't know what the next stage at Aberdeen would have been; whether he would have taken them on to the next level. So it was a very tough decision he had to make,' recalled Bryan.

His own decision-making process was hardly eased by events at Ibrox, where his Scottish under-21 boss, Walter Smith, was in temporary charge at Rangers.

'There were lots of rumours when I was with the Under-21s that all the big clubs were watching – the Arsenals, the Tottenhams, the Liverpools. You'd end up picking up the Sunday papers after playing for the Under-21s in midweek and your name would be linked with someone else.'

But Fergie had a plan – one designed to ease Bryan's disappointment at Leighton's sudden and untimely return to favour. 'The day before the Cup Final he said: "Look, I'll get you a club – don't worry about that! Walter Smith has been on the phone, he wants to take you to Rangers."

'I thought: "Great – a move to the second, third biggest club in Scotland!" For that's what they were at the time because Aberdeen were the best. And I went away on holiday thinking: "Right, I'm going to be playing for Rangers next year!"'

Of course, football is never that simple. Cue the arrival of Graeme Souness at Ibrox. Revolution was in the wind.

'Souness had come in and there was something of a cash revolution,' said Bryan. 'Sure enough, the first Scottish paper I pick up on holiday – I think it was the *Daily Record* – and Peter Shilton was linked to the club.

'Next day I picked up a Scottish paper and Chris Woods had actually signed for Rangers – £600,000 or whatever it was. So there's me in the middle of Greece or wherever I was at the time not knowing what was happening until I got back to Scotland and spoke to Sir Alex.'

What Sir Alex did next was simplicity itself – pick the phone up to Ken

Brown and put his boy forward for the newly-created vacancy at Carrow Road.

'I thought: "Not a bad move – just got promotion into the First Division", as it was at the time. And I was all set to come down, we'd spoken about terms – no problem about that – and then unfortunately Jim Leighton got injured in the match the week before I was due to come down so I ended up playing the first ten games of the Scottish League. Hence the reason not coming here until October.'

It was, it seems, very much a joint decision as Ferguson continued in his mentor role. 'It was a personal decision but one made with the help of Sir Alex,' admitted Bryan. 'I suppose he played a big part in it; he didn't just find me any club, he found me a good club who looked after their players in a very similar way to Aberdeen. Obviously he knew Ken very well; knew that Ken would look after us and that was it.'

Even then football's ability to spin "If only…" circles with people's lives continued. For by that autumn of 1986, Fergie had his own irons in the fire. He was, however, not revealing all. Not yet.

'So I signed here in October 1986. But I'll never forget it. He did ask me: "Are you sure you want to go?"

'At the time I didn't read anything into it and said: "No, I have to go and improve myself!" And he said make sure you move on from there, probably thinking that Norwich wasn't going to be the major club that it turned out to be.

'It was just the way that he said it, you know, make sure you try and achieve more. And a month later he joins us in England. I always wonder whether if I'd stayed at Pittodrie an extra month I might have played in a different shirt. I don't know. I'll never know that one.'

By then Mel Machin had been despatched north to do a spot of home-work on Fergie's top tip.

'According to the story that Ken tells, he sent Mel up to watch me in an early game and I think I didn't have hardly anything at all to do in the game. Apparently Mel recommended me on the warm-up! Ken got a phone call from Mel and he says: "Well, he didn't have a lot to do in the game, but I tell you what, he looked good in the warm-up!"'

Needless to say, Bryan's departure south was accompanied by the odd, wee dram to send him on his way – a "lively" occasion he, briefly, came to regret less than 24 hours later as his Canary career opened in the unlikely surroundings of Tooting & Mitcham.

'I was due to be on an early flight down which unfortunately got cancelled. So I got the afternoon flight and was picked up by Ken at the airport. And he says: "Right, big man, straight down to Carrow Road to sign your forms and then we're off to Tooting & Mitcham!"'

Where Crystal Palace reserves awaited. And 'the worst floodlights you can ever imagine'.

Bryan Gunn

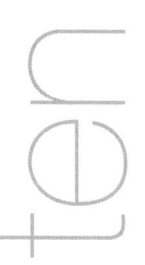

Coupled with the after-effects of the night before, Norwich's new arrival proved a rather hungover starter.

'I don't think I had the best preparation for my first reserve game for the Club and proceeded to give away a penalty kick in the first ten minutes. A short back-pass from Shaun Elliott, of course!' said Bryan, about to repeat the feat – albeit minus the alcohol – on his full debut, a Full Members Cup tie against Coventry City on 4 November 1986. He was not the only debutant that night. A young Ruel Fox also lined up alongside the likes of Ian Crook, Steve Bruce, Tony Spearing and Kevin Drinkell.

'Once again I gave away a penalty after ten minutes and Dave Phillips was the scorer – as he kept telling me once he signed for us,' said Gunn. Phillips would later play a part in one of the most traumatic nights in Bryan's Canary career. For now, however, it was all smiles as the 22-year-old took full advantage of Graham Benstead's dislocated collarbone to make that No.1 spot his own.

'I made my full league debut on the Saturday against Tottenham which we won 2–1 and I remember making a save from Nico Claesen in the last minute down at the then River End, now the Norwich & Peterborough Stand, and I think from there I really hit it off with the fans.'

For the Barclay's new hero had more than one string to his goalkeeping bow – as Norwich's new sweeper was about to demonstrate in his second home game against Manchester United on 15 November 1986. A United side now managed by Sir Alex Ferguson.

'One of my trademarks in Scotland was to sweep up behind the defence – it was something that Fergie and Archie Knox had developed into my game. I think that was a bit of a shock-horror to the Norwich fans at the time,' said Bryan, about to delve into his bag of outfield tricks for the reunion with his long-time mentor.

'The week after the Spurs game we played Manchester United at home – Fergie's second away game, he came here,' said Bryan, relishing one of those sweet coincidences that only football can organise...We drew 0–0 and I picked up my first Man of the Match award. I suppose the highlight of the game for me was my tackle on Remi Moses on the halfway line,' said City's hero that day, as a thin yellow line was drawn across Carrow Road.

For with both Dave Hodgson and Ian Culverhouse off injured and the one permitted substitute Wayne Biggins already on, it was a ten-man Canary outfit pinning United inside their own penalty area.

'I remember we were down to ten men for much of the second half; pressing quite a lot and a corner kick was put in, it got knocked out and I spotted Remi Moses coming steaming through the middle and I just managed to get to him in the centre-circle.

'I think he was more shocked than anyone in the stadium; he tried to shoot it round me and it hit me in the chest. There were a few heart attacks, on the pitch and in the stands around, but I kept a clean sheet and got all sorts of expletives from Mr Ferguson after the game – with a smile on his face!'

It would, it seemed, not be the only occasion that his one-time babysitter enjoyed the last laugh.

'It actually continued like that for the next few seasons. We had a great Indian sign over Manchester United. Looking back, I think that year we went up to Old Trafford and I saved a Brian McClair penalty in a narrow 2–1 defeat.

'I think the next year we went up there and I saved another penalty in a 1–0 victory and the likes of Gordon Strachan, who he'd also signed from Aberdeen, was giving me all sorts of abuse – from time-wasting to being a big, blond-headed so-and-so, but those are some of my best early memories of my time at the Club.'

At that stage there is little doubt that the life of Bryan was very much the life of Reilly as Norfolk's Scottish import found Norwich very much to his liking. It was, after all, not wholly different to the city he'd left, in its splendid isolation and rich, agricultural hinterland – all coupled to the residents' ardent passion for the local professional football club.

'There was a very similar make-up to my lifestyle,' said Bryan, whose brief flat-share with Dave Hodgson at the top of Rouen Road produced 'more parking tickets than anything else'.

Times were good. 'We were doing very well in the league. We were going to places like Old Trafford and winning; going to places like Liverpool and coming away with a result; going away to London, to Highbury on the last day of the season and getting a result to finish fifth.

'We were the highest any Norwich team had ever finished in Division One and we were heroes.'

The side that Ken had built and Mel had coached was 'built around players who were very good reserve-team players at big clubs, i.e. Tottenham, with the likes of Crooky, Ian Culverhouse in that first year.

'The Club also developed players like Kevin Drinkell who'd done well in the Second Division, moved up to the next level and scored a lot of goals. They gave Wayne Biggins the opportunity to play. And we had a very solid defence – Culverhouse, Butterworth, Bruce, Spearing – at the time very solid, committed players. We had Micky Phelan in midfield; youngsters like Ruel (Fox) and Dale (Gordon) coming through. It was just a good team.'

One that would have earned a ticket to Europe that year, but for the Heysel disaster.

As the good times continued – marriage to Susan was next on the list – the dark clouds were few and far between.

In fact, the only real hiccup in those early years was Ken Brown's departure. 'That was my biggest disappointment – not spending enough time with Ken Brown as manager,' said Bryan, as internal politics at Carrow Road began, bit by bit, to gnaw away at the Club's foundations.

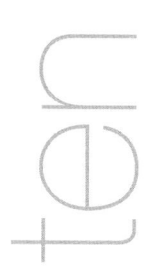

'I felt he was very unfortunate at the time to lose his job. We were not in a good position in the division, but for a man that had previously got the Club up there and won the Milk Cup a few years before I thought he was quite harshly treated.

'We moved on, but that's one thing I would like to make public – my disappointment that I didn't get more time to work with him.'

Not that Brown's replacement proved any sort of slouch. Far from it. The wind stayed in Norwich's sails as the Gunns, the Crooks, the Bowens, the Culverhouses and the Butterworths headed, almost as a single unit, towards the peak of their powers. Bryan also had a fellow Scot in his midst, Robert Fleck, to light the Canaries' fire.

'Dave Stringer came in and did a fantastic job; he got us into the top four which, again, was the highest that we'd ever achieved, and to an FA Cup semi-final at Villa Park against Everton,' said Bryan. Not for the last time, City would fluff their lines on the big, FA Cup occasion – though their no-show was rendered wholly irrelevant by events unfolding at Hillsborough.

'Looking back at it now we didn't play on the day and it was a big disappointment to us, but you look back now and the disaster at Hillsborough put it all in perspective…If it was right for any team to play at Wembley that year it was Liverpool versus Everton.'

Come City's second chance of a trip to Wembley and injury was starting to rain on Bryan's parade as a serious back injury sustained in the away trip to Sheffield United gave Mark Walton a free run through the latter part of the 1991–92 season.

'That was the start of on-going back problems,' said Bryan. 'I was actually diagnosed as having Ankylosing Spondylitis, a degenerative disease of the spine.

'I set my sights on the semi-final, but it just wasn't to be. I remember training with Mark Walton the week before and though I was diving about, it was very much a token gesture. It was another big disappointment. I think I did the radio on the day and I really wasn't expecting us to get beat – we'd done so well in the build-up to it.'

Roll the clock back 12 months to the summer of 1991 and far from football's incessant glare Francesca Gunn was diagnosed as suffering from leukaemia. She was not yet 18 months old.

'I'm not sure when it became public; when it became public knowledge. Initially I'd spoken to the manager, Dave (Stringer). Let him know the situation. I was allowed time off during the day when I needed to take Francesca off to Cambridge for treatment.

'We were quite fortunate that a lot of the treatment was done in the summer; so a lot of the initial worry was then.

'The football season became a bit of a relief for me – the training, the build-up, the pre-season. For me, personally, it was my chance to go to the training ground and train. I think I used training as an escape from it.

'I don't think I sat down with the squad and said: "Look my daughter has leukaemia…" but each person knew. Dave had obviously mentioned it to different senior players, the lads had talked about it and each, at different times, would come up and have a chat about it. Particularly the ones that had children at the time, Ian Butterworth, Ian Crook, Flecky from afar – he was on his travels at that stage.

'It was very much try to get on with life as normally as possible. We were taking Francesca to matches as well and at that stage the press would find out, we'd do a couple of different TV interviews when things looked like they were going well.

'At one stage we thought there was good hope for a cure, that's when we were speaking to people about it.

'I remember the dark day. We were playing Blackburn away on the Saturday, got beat 7–1. Just that week we found out that Francesca was not very well…I decided to play in the game. I remember being in the darkest, bleakest hotel we could have ever been in, in Blackburn…Dave Phillips was my room partner and it must have been a very awkward situation for him. Susan and I had been speaking on the phone and I'm not sure what my mood was.

'It's a bit of a blank now. I remember flying back on the plane after the game; there was a seat kept for me – it was Robert Chase's plan – to get me back to Norwich as soon as possible. I must admit it's a bit of a blur round about that time.'

Francesca Gunn died late that Sunday night – 4 October 1992. She was two and a half years old.

'Susan's very different from me; she was very private about it,' said Bryan, as his own two worlds collided – the father with a need to grieve, the footballer with a public to serve.

'Obviously when Francesca died it put a completely different picture on everything. Then you have to say to yourself: "What do we do next? Where do we go from here?"

'As I say, Susan was very different from me. She would probably do most of the crying, whereas I would have my moments, but everything was a release to me. If I could go somewhere, do something. It was just my way of trying to cope with it.'

A new addition to the Gunn household provided a light in their darkness.

'Susan was pregnant when we found out initially about Francesca. Melissa came along and then you've got someone else to look after for the rest of their life as well. But obviously there's a big part of you missing,' said Bryan, getting by with the help of his friends.

'Susan and I sat down and tried to talk it through the best we could. Again I'd come in and speak to Mike (Walker) who was the manager by then and John Deehan was fantastic.

Bryan Gunn

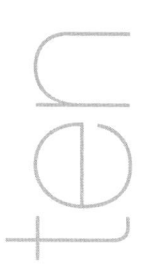

'He'd come back in the afternoons and we'd do training sessions; just one-on-one sessions, just to keep ticking over.

'There was a cup-tie against Carlisle which I missed and then I think there might have been an international; there was a week's grace; no game on the Saturday. The funeral happened within that time and then the next decision was: "Where do we go from here? How do we do it?"

'I spoke to Mike – at the end of the day it was his decision. But I did tell him I was in the right frame of mind. I'd done a few sessions with Dixie during the week and had joined in with training in the middle of the week with the rest of the lads.'

And when the next Saturday came, the Big Man was there for the home clash with QPR.

'Playing the game against QPR was, I don't know, one of the bravest things I've ever done. I don't know. If I hadn't done it then, then it would have had to have been the week after or the week after that.

'It was just making the decision. It was a family decision and one that we felt that Francesca would have wanted. She was just starting to come to football and enjoying it. She thought her daddy was fantastic, his picture was in the paper, he was on the front page of the handbook that year – those sorts of things help you make the decision.'

Besides, Francesca was never far away. She would, after all, still go to the football every week with her father. For there, in Bryan's glove bag, lay a lock of blond hair.

'It definitely did create a very special bond between myself, the football club, the city, Norfolk. Most definitely,' said Bryan, as the Norfolk public rose to salute the man in their midst.

It wasn't long before the seeds of an appeal were sown. Ten years on and the Francesca Gunn Laboratory at the University of East Anglia continues to take a lead in the fight against childhood leukaemia.

'It was incredible, the response to it all,' said Bryan. 'Initially I think we felt that we didn't want to do anything. But Keith Colman chatted through a few things and came up with the idea of a football auction. It was on the same night as the Lord Mayor's procession, at the Norwich Sport Village.

'Actually before that it was "Gunn's Golden Goals" in the *Evening News* – asking fans to pledge money for the goals scored in the remaining games of that season. If I remember rightly the game that kicked it off was the 5–1 defeat at Tottenham. But although we didn't win any points on the day, the appeal had started and we'd scored a goal.

'We were hoping to raise £10,000 – that was the target set at the time. In the end it was £14,000, £15,000 because we had some high-scoring matches – in fact, we finished with a 3–3 at Middlesbrough. It was just a tremendous end to the season.'

The football auction night would eventually raise another £10,000 and with the *Evening News* busily publishing people's pledges, the Bryan Gunn

Leukaemia Appeal was swiftly gaining a life and momentum of its own.

'Initially I did try to get out to as many different functions as possible – open this, cut a ribbon here, shake hands there, but it just got incredibly demanding and too difficult.

'You were saying "Yes!" to some and "No!" to others, so you just end up upsetting people. So we felt the way to combat it would be to let people do their events and then invite them to another do when they could hand over the cheques.

'There was no way I could get out to every event particularly at that time, January '95, when I'd just broken my leg and Susan was expecting Angus, so we made a conscious decision round about then that we'd done, as individuals, as much as we could in terms of going out and supporting the appeal.

'I can't remember now whether it was when we got to five hundred grand – there was some target we got to and we said: "We can't do any more, but people can continue to raise money…"

'We still haven't found a cure for leukaemia, but with the equipment that we can fund in the Francesca Gunn Laboratory at the UEA and in the hospitals; the students that we can put into the James Paget at Gorleston or the Norfolk & Norwich, it'll all help to one day find a cure.'

There was, it seems, a further consequence of those heroic fund-raising efforts in the difficult months that followed Francesca's death – particularly once the appeal began to gain a more formal structure by the summer of 1993.

It is an interesting side-effect that has probably dipped under the radar in terms of what made that Canary side tick, what bound that team together, as Norwich flew into the new Premiership season and prepared to storm one of the greatest footballing citadels in Europe.

Yes, it had Mike Walker's unique man-management skills; sure, it had a core of eight or nine senior players hitting the peak of their powers together; of course, it had the emerging talent of Chris Sutton at its head. But it had something else. It had a common cause born from a shared loss. And, now, it had an appeal to rally round.

'I think the Leukaemia Appeal helped that Europe team to gel because the lads were all part of that,' said Bryan. 'The amount of fund-raising, the amount of functions that we did around that time – whether it be Chris Sutton serving pizzas at Figaros to bowling nights at Solar Bowl against Ipswich Town; the golf days we had; we did a lot of things together in that year and it sort of built the spirit, the team spirit up.'

It is a fascinating theory. The Canaries already had the three 'Bostik Boys' – Sutton, Ruel Fox and Lee Power – so named because "they all stuck together". But to find Sutton serving pizzas on his night off merely reinforces the distinct impression that the side were glued together by something rather more than your traditional dressing room fare.

It would explain a lot. It would offer that trace of "X-factor" which separates the truly great sides from the merely very good.

It would also, for example, part explain how a small provincial city side found the depth of character and conviction to not only become the first – and only – British team to beat Bayern Munich in the Olympic Stadium, but also to withstand the might of Munich for a second time after Adolfo Valencia's early strike had levelled the tie at 2–2 back at Carrow Road for the second leg.

'I think the home game against Munich probably summed up that team, that spirit,' said Bryan, who pulled off one of his all-time great saves to foil Valencia in the away leg.

'That game, at home, was a great achievement. We'd obviously done fantastic away from home – that game will probably be the best result we'll ever achieve in a one-off game.

'When Valencia scored that goal after four minutes – that was the night where everyone got together and got us through a match.

'The whole place went into a hush and obviously the German fans started celebrating. But then the noise generated by the fans and the reaction of the players – it was just one mammoth effort to get back into the game.

'Whether it be the goalkeeper making saves, defensive blocks, tackles in midfield and those nervous moments at the end of the game when you're looking to hold on to what you've got – it was just a tremendous occasion.'

One which almost passed him by after the league trip to Highbury left the City 'keeper nursing a semi-dislocated shoulder and sporting a sick note from matron when it came to a Scotland get-together that week.

'I think we played at Highbury two weeks before and drew 0–0. I pulled off one of my best saves ever; unfortunately I had to pull out of the Scotland squad because I didn't think I was fit enough to train. It probably cost me my Scotland career and all in order to be fit for the match against Bayern Munich.'

From Munich to Milan, the Canaries were seeing the mountain top. From there, however, it would be a long and painful descent as Walker's request for further strengthening fell on deaf ears and a frustrated City boss registered his protest by walking out of Carrow Road one January morning and walking into a new job at Everton.

Come the summer and the Club's growing financial crisis was prompting the first visit to the sales as Chris Sutton moved to Blackburn Rovers for a then record fee of £5 million. More departures would follow as the Canaries' descent from the summit gathered pace.

'It was disappointing,' admitted Bryan, his diplomatic guard dropping slightly. 'We finished that season; Chris went that summer; Foxy went. There was a lot of things happening; a lot of money coming into the Club, but not being reallocated.'

Cue Christmas, 1994, and seven days that, arguably more than any other, shaped the recent fortunes of Norwich City Football Club.

'I remember that season with Dixie as manager,' said Bryan. 'We started off reasonably well; went to Forest when we were sixth or seventh and I broke my leg that night. And the first thing that Dixie and Meggy wanted to do was buy a new goalkeeper.'

In the meantime, City's Premiership fortunes were entrusted to an untested 18-year-old, Andy Marshall. With then chairman, Robert Chase, maintaining a vice-like grip on the purse strings as the Club haemorrhaged money, Marshall was about to give Chase the perfect excuse to ignore the management's urgent pleas.

'Possibly the worst thing to ever happen to the Club then was for its 18-year-old goalkeeper to come in and play the game of his life against Newcastle on Boxing Day,' said Bryan, as an increasingly embattled chairman battened down the hatches and gambled on the teenage 'keeper riding out the gathering storm.

'It just needed that someone with a bit of experience to come in on a two or three-year contract and it would then have put me under pressure and you'd still be developing a young goalkeeper and not exposing him to the rigours of Premiership football at 18…What Chase was looking at was the fact that I'd be fit and he'd have another goalkeeper on his books to pay as well.'

With hindsight, the decision to ignore Deehan's plea for reinforcements in the false belief that Norwich already had enough points on the board to somehow scramble to safety that season proved a disaster.

So much for the future fall-out. In the meantime, there was another drama unfolding at the Queen's Medical Centre in Nottingham as the extent of Bryan's injury became clear.

'As well as breaking my leg, I dislocated my ankle so obviously all the ligaments moved and that's an injury in itself,' said Bryan, with worse about to follow.

'What I did have as well and got little attention at the time is Compartment Syndrome; I had a pin in my ankle, here, on the right leg and then one evening in hospital in Nottingham it just started swelling up inexplicably and I was rushed in for an emergency operation.

'They cut it open and said if it did get infected there was a chance of losing the leg, which gave me a little bit of extra anxiety.'

If you buy into the theory that the Francesca appeal helped to bind that Walker team together, by the time Deehan and Megson were desperately trying to fend off relegation in the spring of 1995 the deep, emotional ties that had served City so well in Munich and Milan had long been loosened.

Phillips, the room-mate that desperate night in Blackburn, had long gone as, of course, had Sutton, Fox, Ekoku and Robins – all flogged to the first bidder as the Club's financial foundations began to give way beneath the chairman's feet.

Bryan Gunn

Of those that remained, Butterworth's own injury nightmare ripped another dressing room leader out of the manager's survival plans, while those that did arrive – the Newsomes, the Adams', the Milligans and the Sherons – were, in a sense, "outsiders". They hadn't served pizzas in a little girl's cause.

Sidelined by his serious injury, Bryan could only watch as the team that Brown bought, Stringer nurtured and Walker inspired slipped out of the top flight just as the Sky TV money began to pour in.

In theory the arrival of Martin O'Neill as manager that summer should – and probably would – have led to the Canaries making a swift return to the top flight. In practice, such fond hopes soon foundered on the Club's fearful financial position and, in particular, the disintegrating relationship between manager and chairman.

The question of whether or not Norwich needed to buy an experienced 'keeper ahead of O'Neill's promotion push still loomed large.

'I got a phone call when I was on holiday in Spain to say that I was needed back for a rigorous fitness test just in case Martin needed to go out and buy a new goalkeeper because even he was thinking down those lines as well,' said Bryan.

'Fortunately I came back and proved my fitness; I'd been doing rehab at Lilleshall and working quite hard during the summer. Not having known Martin before, I had to come back and impress.

'I had a fitness test at Colney and the decision was that I was fit; there was still a bit of work to be done on the kicking aspect, but there was still six weeks to go until the beginning of the season so there was no major worry there and I started the season as Martin's No.1.'

Though O'Neill's tenure of office proved wretchedly short-lived, as for the one and only time in his career the future Celtic boss walked out on a managerial contract, there was still enough time to spot "a touch of greatness" in his thoughts and deeds in the City hot seat.

'I didn't make my first save – he told me this – until we beat Oldham at home 2–1 in late August. He patted me on the back and said: "Big man, you were brilliant tonight – that was the first save you made for me!"

'That was just the way he was, the way he went about things, boosting you at the right time; saying things that you wouldn't expect. A manager with a difference, no doubt.

'Like Fergie he had the will to win, the want to win. For Martin, how he wins is not a problem; he's going to win the game. If he wins it by playing Brazilian-style football, then that's fantastic; if he wins it by getting the ball into the box and the centre-forward heads it in from the penalty spot, then that's just as good.'

With O'Neill bound for Leicester and the angry masses at the gates, in his desperate hour of need an embattled Chase turned to Megson for Norwich's next managerial appointment.

Ten years on and nigh-on every party involved now concedes it was the wrong move. Not that anyone ever stood much of a chance as the chairman reached for the financial panic button and began auctioning off what remained of the Carrow Road silver – with or without the manager's blessing.

'I think Meggy was the wrong manager for this football club at that time and I don't think you can blame Meggy for that,' admitted Bryan.

'He was put in at a very volatile time at the Club. The finances were going through the mill and he didn't have a lot to play with. It was a tricky one for Gary.'

And then there was the issue of style. Playing football the Megson-way never sat easily with one or two influential players in that troubled dressing room. Leaving Mark Bowen high and dry on 399 games for the Norfolk club, as his illustrious Canary career came to an acrimonious end, merely made public the private tensions afoot.

'At the time I had built up a good relationship with Meggy. He was an experienced player; we'd played a lot of golf together; his attitude to football, his moans and his groans on the pitch was something I'd been used to doing. Moaning and groaning trying to get the best out of people – so I knew where he was coming from in that respect.

'But, yes, there were different areas of the team where they disagreed with his ideas on football and the way it should be played. It was unfortunate again that it didn't last – it seemed to be a merry-go-round at the time and it didn't end there.'

For come the summer and as Chase finally fell and the luckless Megson departed, so Walker made a triumphant return. For the first season at least, the odd ache and pain apart, the Gunner was in.

Come the following summer, however, and the end was drawing nigh. There would, however, be one more twist to the tale before the Carrow Road curtain finally fell.

Locked in combat with the maturing Marshall for the No.1 jersey, Bryan's pre-season preparations had taken a rather interesting turn courtesy of a phone call from Parkhead.

Having been pipped to the post at Rangers by Chris Woods some ten years earlier, the opportunity to see out the final years of his career in a "Bhoys" shirt appeared to be knocking loud and clear.

'At the start of that season I ended up getting a phone call from Scotland to say that Celtic were looking for a goalkeeper,' said Bryan, with matters reaching a head one summer night in Peterborough as the Canaries made their traditional pre-season trip across the Fens.

'It was the night of Peterborough away and Mike had received a call from the agent saying that Celtic were interested in taking me. And I thought I was going to Celtic. The agent said that Mike's not going to stand in your way,' said Bryan, about to give the boys his farewell speech.

'So there I was, Peterborough away. I've handed out all the bibs to the rest of the players and, as I did so, told them all I was going to Celtic and the only thing that would stop me from going to Celtic was the manager.

'And he named me in the team to play Peterborough that night. And I thought: "What's he doing? I'm meant to be going to sign for Celtic!"

'He could have easily named Marsh; he was his No.1 the week after; I played in the Peterborough game and I think we drew 1–1; Marsh played on the Tuesday night and we got beat six by Arsenal and then he started the season. I've only spoken to the agent once after that so I've no idea how true it all was, but they ended up signing Jonathan Gould. So they were on the look-out for a goalkeeper.

'I've never held it against Mike – that was his decision again. But I could have ended up playing for Celtic – and in the end that season I played against them for Hibernian.'

Well aware that another Carrow Road contract would be hard to come by that summer, when Bryan finally did squeeze in ahead of Marshall, he arrived back in a side short of both form and fortune. Walker was struggling to weave his magic for a second time – particularly once Chase's years of financial mismanagement had left him with so little in the larder. A typically "epic" FA Cup third round performance away at Grimsby Town the week before heralded Bryan's final fling in a Canary shirt.

'I came in and played a few games. Unfortunately the first one was away at Wolves – a 5–0 drubbing. Came into the dressing room at the end of the game and said: "Sorry lads, my fault for the fifth one…"

'It was just one of those days that a team will have and unfortunately I was the goalkeeper who suffered from it on the day. But I came back from that, showed a lot of character and we beat Forest 1–0 at home, coming off the pitch clutching the champagne again.

'We then beat Sunderland 2–1 on the Tuesday night – that was my final home game.

'I played well, but unfortunately let in a bad goal. Late in the game, it was slippy, it was a wet night and a Lee Clark shot went through. I'd saved everything else apart from that one.'

Cue the final game of a long and illustrious career. Away at Crewe Alexandra on 31 January 1998.

'We went to Crewe on the Saturday and I remember getting beat 1–0 and that was an Erik Fuglestad own goal.

'I think we were playing Manchester City at home the following week and Mike took me in and said Marsh was back in, he was his No.1. As I say, that was his decision. If you're a No.1 it's great, if you're not a No.1 it's a difficult scenario.'

In the end, one of Bryan's long-time pals from their Aberdeen days together took the Big Man back up north – to Edinburgh and Hibernian where Alex McLeish was now manager. Even then, fate conspired to deny Bryan one last way back to Norfolk.

'Initially Hibs took me on loan for the final three months of the season, but due to an administrative cock-up in Scotland they'd already signed two loan players and couldn't have three so I think I ended up signing a three-month, full-time contract, with Norwich releasing my registration for a small fee.

'And that was my ties severed with Norwich. Who knows? Had I got to the end of that season, had I still been registered then, you never know, I could still have been a Norwich player.'

A second broken leg cut Bryan's Hibs career short just six months into a new, two-year contract.

It was not long, with a little help from their many friends, before the family was moving back home to Norfolk.

'At the time Gordon Bennett was very generous in saying to me when I left the Club that there would always be a role somewhere in the Club for me, which was fantastic to know,' said Bryan, still a commanding figure at Carrow Road in his role as sponsorship sales manager. He's also got a matchday hospitality club to run and as Gunn Club regulars will no doubt attest, he remains the most hospitable of hosts.

They are, after all, very much his people. Norwich City remains very much his football club. As the Sheriff of Norwich for a year, he even had a city to call his own.

For there are certain ties in the life of Bryan Gunn that will never be broken. Ties that not only brought the Big Man home but, in the darkest of times, bound both a football club and its team together.

'I did have to make a decision because I got the same offer to stay at Hibernian – even though I'd only been there for six months.

'We were always planning our route back. When we moved to Scotland we already had Angus's name down in the school in Alpington. Can I imagine living anywhere else in the country? No, I don't think so. Francesca is our tie.'

11 Iwan Roberts

Despite a disappointing first campaign with the Canaries, Iwan went on to become the darling of the Carrow Road faithful during his next six seasons with the Canaries.

After 306 appearances for the Club Iwan ended his Norwich City career with 96 goals to his name and sits proudly in third position in the Club's all-time scoring charts.

Goals make heroes and once they started to flow for Iwan his popularity grew and grew. His wonderful brace at Portman Road against arch-rivals Ipswich Town in March 2000 will always be remembered fondly by all at Carrow Road. The delight expressed on that gap-toothed face once the ball hit back of the net yet again will never be forgotten.

Norwich City and Iwan Roberts were simply a match made in heaven – and how fitting it would have been if his goal in the 2001–02 play-off final had seen City promoted.

Twice voted Player of the Year, Iwan's aim of getting Norwich back into the Premier League was achieved in his final season at Carrow Road. Seeing their hero on the balcony of City Hall with the First Division championship trophy almost brought tears to the eyes of the Canary faithful as they bade farewell to a Canary legend.

Iwan Wyn Roberts

Born: Bangor, 26 June 1968
City Debut: 9 August 1997, Wolverhampton Wanderers (h) 0–2 Division One
Final Game: 9 May 2004, Crewe Alexandra (a) 3–1 Division One
League appearances: 278
League goals: 84
FA Cup appearances: 7
FA Cup goals: 1
League Cup appearances: 18
League Cup goals: 10
Others appearances: 3
Other goals: 1
Total appearances: 306
Total goals: 96

Right. Where on earth do you start with this one? It is, after all, hardly any time since there wasn't a dry eye in the house at Gresty Road, Crewe, when Iwan Roberts finally brought the curtain down on his illustrious Canary career 306 games and 96 goals after it all started.

In amongst those simple statistics lie so many stories, so many headlines, so many still-fresh memories.

His beaming face on the balcony of City Hall as the old Football League championship trophy was first introduced to the vast crowd gathered beneath; the wheel-away, arms-outstretched run and dive onto the half-way line at the Millennium Stadium, Cardiff, after his extra-time goal put the Canaries within touching distance of promotion via the play-offs; that famous, gap-toothed grin and joyous salute to the Barclay that would greet his latest Carrow Road strike.

Even that final outing in a Canary shirt managed to add another short chapter to his story of legend as Iwan's last appearance in front of the travelling City faithful produced two more goals for his album – the first of which was an utter peach.

'I've never scored a goal like that in my life,' said Iwan, as strike No.95 in Norwich colours took him one step nearer that magic 100 mark and merely confirmed his lasting place in the Club's hall-of-striker fame – third in City's all-time list of goalscorers behind the fiery Irishman Johnny Gavin (132) and Chris Sutton-in-disguise, the great Terry Allcock, on 127. A twice-taken penalty later, to really push the Gresty Road party button, and there was goal No.96 to complete the Roberts collection.

Of course, for anyone who missed City's 2003–04 title-winning season there is also the small matter of his own book to ponder – '*All I Want For Christmas*' which topped the local best-sellers chart for many a week.

So when all else fails, go back to basics. Begin where any great story should – at the very beginning. In a small, close-knit village in the Welsh-speaking depths of North Wales. It was there that the lasting character of the man, both as a player and a person, was first shaped and formed. Even 20 years later, travel to any game in the North-West and afterwards Iwan could always be found locked in conversation with proud family and friends in a language all their own.

For the rest of us, waiting patiently for a quick, post-match quote, trying to decipher even a word of the fluent Welsh that greeted you was next to impossible. As any number of struggling centre-halves discovered once the young Iwan Roberts first started to make his way in the game at Watford.

How he got there and which other young dragon was there at Vicarage Road to greet him made for a memorable start to Iwan's 20-year professional career – one that continues to this day as the 36-year-old adds his influential presence to Gillingham's championship cause.

'I was playing for the Welsh under-18 Schools team and their manager was best friends with a guy called Tom Whalley who was the youth-team manager at Watford,' said Iwan, about to forge a lasting link with another future Canary – Malcolm Allen.

'Tom's from North Wales, from Caernarvon. So I sort of knew Tom and I knew Malcolm playing against him in the local leagues in North Wales. And Malcolm was down there too.

'That's really how I got to go to Watford. I went to Manchester United for a trial – they wanted me to have an apprenticeship there. I went to places like Villa, Leeds, Bristol Rovers, but because Watford had the Welsh connection I knew that although it was a long way away, the Wales connection would make it easy for me to settle.

'And at the time it was a massive decision for me to leave home and go to Watford, but it made it so much easier knowing that I had two Welsh-speaking people there.'

What also made Iwan's new life easier was the fact that even as a 14-year-old he had more than held his own in the company of grown men. He had already met and mastered the physical challenges that life as a professional footballer – particularly that of a 6ft 3in target man – brings.

'It helped me a hell of a lot – actually playing in a men's league in North Wales when I was 14, 15,' said Iwan, swiftly learning the darker arts of being a big and bright centre-forward, especially once a dim-witted centre-half loomed into view with his bulging eyes, keen on adding the legs of a teenage prospect to his trophy cabinet.

'I was always a big lad,' said Iwan, with a son fast following in his father's footsteps. 'I was one of the tallest lads at school – like Ben now really. Big and tall, but all skin and bones. I didn't carry any weight until I was about 23, 24. So, yes, being a big lad definitely helped me.

'But the place that I'm from is a small community so everyone knew I was playing for the Welsh Schools team – big things were made of that. And there were a couple of known, so-called "hard" men that played in the league and they tried to intimidate me when I used to play against them, but even at that age – and I must have been about 16 – I wouldn't let them get to me.

'I think one of them said the same old thing: "I'm going to snap your legs…" that kind of thing and I can remember in that particular game I actually scored two goals. I've always thought since then that that's the best way you can shut anyone up. So, as I say, playing adult football at such an early age definitely helped me.

'Probably just the physical aspect of the game, really. I got used to it at an early age – playing against grown men when I was 14 – and it's carried me in good stead up till now really.'

As for what served him well at Watford, a blossoming friendship on and off the pitch with Malcolm Allen obviously helped. It is also worth bearing in mind that the Watford of Iwan's vintage – Graham Taylor's side of the mid- to late-80s – was far removed from the Hornets side of today.

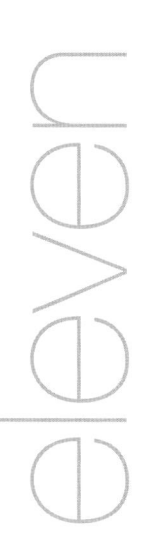

As, indeed, was the place itself compared to the Roberts' family home.

'It was a huge culture shock going from this small Welsh village to Watford – especially given that Watford is there, on the outskirts of London. It's four and a half, maybe five hours in the car.

'And I am literally from a village that's got a shop – it's got three garages believe it or not – it's got a pub, a little primary school and that's it. I wouldn't have a clue what the population is, but it wouldn't be more than a couple of thousand, maybe.

'Everybody knew each other. It was back in the days when you can leave your door open and nothing would get stolen and stuff like that. So it was a massive culture shock for me – even clothes-wise.

'You've gone down and seen what the other apprentices are turning up in and you're thinking: "I'm well out of date here!" It took me a bit of time to settle in, but I was an apprentice with people like Tim Sherwood, the two Holdsworth boys and Paul Franklin was there as well – Franko was having problems with his knee.

'They'd just finished second or third in the First Division; they'd been to the FA Cup Final; Graham Taylor was doing really well. So it was one of the top clubs at the time. So it wasn't as if I was going to a Second Division club. I was going to a good First Division side.'

And one where the forward line, at least in the reserves, spoke Welsh.

'Malcolm and I hadn't played with each other until we went to Watford. I knew of him. He lived about half an hour away from where I was brought up. He was probably playing for the best team in that league at the time and everybody knew him, everyone knew that Malcolm Allen had gone to Watford and done really well. And he's a fluent Welsh speaker as well.

'Even in reserve games we'd talk Welsh up front. And you could see the centre-halves looking at each other and saying: "What are they on about?" You could talk tactics, what are you going to do… Yes, we used to speak Welsh all the time.'

Allen had been and gone from Carrow Road by the time Iwan finally arrived in Norfolk at the start of the 1997–98 season, but the Welsh theme would continue to underpin his career. After all the man who brought him to Carrow Road, Mike Walker, was born in Colwyn Bay, North Wales, while before the arrival of Darren Huckerby to light the blue touchpaper in City's title season Iwan's most prolific strike partner in Canary colours was a right Welsh firebrand – Craig Bellamy.

'I think it did, it also underpinned my relationship with Bellars (Craig Bellamy). It's probably the same with the Scottish, the Irish. I hit it off with Bellars, I hit it off with Izzy (Chris Llewellyn) – we've got a young boy down at Gillingham now, Andrew Crofts. He's with the Wales under-21s and I get on really well with him.

'I don't know. Maybe you make more of conscious effort because people are from your country. Don't get me wrong – I fell out so many times with

Bellars. But we were good friends and I think that's probably why we played well together.'

The two even played together for Wales as the great steel roof of the Millennium Stadium, Cardiff, glided together for the first time and the Principality played host to the boys from Brazil.

'I know we lost 3-0, but it was one of the highlights of my career. I played the full game, played well; the Millennium Stadium; they'd closed the roof for the first time; sell-out crowd; playing against the best players in the world. It's definitely up there.'

As, in fairness, is his very first Wales cap – a World Cup Group Seven qualifier against the mighty Dutch in October 1996. It was somehow entirely fitting that the game that night should be played in North Wales at the Racecourse Ground, Wrexham, given the two strikers on view. 'Me and Malcolm Allen – my first cap, in a World Cup qualifying game against the great Holland side – when they had Rijkaard, Koeman, van Basten, Gullit. That's right up there, too.'

By that stage, Iwan was at Wolves, having made a £1.3 million switch across the Midlands from Leicester City where, he admits, he'd had the time of his life until the then chairman, Martin George, managed to sour the atmosphere on the eve of one of the Foxes' seemingly endless Wembley appearances, under someone well know in these parts, Martin O'Neill.

'Before I came to Norwich, I guess the club I felt most at home at was Leicester. Up until my time here, that would have been the best time of my career – I was only there two and a half years – but football-wise that was probably the best time in my career. Both what we were achieving on the pitch and the bunch of lads off it,' said Iwan, whose spell at Filbert Street yielded 41 goals from his 100 league appearances.

'I finished top scorer in the three seasons I was there. I joined in the November from Huddersfield; finished the top scorer that season; finished top scorer in the Premier League when we got relegated; finished top scorer again when we won the play-offs against Crystal Palace.'

That was a game that Iwan would miss as he struggled with a rib injury sustained in the run-up to Leicester's play-off charge. It cut little ice with George – a man who managed to rub many people up the wrong way, Leicester's saviour, O'Neill, among them. A typically ill-timed remark duly found the club's top scorer packing his bags that summer as Mark McGhee renewed his acquaintance with the Foxes' front man.

'Brian Little brought me to Leicester; McGhee was there for sixth months – he'd tried to sign me for Reading a few times – so I knew he fancied me as a player. But if I had my time again I wouldn't do the Wolves move, no.

'I fell out with the chairman at Leicester – Martin George. He wasn't the most popular person there and he said something on the day of the play-off game.

'I wasn't on the bench that day – it was my decision. Martin O'Neill said: "I want to put you on the bench, but you've got to be honest with me. If you had to come on after five, ten minutes, do you think you'd be able to last the game?"

'"And Julie and a fella' called Alan Birchenall – The Birch – were talking in the stands and he was saying: "Is Robbo on the bench?" and Julie was saying: "No, he's not!" and the chairman was ear-wigging for some reason and all of a sudden he's come out with: "Well, he doesn't deserve to be on the bench. The people that deserve to be on the bench are the people that have got us here…"

'We'd had a great run with about six games to go – we must have won at least five because we left it late to get that sixth place – and I'd got 20 goals that season. So that really, really hacked me off, to be honest. Plus, at the time, Wolves were a bigger club.'

A bigger club with a big, big star in the shape of Steve Bull. Iwan's Wolves debut, with hindsight, might have marked his card as the one-time England striker bagged himself a hat-trick in a 3–1 away win at Grimsby Town on the opening day of the 1996–97. Bull was about to become the immovable object that would hasten Iwan's arrival in Norfolk a summer later.

'Bully was always first pick and then it was always me or Don Goodman who was going to partner Bully. Me and Don had two games together – we won one and drew one. It was not as if we couldn't play together.

'I can understand why Mark McGhee did it because Bully's a massive, massive cult figure, a hero, a legend – all those things up there. And he was still banging the goals in, to be fair. So he didn't really want to upset the punters by putting Bully on the bench. Because he had a bit of a sticky patch, he stuck with him and I can see that. Graham Taylor did it and paid for it, really.'

Hence the move to pastures very new in the summer of 1997. Iwan was unveiled alongside Oldham defender Craig Fleming as the two, principal planks in Walker's push for the play-offs and promotion that season. It says much about Walker's enduring eye for a player that the pair would – first in the run to and final at Cardiff in 2002 and again en route to the First Division title in 2004 – play such key roles in Norwich's success.

'I hardly knew anything about Norwich before I got here. I'd played here a few times. I knew that they tried to play the right way. I knew Mike Walker – the Welsh connection again – Gossy was here, people like Mark Bowen. Malcolm had been here – so I knew that they played the game the right way. But didn't know anything as to how nice the area was to live.'

That first season, by Iwan's own admission, wasn't a runaway success. An opening day defeat to – of all people – Wolves set the tone for a difficult campaign in which both form and fortune would desert Walker as injury after injury, and crucially to the wrong players at the wrong time, chipped away at City's play-off prospects. A badly bruised toe, courtesy of a night out with Martin "Mad Dog" Allen in a 1–1 draw at Portsmouth on 2 September 1997, hardly helped Iwan's cause as he found himself sidelined for six weeks. February brought another month-long injury absence.

In the end he finished his first season at Carrow Road with five goals from his 31 league appearances – a lean return for Norwich's £850,000 investment.

'That first season here under Mike was probably the toughest year of my career – especially the start of it,' said Iwan, about to find himself in the firing line – never a nice place to be for someone so keen to make a good impression.

'I could understand people's frustrations. We were talking about getting into the play-offs, I was the final piece in the jigsaw because they had a good side here anyway and I didn't perform. I didn't score the goals; looked sluggish, looked slow, looked overweight and I can see why people might be thinking: "This is the worst signing the Club's ever made..."

'I can remember some of the letters in the paper saying just that, that this is the worst signing that the Club's ever made.

'The transfer fee didn't weigh on my mind. Not really. I wasn't the record fee for the Club – that was Jon Newsome. I think if you go somewhere and you're the record transfer buy price-wise, I think that's a bit of a burden really...So, no, the transfer fee didn't bother me. I knew it was a lot of money for the Club with the financial situation it was in and, if I'm honest, I think if they could have sold me that season, after my first season, I think they would have.'

There is a very real regret there that it didn't work out under Walker. The respect and affection were there – just not the luck, perhaps.

'Mike's a top man. He's a really, really nice fella' and the way that I feel is that I let him down. I let him down with my performances. And that's not why he left the Club, but I do feel partly responsible.'

Looking back now on that opening day defeat by Wolves, it was a two-goal blast by 17-year-old Robbie Keane on his Wolves debut that grabbed all the headlines. More significant perhaps in terms of the Iwan Roberts story is the young man making his fourth City appearance that day – 18-year-old substitute Craig Bellamy.

If Walker's final season at Carrow Road achieved anything it was to pair those two together – two players who, but for untimely injury, could have delivered promotion to Norfolk way ahead of schedule – above all in the following season when the Bruce Rioch-Bryan Hamilton show began to gather steam.

'If I had to design an ideal striker for me then I think Bellars does tick most of the boxes. It's easy for me to say because we did hit it off. I could say the same about Hucks (Darren Huckerby) really. They're both quick, bright footballers. The difference between the two is that Hucks probably isn't as greedy as Bellars.

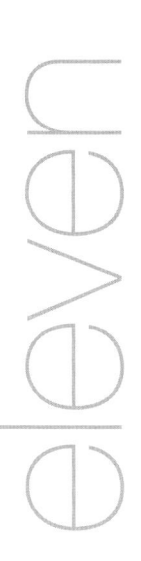

'There's a few situations where Hucks had put them on a plate for me; Bellars probably would have shot. That probably comes with age as well – age and experience. But my ideal partner would be one of those two.'

Bellamy also had attitude. With a big capital 'A'. Be it confidence or cockiness – call it want you want – the Cardiff-born teenager had it. In spades. Still does. It is one of the reasons why he is where he is. At the top.

'You could see that there was definitely something special there. He's so confident, so quick, he works his socks off in training every day.

'And if you didn't work that was when he would get on at you – and rightly so. I don't care how old you are, if you're 17 and if you're working your socks off and someone else isn't then you've got to dig them out. And Bellars wouldn't be scared of telling whoever it was, Gunny or whoever, Flecky, he wouldn't be scared of telling them that they weren't pulling their weight.

'And that's probably why he has got to the top. All the top players – people like Alan Shearer, Michael Owen, Beckham, whoever – they have got that little bit of attitude. They probably don't bring it out as much as what Bellars does and some of the things he says on the pitch, but I think they've all got it.'

It wasn't simply having the young Welshman as a sidekick that brought the best out of Iwan that season. Both Rioch and Hamilton were bringing new ideas and fresh approaches to his game. A stricter fitness regime was also turning Iwan into a leaner, meaner machine as his 30th birthday loomed.

'I learned a lot off Bruce. I never used to get on people's shoulders like Bellars does all the time until he came to the Club. I was just back to goal – play the ball up to me. And Bruce has come into the Club and said: "Robbo, why don't you try this...Get on people's shoulders and you'll get more goals – especially in the box..." And I'd never really done that before.'

From Hamilton came a better first touch. Iwan was fast becoming far more of a footballer than many ever give him credit for.

'Because of my size, I've scored so many goals with my head, the lack of teeth as well – they do probably label you as this big lump up front. I can imagine opposition managers saying: "Oh, yes, Roberts – he's a big lump. He puts himself about and that..."

'But I do have a bit of pride that I have got a decent touch. If you knock the ball up there I can bring things down.

'To be fair, it's something that I had to work on and a lot of credit has to go to Bryan Hamilton – believe it or not. He brought head tennis up to Colney. We hadn't played it since I joined the Club and that improved my touch so much – two-touch head tennis. I was actually talking to him before the Northern Ireland–Wales game at Cardiff and I said to him: "You improved my touch so much by bringing that head tennis up..." Just a simple thing like that. But I had to work at it.'

As he did on his weight. Once again, the introduction of fitness weights to the Roberts regime worked wonders.

'I didn't really start doing weights up until four, five years ago. I don't know why. It hadn't really appealed to me – if I bulk up I don't want to be too muscular and all this but I tell you what, I wish I'd started doing them when I was 18. Because they improved me – they made me a little bit quicker. But you live and learn, don't you?' said Iwan, as he finally found his ideal playing weight.

'I would say my ideal "fighting weight" would be between thirteen-ten to fourteen stone. Between that I'm happy.

'In that first season under Mike I would have been around fourteen-ten. And then the second season when Bruce took over on my first day back in training I was fifteen-three.

'But it is hard work in the summer when you're away with the family. You do get used to it though. When I'm away I will go for a run every other day. Otherwise – especially if you're in America – the food that you get out there, I'll soon pile it on. And I hate myself when I do it.'

Come the end of October 1998, and the Roberts-Bellamy show was flying. A 4–1 home win over Huddersfield Town on 24 October finds the pair scoring a pair apiece to take their total in the league to 18. And the season was still little more than ten weeks old.

By the time Norwich travelled to Wolves on 12 December, that total stood at 22 – well on course to hit that magic 40-mark. With two, 20-goal strikers to your name and the likes of Darren Eadie and Keith O'Neill enjoying a vaguely injury-free run, Norwich looked the play-off part.

And then came that tackle. Kevan Muscat wrote himself into Norwich City legend for all the wrong reasons with a scything lunge unspotted by the referee that left Bellamy needing ten stitches in a gaping wound on his knee. Though Bellamy would return six weeks later at the end of January and, indeed, added three more goals to Norwich's faltering play-off push, the momentum was lost that day at Molineux. City finished ninth – 14 points short of sixth spot.

'That season, had he stayed fit, we would have had enough goals between us to get us to the play-offs. Definitely,' said Iwan.

'I think Kevin Phillips and Niall Quinn at Sunderland finished the top pairing that season and I think Bellars and I were only five, six goals behind them – and Bellars missed about six or seven weeks. So he missed a lot of games otherwise we would have definitely have got into the play-offs. We would have finished the top pairing in that division.

'And, I think, he would have got the Player of the Year that year if he'd have stayed fit. I won it, but I think had Bellars stayed fit, he would have scored the more goals.'

Still there was always next year, until one summer's night at Southend United, in a pretty meaningless pre-season friendly, City's young strike jewel crumpled to the ground, his cruciate knee ligament ruptured.

He would not reappear until the very tail end of the 1999–2000 season – at home to Port Vale on 22 April. By then the Rioch-Hamilton dream ticket had fallen by the wayside. Rioch exited after a dispiriting 1–0 home defeat by Crystal Palace on 11 March. A Roberts double in the derby trip to Ipswich Town a week later at least got the new Hamilton regime off to a flying start, but the dark clouds were descending. Bellamy's two goals before the end of the season merely underlined what everyone had been missing for the previous eight months. One week into the new, 2000–01 season and he, too, had gone – sold to Coventry City for a potential £6.5 million.

Still, time enough for a wholly shambolic 1–0 defeat away at Barnsley on the opening day of the season – a match that featured a ten-man home side conjuring up a winner from a ghastly error from new Dutch defender Fernando Derveld and a dressing room bust-up afterwards as both the recriminations flew and the tempers frayed.

'When he left for Coventry it was deflating,' admitted Iwan, sharing an emotion with the rest of the City faithful. 'If we'd have kept him I think we would have had a great chance that season. But it was too good an offer for the Club to turn down – especially in the financial situation that they were in. But we were selling our best player. I think that's the way the majority of people were looking at it.

'At that time there were little signs that things were starting to unravel a bit. Bryan had brought players in and they weren't good enough for the First Division. And as optimistic as you want to be – you want to say the right things for people that come and watch and pay your wages – you could tell that we were going to struggle.

'We lost to Barnsley, they only had ten men, the fight in the dressing room after – there was unrest in the camp.'

The arrival of two real old warhorses in the shape of Tony Cottee and Steve Walsh that September could, in all fairness to the under-pressure Hamilton, have worked a treat. Cottee would have given City the craft and experience that they sorely lacked in the hole alongside Iwan at one end, while at the other Walsh – an undoubted leader of men – would have stiffened Norwich's resolve for the bruising fight ahead.

But – and it was a fatal but – the two new arrivals had to play games if they were ever to take the dressing room with them. Both struggled fitness-wise. Walsh started twice that troubled autumn – in the 3–3 Worthington Cup second round draw with Blackpool on 19 September and the painful 4–0 defeat at Wolves the following Sunday. He would finish neither game.

Once word started to circulate – as it always does in a dressing room – as to what the pair might be being paid for their ineffective services, it merely sowed further dissension in the ranks. Iwan, the senior statesman and big-time pal of Walsh from their heady Leicester City days together, felt the gathering storm break around him.

'They were both great players in their time, but we probably got them too late really,' said Iwan, as Hamilton's big gamble failed. He needed them to play games; needed them to prove their worth – to the board, the supporters and, above all, to the rest of the players.

'Big Walshy he was struggling with injuries; TC's come and it didn't work for him. I think he'd lost his sharpness in front of goal. Time had caught up with him. So looking back they weren't the best signings that Hammy made and probably cost the Club quite a lot of money as well. It's easy to look back, but it could have worked. It could have worked.

'We did need another centre-half. When Walshy first came I thought: "Wow, what a great signing!" because I knew what he was like at Leicester. But I knew that his knees were shot to bits and that he would struggle to play at that level consistently.'

Events would finally come to a head away at Portsmouth on Saturday, 2 December. Cottee had spared everyone's further embarrassment by exiting swiftly for a new role at Barnet. Walsh soldiered on – out of the first-team picture completely.

A dire 2–0 defeat at Fratton Park made it five defeats on the spin and Norwich, now without the seriously injured Gaetano Giallanza, were heading south for the winter. Plummeting south, to be accurate.

'I think we would have got relegated if he hadn't have left,' said Iwan, as the word "Crisis" in six-foot, fluorescent letters lit up the skies above Colney and Carrow Road. Hamilton was, in the public's view, also the chairman's right-hand man and without him Bob Cooper's position in the boardroom became all the more vulnerable.

'I think Hammy had lost all the respect in the dressing room and I think there was only one way we were going, to be honest,' said Iwan.

Come the Monday, and the manager felt obliged to call a senior players' meeting in his office. Whether it was always designed to clear the air; whether it was always Hamilton's intention to let everyone lay all their cards on the table; or simply a "Come on boys, be honest with me…" chat that somehow got out of hand, perhaps we'll never know. Given what and who followed Hamilton's exit, I suspect history will see that day as one of the Club's great turning points. Monday, 4 December 2000, for those who want it for the record books.

For others it was also the one day in recent times where you would have loved to have been the proverbial fly on the wall. For his part, Iwan was all too aware of the political minefield into which he was now straying.

'If you come out and say what you really want to say and then he stays, then while he's here it could be the end of your time at the Club, sort of thing. It's either you go or he goes.

'But we knew that something had to be done. So he called the six of us in – I think it was six of us – and the way we thought he'd settle it was that he was going to go upstairs.

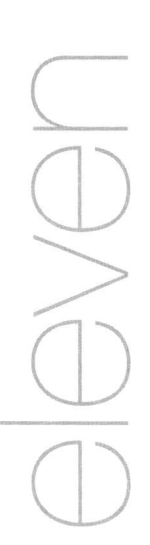

'We didn't have a problem with that, but obviously one or two had said: "Well, I think it'll be better if you left the Club completely…" And we left it that he hadn't come to a decision. I'm driving back from somewhere, I put the radio on and he's left the Club.

'I think it was the right thing to do. To be fair to Jacko (Matt Jackson) and Marshy (Andy Marshall), they put their heads on the line, if you like, and said: "Yeah, gaffer, I think it would be better if you left…" I think he had to. I do believe that if he hadn't, we would have gone down.'

Likewise, in the judgement of history – with hindsight sitting firmly by her side – the board's move to appoint Nigel Worthington as Hamilton's replacement, first on a caretaker basis and then full-time, proved a master stroke. It certainly had the players' approval, with the hapless Dutch pair of Raymond de Waard and Fernando Derveld making a sharp exit within almost hours of the new manager's arrival.

'The lads liked Nigel – he had that discipline that I think everybody needs,' said Iwan. 'OK, he'd had a bit of a bad time at Blackpool, but I think it was a really bold move from the Club and it was the right decision.

'We'd gone from one manager to the next and the next and I just think that it needed that stability for a couple of years to get ourselves back on an even keel. We were in the doldrums; they were dark days. We were scraping for points. With three games left we still could have got relegated and things like this. They were bad times, so fair play to the board for giving him a chance.'

It wasn't the only smart move of the winter. 'I think they did well as well to promote Stevie (Steve Foley) to first-team coach because he's a great coach, so there wasn't that massive change that you normally get when a manager leaves and someone fresh comes in and brings different people in.

'I don't think we had that sort of time.'

Saved from relegation, City went into bat the next season with hope, confidence and discipline restored. Few – even Worthington himself – ever expected the 2001–2002 campaign to end where it did. A couple of penalty kicks away from promotion to the Premiership.

In getting to the First Division Play-off Final at the Millennium Stadium, City also racked up one of the sweetest moments in Iwan's Canary career – that play-off semi-final success over his old employers, Wolves.

'I can't put my finger on what clicked that Cardiff year. It seems like ages ago now, it really does.

'The spirit was great here. I don't know, really. I missed quite a big part of it with my knee and my hamstring – about 12 weeks of it. What was our secret? I couldn't tell you.

'But the Wolves play-offs – especially the one here – they were big, big games. We were so determined. Paul Butler had come out in the paper and said how it'll be all over after the first leg and the gaffer had that all over the dressing room, at Colney, down here. We won the game 3–1, but I personally knew that it wasn't over. I knew what the atmosphere would be like at Molineux. I'd played for them in the play-offs when we lost to Palace and it was so hostile up there, but again that comes down to the character we had here.

'Defensively that year we were solid – well, we have been for the last two or three years – we didn't concede many goals, so I knew after the result here, after beating them 3–1, I knew that we had a great chance of going up.

'But that night at Wolves – even though we lost the game 1–0 – that is one of the highest highlights of my playing days here. And, indeed, my career as well.'

All eyes now turned to Cardiff, to the land of Iwan Roberts and his fathers. Still short of match fitness after his spring injury, Iwan was never a likely starter. This time, however, he did make it to the bench for a play-off final. There were no barbed remarks from the chairman to spoil everyone's day – even if the final prize just slipped through City's fingers.

'So many people had said: "You know what's going to happen – you're going to come on and you're going to score the winner!"' said Iwan, as he rose off the bench and met Alex Notman's inviting, extra-time cross with a textbook Roberts header.

'When it went in I didn't know whether it was golden goal or what. And I was thinking: "Have we won? Have we won?"

'And for eight minutes we were there weren't we? Going back to Wales, going back to play in the Millennium again, it's something that will live with me for ever. Walking out with yellow and green everywhere, the atmosphere and just the whole occasion really.'

Even the pain of losing that penalty shoot-out fades – particularly now Norwich are mixing it with the big boys.

'Now that we're up I think the pleasure does overtake the pain – it does ease it, definitely,' said Iwan, still left with the odd what-might-have-been.

'I'd never scored there – that would have been the most important goal of my career. Financially, for the Club, they would have been safe for evermore.'

Suggestions that City possibly over-achieved that year may be borne out by the fact that, a year later, Norwich had slipped away off the play-off pace. Bits and bobs were working well, but all too often the weight of responsibility for scoring goals – or if not that, then holding the line – fell squarely on Iwan's thirty-something shoulders. Paul McVeigh would ease some of the Big Man's burden, but again it was a case of trying to make do and mend in the absence of an obvious Bellars. Was McVeigh an out-and-out front man? Or was he better suited to ducking in from the left?

The fact that that debate was being had at all, in itself pointed at the gap in Norwich's armoury. In the end, when it comes to scoring goals on a consistent basis, quality counts. It also costs.

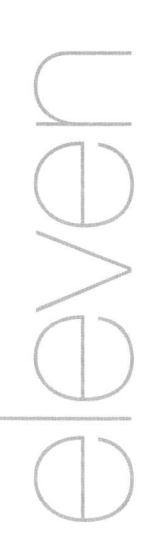

'I think, if we're totally honest, we didn't deserve a play-off position that year because we probably weren't good enough,' said Iwan, as the Canaries finally bit the striker bullet on Saturday, 13 September 2003 and unleashed the on-loan trio of Darren Huckerby, Peter Crouch and Kevin Harper on a frankly unsuspecting First Division. It was a big, bold gamble – one that left rather less room at the inn for Iwan.

'People have asked me that a few times, how did I feel when Crouchy (Peter Crouch) came in, and it was not a problem. Not a problem,' said Iwan, in full elder statesman mode.

'It's not about an individual, it's about the team. Our biggest goal was getting promoted and I knew that by bringing Hucks, Crouchy, Harps (Kevin Harper) in it made us a better squad and a better team.'

Bolt their quality on to a team famed for its "togetherness" and add a young, ambitious boss fast proving himself to be both a shrewd operator in the transfer market and a fine manager of men and Norwich started to really motor.

'I think the lads have got to take a lot of credit for that togetherness,' said Iwan, swift to pay tribute to the Worthington way of doing things.

'His discipline – that's a massive, massive thing for me. The lads have got so much respect for the gaffer and, to be fair, none of the lads would ever cross him. You wouldn't get anyone going out two nights before a game – they just wouldn't do that because they know what he's like.'

As good a manager as Iwan's had? 'I think for what he's done here in a short space of time, he's got to be right up there, to be fair. He's young. He's still learning. But he's got the Club back in the Premier League and fair play to him – the majority of his signings have been successful.'

None more so than Huckerby whose permanent signature – announced to wild delight ahead of the Boxing Day home win over Nottingham Forest – did so much to fire Norwich into the top flight. Here, at long last, was someone to fill Bellars' boots.

'If he'd been here for a couple of seasons – even if I'd had a chance to play more games with him last year – I would have got 100 goals. I'm positive I would have got 100 goals. I was only four away.

'There were a few occasions when I was on the bench and we'd got penalties – if he'd been here for maybe two, three seasons I think I might even have got 150!'

In the event, Iwan signed off with eight goals from his 42 league and cup appearances – strikes that would still play an important part in shaping Norwich's championship destiny.

'I only started 14 games and I got eight goals,' said Iwan, rightly pointing to the games where he made a big, big difference.

'The Sheffield United one got us three points at a critical time – in fact that was probably one of the most important goals I've ever scored for the Club,' he said, as Norwich nipped a little wobbly bubble in the bud on the back of the shock 1-0 home defeat by Bradford City three weeks earlier.

'But even the penalty against Derby at home – where we're 1–0 down with ten minutes to go – no one really fancied taking it. I'd just come on as sub or whatever, missed the first one and I thought: "Right, I'm taking that one again..!" So I would have said that was an important goal as well.

'And even the two at Crewe – they were important to me. Especially the first one. So it was, it was a great season.'

Breaking up is never easy, but at least that day at Gresty Road gave Iwan a richly fitting send-off – made all the more sweeter by his two, final farewell strikes. Age, it seems, was just against him when it came to a ticket to the top flight. One of his few regrets is that another of Norwich's play-off and promotion giants, Malky Mackay, never got his chance to say his goodbyes before his switch to West Ham United earlier this season. Football can be like that – a bit of a heartless cow at times.

'With me not getting another contract, I couldn't have gone out in a better way really. That's why I do feel for Malky a little bit because he didn't get the send-off that he deserved.

'I had the last home game – the great reception at the end. Crewe away, the civic reception, I had three great occasions to say: "Farewell!" That's why I do feel for Malks – he hasn't really had that. But he'll definitely get a chance to come back and play against Norwich – I've got no doubt about that. But I felt for him when he left.'

Iwan, of course, swiftly found new employment through the Watford connection with Gills boss Andy Hessenthaler. It says much about the man that for all his many triumphs in a City shirt, there were still a few, first-night nerves as he arrived at the Priestfield Stadium for the first time this summer as a Gillingham employee.

'I was always quite a shy lad. I've never been outspoken. If I'm put in a room and have to talk in front of people I find that quite hard, to be honest. Granty (Peter Grant) used to be brilliant at it. You could put him in a room and he could talk to people all day.

'But I am a little bit shy and a bit reserved and it's the same now. As daft as it sounds, when I first went to Gillingham, July 1 – I've played for six different clubs; played nearly 600-whatever games; got a championship medal – and there I am, still a bit wary of going into a new dressing room and a new environment.

'I thought I'd never do it again, really. I thought I'd be here for the rest of my career..'

Age was the key, it seems. 'I think he (Nigel Worthington) definitely has got something about people's ages,' said Iwan, who celebrated his 36th birthday this summer. 'I think he has got something in the back of his mind that once you're 33 or 34 then you are coming to the end of your career, but I'm still playing and I'm enjoying playing again. I didn't play that many games last year so I still feel quite fresh, to be fair.'

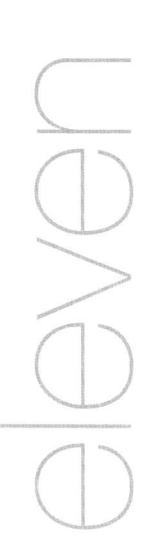

But if the Welsh dragon was, on occasion, slightly shy, there was also a deep-seated fire in the Roberts belly – one that, in many ways, would underpin his seven years at Carrow Road. He had a point to prove. And, boy, did he go out and prove it.

'I don't think there's one thing I'd change about my time at Norwich – even that first year,' said Iwan, as he looked back on a difficult start to his City career. One that could so easily have ended in a swift trip to the summer sales.

'Because had I not realised that year that I was overweight, I was slow then, I wouldn't have had the success that I've had after that. That first year gave me a massive kick up the arse.

'I had the same sort of scenario when I went to Huddersfield. Not overweight, but didn't settle in straight away. I was their record signing so that was a bit of pressure. As I say, I didn't really settle in properly for the first few months and I could hear people say: "What a waste of money, go back to Watford…" and things like that.

'And it was the same here. "You donkey, Roberts!" You'd read letters in the paper, things that people would write in and it does spur you on. You have to be a strong character and strong-willed and the only way that you will win them over is by working your socks off.'

Few, if any, City supporters now need any convincing that Iwan Roberts was a great player. Someone who gave his all in Canary colours. The respect and affection – for both the city and the supporters – remains mutual.

'I've lived here seven years and Norwich is a fantastic place to live. The people are friendly – I've probably got more people stopping me in the street now, now that I've left, than I did when I was playing here.

'It's not my club, but it'll always be my club – if you know what I mean. It will always be the first result I look for,' said Iwan, who returned to the warmest of welcomes from the supporters for Norwich's Carling Cup clash with Bristol Rovers earlier this season.

'I came back the other night and it was if I hadn't been away – the welcome that I had. People coming up and saying: "Oh, I've read the book – really enjoyed it, blah, blah, blah…" So it'll definitely be a big, big part of myself. It'll always be in my heart.'

12 Nigel Worthington

Nigel joined the Canaries in June 2000 as first-team coach during Bryan Hamilton's short spell in charge at Carrow Road and will certainly go down as the best signing made during the brief Hamilton era.

When Hamilton resigned in December 2000 – with the Canaries fighting for their First Division survival – Nigel was asked to take the reigns on a caretaker basis. After an impressive six-game spell, which yielded two wins, three draws and one defeat, Nigel was handed the manager's job on a permanent basis.

After keeping City up in 2000–01 he then proceeded to lead the Canaries to the 2001–02 First Division Play-Off Final at Cardiff's Millennium Stadium. And then in 2003–04, after a nine-year absence from the top flight, he took Norwich City back to the Premiership as First Division champions.

An impressive playing career saw him play for Notts County, Sheffield Wednesday, Leeds United, and Stoke City plus win 66 caps for Northern Ireland, then cutting his teeth in management with Blackpool before joining the Canaries.

> **Nigel Worthington**
>
> **Born:** Ballymena, 4 November 1961
>
> **Norwich City Managerial League Record:**
>
> **2000–01** P26, W9, D7, L10 Final League Position 15th Division One
>
> **2001–02** P46, W22, D9, L15 Final League Position 6th Division One & Play-Off Final
>
> **2002–03** P46, W19, D12, L15 Final League Position 8th Division One
>
> **2003–04** P46, W28, D10, L8 Final League Position 1st Division One

The trick with this one is to read the chapter on Dave Stringer first.

Pick out the bits on who and what shaped his football thinking. How, be it first with City's 1983 FA Youth Cup-winning side and then subsequently with the Canary first team, as they came within an inch of winning the old First Division title in 1988–89, he tried to bolt the best of Ron Saunders on to the best of John Bond. In short, to find that middle way.

From Saunders would come such keystones as fitness, organisation and discipline; from Bond, Dave would borrow the football and the flair. Likewise, in the two men's contrasting personalities, Dave could find further inspiration.

Perhaps that was just where his own character as an individual would naturally lead him. But both as a man and a Norwich City manager, Dave would pitch his tent firmly between the two – never as hard or as remote as Saunders, nor was he as flash and flamboyant as Bond.

Nigel Worthington's formative years were at Hillsborough, the home of Sheffield Wednesday Football Club. In the course of ten very successful years, he would make 338 appearances for the Owls under principally three different managers – his long-time mentor Howard Wilkinson, Ron Atkinson and Trevor Francis.

Wilkinson and Atkinson, in particular, would make a lasting impression on the young man from Ballymena. And – just as Stringer found with Saunders and Bond – in the publicly taciturn "Sergeant Wilko" and the champagne-swilling, camel-coated "Big Ron" Nigel found himself caught between two similarly contrasting figures.

And just as Dave did 20 years earlier, as the Saunders boot camp made way for the big smiles and ready laughter to be had under Bondy; as Wilkinson left to mastermind Leeds United's 1991–92 Division One title triumph and Atkinson arrived with the party poppers and Havanas, so Nigel left Hillsborough with the same lessons learned. Wilkinson was his Saunders; Atkinson his Bond.

'Things that I'd say I picked up from Howard (Wilkinson) were organisation – both in a football club and in a team – professionalism and discipline. Those three things are very, very high on the agenda,' said Nigel, with a fourth Saunders-Wilkinson mantra – fitness – never far away.

'Things I picked up from Big Ron? Banter with the players. He could have the banter with the players, but then the manager and the player thing came in – when it was the right time. I learned that from him. The lighter touch. Yep, we'll have a bit of fun, a bit of playtime. Now we're working. And that was something that I thoroughly enjoyed and, as I say, picked up from him.'

Other traits, however, you wonder whether they're not in the man himself. Like his ability to spot a moper. 'If people are not adding to what you are doing, you cannot have them lingering around. Then they mope – their body language is all wrong and that's not helpful.

'I can walk through a dressing room in a morning and I can feel the mood. I know what the mood is. Whether we need picking up, wakening up or we're in a good frame. I get that feeling straight away and I do it every morning. I walk through deliberately to see where we're at.'

That's not Wilkinson; that's not Atkinson. That's Worthington.

Nigel was just 19 years old when he first bumped into Sergeant Wilko – a man who would come to play a pivotal role in the Canary manager's professional life. First impressions were not good.

'It all started off at Notts County in 1980 where Howard was assistant manager to Jimmy Sirrel. He gave me a hard time as a young player, but now you look back and think: "He probably made me..."

'Because he demanded. He could see something there ability-wise, enthusiasm, commitment-wise. He'd have to work on the quality side and through a lot of hard work, determination and something in my head to say: "Right, I'll show you!", working with him in the afternoons, it worked. And that's something that I'm grateful to him for.'

Wilkinson's young charge would follow him to Sheffield Wednesday and on to Leeds in July 1994, as Nigel blossomed into a highly accomplished left-sided defender – one equally adept at switching to a more forward role as and when his regular Owls partner on the left, Phil King, demanded.

Come the summer of 1997 and with 66 full international caps in the bag, not to mention the small matter of two World Cup finals appearances and a clutch of domestic cup trips to Wembley to his name, time was starting to catch up with the 35-year-old, then 12 months into a two-year deal at Stoke City. If the legs were still willing, it was the shoulder that was weak.

'The summer that I got the phone call, I'd just got through the tail-end of a second dislocation of my right shoulder. I've got to say that the different injuries that I've had – and thankfully there have been no breaks – the two dislocations of my shoulder were the worst pain that I've ever experienced.

'I must admit I'd got to the stage where I thought: "Do I need this pain?" And at the age of 35, 36 it was a case of: "No, I don't!"

'It could have very easily popped out for a third time. It's one of those where as you get older they tend to do less with you. If I'd been 21, 22 they'd have probably have pinned it to make it that more secure, but they leave it when you get that bit older.'

The phone call in question was from Radio Five football expert Jimmy Armfield. The former Blackpool and England defender had been charged by the Bloomfield Road board with identifying a potential successor to ex-Canary manager Gary Megson – then en route to Stockport County. Armfield's enquiry was quite simple – would Nigel be interested?

It wasn't, it seems, the first time that Nigel's name had cropped up in a conversation with Armfield.

'I know he got a tip-off from Howard Wilkinson to say: "Give Nigel a ring!" Not knowing what my response would be because Howard had never spoken to me about the situation at all – and he never does.

'But he put my name forward; Jimmy gave me a call; I asked Stoke if I was alright to go for an interview; they said yes; went for the interview; felt that went very well; there was a good response around the table; back to Sheffield; two hour drive back; within an hour of being back in the house, got the call to say that I'd got the job – as manager, but with the option of playing as well.'

On and off the pitch, Nigel's two-and-a-half year managerial apprenticeship at Blackpool would leave him well-armed for nigh-on anything and everything that football could ever hope to throw at him.

Outwardly at least, it was not your normal, run-of-the-mill lower league club. After all, it's not every club that finds its tycoon owner and chairman facing a guilty verdict of raping a 16-year-old model at the family's castle home, Claughton Hall, near Lancaster.

By the time Nigel arrived, the fedora-loving Owen Oyston was one year into his six-year sentence and in the midst of launching an appeal against his guilty verdict. His wife, Vicki, was left in charge of the football club, with their son, Karl, waiting in the wings to help share his mother's burden.

On the pitch, it was soon clear that being the new player-boss wasn't going to work. Likewise expecting his new charges to perform to top flight standards was a non-starter – as was spending serious money. Despite the Oyston family's media empire being reportedly worth £100 million, Nigel worked on a shoestring. Looking after the pennies became second nature.

'Being player-coach, player-manager was something that I knew was going to be very, very difficult. I think I played six or seven games in all, but at a smaller club, for different reasons, it's harder.

'There's less people about; it's more hands on; you're helping with kit; you're watching games; you're watching players; you're travelling all around and it was hard work, I must admit. So I decided to quit the playing and concentrate solely on doing the management bit.

'I think the players probably knew a bit about me – where I'd been and what I'd done. And, really, I was learning about them because not having played a great deal at that level, you're still learning about people.

'It was a good thing. There was a stand-offish period where we're feeling for each other; seeing how each other works. And I must admit the players responded very well to the situation and they were a couple of very good first years,' said Nigel, with every week providing new lessons in the art of management. One early one was the need to be realistic – to know where you were in the greater scheme of things. And that applied across the board – to the club, to the team and to the individual player.

It is a wariness of trying to think you can run before you can walk that Nigel keeps with him to this day as the Canaries look to find their feet in the top flight of English football. For just as Second Division players don't become First Division ones overnight, nor does everyone take to Premiership football like the proverbial duck to water.

'You had to scale down your expectations of what the players were capable of doing – very much so,' said Nigel, as he looked back on his first early steps in management.

'You're dealing with very honest people; very hard-working people. But there's only so much at that level that you can get out of them. And you've got to be wary of that. If you're expecting them to do something they're unable to do, one, they get frustrated and, two, you get frustrated and nothing happens.

Nigel Worthington

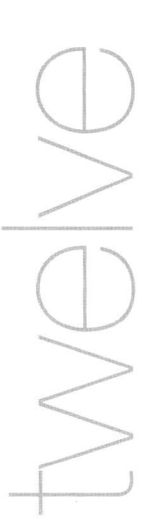

'You're doing a lot of work on the training ground; you cajole them; you try to get the best from each individual; get them to put it in collectively; you've got to monitor where you're at. It's pretty much the same as coming out of the First Division and into the Premiership. You've got to see where you're at – have a look at the situation.'

A further fundamental strand of Nigel's managerial thinking was also emerging in those formative years at Bloomfield Road – the need for discipline. With the lights of the Golden Mile twinkling away on the horizon, all manner of temptations and pitfalls lay within easy reach for the young players in his charge. Time to borrow a page straight out of the Saunders/Wilkinson rule book – a page that, to this day, sits pretty near the top of the manager's in-tray.

'I went in there and the discipline at Blackpool, on and off the pitch, wasn't the best – Blackpool can be a lively place at the best of times and I can honestly say that we got that turned around and smartened that up, which was a big plus and something that I was very, very pleased about.'

Off the pitch and Nigel's education was also coming on apace, as mother and son involved their bright young manager in the decision-making process – tapping into a natural curiosity as to what went on beyond the dressing room door.

'Mr Oyston – the father – was in prison prior to me going to the club. On that score, everything was done and dusted.

'His wife was running the club as their new chairman – Mrs Oyston's a lovely lady and good to work with. Very, very straightforward and honest which is what I like.

'And then 18 months down the line she decided she was getting on in age, decided to step back and her son came in as chairman – Karl – and I've got to say that, to this day, we've got a wonderful relationship. The two families get on great.'

Time to get learning. 'I went into management with a very, very open mind. Very green – but willing to learn. And thankfully the people at Blackpool – and equally so the people at Norwich – involved me in all the business side.

'And, from my point of view as a learning curve, it's great. There's figures, there's man-management, there's the business side of running a football club which I'm very interested in – to see how it's managed.

'At Blackpool I used to go in – and it's very similar to here – and do my half-hour board report and then the people there would say: "Well, why don't you stay for the duration of the meeting? You might have something to offer..."

'I did that and enjoyed that. And exactly the same has happened here at Norwich where I'm in for the full board meeting – at their request. So I know what's happening on the property side, the catering side, the development side of the football club and if there's any small thing that I can throw towards that, that might be helpful, then great. If not, then I'm still learning and picking up.'

Others lessons would also follow – all of which would arm him well for the challenges ahead.

'You've got to learn to delegate to the coaching people around you; let them know what you want but then trust them to get on with the job.'

'Patience. Rome wasn't built in a day. And treat people as individuals. When you are dealing with so many different personalities and opinions – young, old, experienced, inexperienced, whatever – everyone's an individual.

'They've all always got a different little problem and you've got to treat them as that individual. Work with them on a one-to-one – that's one of the biggest things.'

And, finally, a lesson straight out of the Bondy/Big Ron way of working. 'Enjoy it,' he said simply.

For Nigel's gruelling apprenticeship at the lower league coal face was, it seems, starting to take its toll and by the Christmas of 1999 he wanted a break. He knew exactly how Micky Adams felt when the Leicester City boss surprised everyone by quitting the Walkers Stadium in the autumn of 2004.

'I must admit the Micky Adams scenario sounded very, very similar. There'd been a lot going on and it was time for a change; time to step out; have a breather.

'As a first experience in management, it was hands on, head down – "I want to be successful!"

'But it was at a club where it was always going to be difficult for me to try and do it because of the resources – or rather the lack of. I was working on a shoestring, the team was 12th, 14th in the Second Division and I just couldn't see us moving forward. There was no pennies to bring anything a little bit better into the club to try and move it forward.

'I just felt it was only fair that I let someone else pick up the mantle. It might have been a selfish thing, but for me it was only going to be time before I did myself damage health-wise. So it was a case of stepping back from it, recharge and go again.'

First things first, however. Time to enjoy a family Christmas like never before. Worry about what next career-wise in the New Year.

'I spoke at length to Karl (Oyston) about the resignation situation; he didn't want me to go in any way, shape or form.

'But I honestly felt that I'd gone as far as I could with the current group. So I resigned on the 24th of December and I had a wonderful Christmas with the family – where I wasn't looking at the clock to say: "Right, I have to go training..." I can remember it as clearly as ever – it was first class. But, no, I had nothing in the pipeline.

'And after the first three or four weeks, you do start to get bored and think: "When am I going to get back in? What am I going to do?" Then I got

Nigel Worthington

a phone call from Howard Wilkinson to see if I'd fancy being involved with the Under-21s on a scouting level – watching the opposition around Europe. And that meant one or two trips a month. That was a great help because it kept me in touch – and I was recharging at the same time. I was getting my enthusiasm for it back.'

The next phone call was from a real blast from the past – his former boss at Northern Ireland, Bryan Hamilton. With Bruce Rioch deciding that there were three people in an unhappy managerial marriage at Carrow Road, the former Bolton and Arsenal chief bowed out and left Hamilton and the Club's then chairman, Bob Cooper, to run the show.

With Rioch gone, Hamilton had a situation vacant. If only with the benefit of hindsight, snapping up Nigel's coaching services in that troubled summer of 2000 proved to be the smartest piece of business ever done by the ill-fated Hamilton-Cooper regime.

'I got a call – end of March, maybe early April – from Bryan Hamilton to see if I'd fancy coming to Norwich as part of the coaching team. And that was an opportunity that I couldn't refuse,' said Nigel, with the pair's only link being their time with Northern Ireland together.

'Northern Ireland – that's the only connection we've ever had. I got my first 50 caps under Billy Bingham and then from there to 66 it was under Bryan Hamilton. That was the only direct contact I'd had with Bryan – on international games. And no more than that.'

There was, however, an added bonus that, one suspects, neither Cooper nor Hamilton were wholly aware of. As a family, the Worthingtons were already bitten by the north Norfolk bug. Selling his switch to East Anglia to Mrs W and the kids was easy.

'That was the biggest thing of all – my brother-in-law had a property in north Norfolk and he uses that when he's in the country. We used to come down for the odd weekend and so on, so we knew a lot more about north Norfolk than what we did about Norwich as a city.

'And hence we live on that side. We just adore it. It's a wonderful place to live; to bring up your children. So, as far as the family was concerned, moving here was never a hard sell.'

There were other attractions closer to Carrow Road that helped propel Nigel Norwich's way.

'The one thing I knew that over the course of the years coming to Carrow Road was that Norwich had a good football pitch and the atmosphere around the football ground told you that the people were passionate about their football. There was always a good crowd in.

'I came down on the 26th of June 2000, to Norwich City Football Club; joined them; my wife and the three children were backwards and forwards over the course of the summer tidying things up in Blackpool, but I think within six weeks of me being here I moved into my brother-in-law's house until we found ourselves a home of our own. So it was pretty quick.'

Almost as if it was all meant to be. 'Do I believe in fate? Yes, I do. I think there's a map laid out for you and sometimes you take that road and sometimes you're shown that road. Sometimes you've got to make your own luck as well – there's no doubt about that. But it's seeing a good opportunity when it comes and grasping it.'

He arrived in the midst of one of the Club's lower ebbs. For all his own enthusiasm, his own delight at having such a facility as the Club's Colney training HQ to work with, there was poison in the air which the opening-day defeat to a ten-man Barnsley – complete with post-match dressing room bust-up – only hinted at.

'I don't think I appreciated what state the Club was in financially, the feeling within the supporters, where the team was at and so on. But I'm a quick learner and I could see things weren't right within the football club – and I could say that from top to bottom. From top to bottom. Now I think we've got a very settled board with good people who want to take the Club forward in a constructive way.

'And from a football point of view, we've got a good staff who work hard and an honest bunch of players – and that's the biggest thing of all.

'They come in on a daily basis, enjoy their work, but work hard. And that's something that, as a staff, we demand. That's maybe where we've moved on from.

'That people over the last four years are smiling; they're enjoying their work and, as I've always said, if you're enjoying your work you'll always get that extra five or ten per cent which naturally comes out without any effort at all.'

The sweat of a Wilkinson; the smiles of an Atkinson. A bit of Saunders, a bit of Bond.

Matters would all come to head in the wake of a 2–0 defeat at Portsmouth on Saturday, 2 December 2000 – City's fifth straight league defeat. Confidence, humour, spirit and, above all, points were all lacking as Hamilton prepared to end his spell at the helm after just 35 games. His exit came the following Monday.

'Results weren't right – that was as plain as day. Doug and I were in the office one day, Bryan came through and said: "Look, I'm going to pack it in!"

'And that's it. Within an hour, an hour and a half, he's gone. The chairman's come in and said: "I'd like you to take over as caretaker manager..."'

Opportunity was about to knock, loud and clear. Forget the football for a moment. For a husband and father that had just moved his family 'lock, stock and barrel' from one side of the country to the other – and all to a corner of the world that the Worthington clan had long lost their heart to – Nigel had every incentive to stay firmly put. He needed the move to Norwich to work. And not just for straightforward career reasons.

Nigel Worthington

'I was delighted with that situation – that the chairman had asked me to be caretaker,' said Nigel, as fate once again laid out a road before him. Now he had to take it.

'We'd just moved into a new area; been there for just six months; you've got your whole family in; you're a coach under the manager that's just left; where do you stand? Are you in the Club, out of the Club?

'Nine times out of ten if somebody else comes in you could be on your way – unless that person takes to you. So I had only one option. All the eggs in one basket – go for it.'

It was a decision that only came with the full backing of the fledgling "Team Nigel" that was starting to emerge out of the wreckage of two managerial upheavals in the space of nine months, as first Rioch quit and then Hamilton left. Further change would come in the boardroom where Hamilton's exit left the chairman, Bob Cooper, missing his No.1 ally.

Back at Colney, Livermore – with all his connections to the Saunders glory days – and the then reserve-team boss, Steve Foley, signed up from day one.

Four years later, the three are still on the bridge of the good ship Canary as it sails in rather calmer waters than those that awaited that Christmas as Nigel – with a little help from his friends – desperately tried to steer City away from the rocks of relegation.

'Right at the start, during the caretaker spell, my first question to Steve and to Doug: "Does either of you two want the job?" And Doug said: "No!" and Steve said: "No!", so I said: "Right, if it's all right with you I'm going to throw my hat in the ring and see what happens."

'And, for me, that's the way it's been – it's been the three of us all the way through. And Keith Webb. And you've got your kit man and your physios, the sports scientist – they're all part of it.

'We make our decisions as a threesome. As manager you always have the final say, but we have good discussions. There's different opinions which I like – I don't like "Yes!" people for the sake of it. I like different opinions and then I can make my own mind up as to what I think is right or wrong. And if I get it right, we all get a pat on the back; if I get it wrong, then it comes back to me.'

Many suspected that a figure from Nigel's Wednesday past would emerge from the woodwork as he, in turn, put his own men in – a Nigel Pearson, for example. 'It never even crossed my mind about bringing other people into the football club,' said Nigel, with the widely-respected Foley swiftly installed as the new first-team coach, with Livermore proving the ideal No.2.

'Doug and I shared an office for six months and I got to know Doug really well. And when you've got someone like that – someone with a wealth of knowledge; someone who is direct and honest – you've got to have that at your side.

'Again in Steve, you've got another honest person and a very, very good coach. To me, only a fool for the sake of it would say: "Right, out you go – I'll bring my own people in!"

'But, for me, the one thing that Norwich City needed at that time was stability within the football club. And in Steve and Doug you had two good men there already. So it was just a case of fine tuning the staff side of things and then getting the players to believe in what we wanted to do. And then try and take us forward.'

Initially, "Team Nigel" was given a month to prove their worth as the board began to court former Southampton chief Dave Jones. His fateful decision to join Wolves helped, as did Norwich's results. A 1–0 home win over Gillingham in their first game in charge found City digging rather deeper for victory than had been their way under Hamilton. And while a 2–0 defeat at Grimsby Town hardly cheered the soul the following week, a 3–2 win at Queen's Park Rangers on Boxing Day did much to suggest that the team were responding to the new man at the helm.

Come the 1–1 home draw with big-spending Blackburn Rovers on New Year's Day and Nigel delighted the post-match press conference by dropping the traditional manager-fare of "The boys done great today..." in favour of boldly announcing he was off to the boardroom to get some answers. Within a couple of hours, the job was his and "Team Nigel" was in business on a full-time basis.

'I can remember going into the boardroom after the month was up – after the Blackburn game on New Year's Day. The three of us went in and we said: "Look, you've had your month – it's crunch time. Where do we stand?"' said Nigel, with the impression remaining that – as ever – he pulled few punches.

Changes needed to be made at board level, too. In particular, Cooper's close working relationship with the now-departed Hamilton had left many people feeling uneasy. It was also the public's perception that it had, in part, contributed to Rioch's exit.

'I said to the board that day that you've got to sort yourselves out first – if you sort yourselves out first, then the football club will have a chance – regardless of who's manager.

'And I think we can clearly see that has happened – for the good of the Club. Thankfully, I got the phone call a couple of hours later when I got home to say that I was going to get the job.'

The whole episode is instructive in many ways – not least in the way it demonstrated Nigel's capacity to make the bold move; to put his head firmly on the block; to seize the day.

'I'm one of those people who, nine times out of ten, will go for it. Come hell or high water. And if it's high water, I'm one of those that lives with it. I get on. I made a mistake, but I get on,' said Nigel. In short, he's not averse to taking risks. And that's no bad thing. Better, in many ways, to have a manager who makes a decision – be it good, bad or indifferent – than a manager who makes no decisions at all.

'I just think that opportunities are there to be taken and all I can do is – if it's right for me, right for the football club – grasp it when it comes,' said Nigel.

Having made a decision – be it to sign this player or sell that one – the trick is then to persuade the board to jump at the same time – for them to make that final leap of faith and back the manager. And that only comes with success.

That having got Norwich to a First Division play-off final at Cardiff in his first full season in charge, 15 months later they were not only prepared to sanction the loan moves for Darren Huckerby, Peter Crouch and Kevin Harper, but then to back their boss again when he asked for Huckerby's signature on a full-time basis – big, bold, almost out-on-a-limb decisions that came at a tough financial price. But they made them – and would come to reap the reward in stunning style.

'The biggest thing of all is that I've got to give them that confidence in me to say: "Right, we've got to make a decision. Do we back him or not?"

'And I think that comes as part of the success – if you instil confidence in others then there's a mutual feeling there that we're on the right track.'

From day one, big decisions were made. Out went the hapless Dutch pairing of Raymond de Waard and Fernando Derveld, paid up and shipped out – almost within hours of Nigel getting his feet under the table on a full-time basis. At a bigger financial cost, Steve Walsh would follow. They were the easy decisions – chucking out either the dodgy or the ageing apples from within the barrel.

'You had groups in the dressing room and you cannot have groups; you cannot have different factions; that dressing room has got to be as one. And that's something that, as soon as we were in place, that we moved quickly on,' said Nigel, picking up the kind of axe long favoured by a Saunders or a Wilkinson.

Go back to the Dave Stringer chapter and re-read the bit where he describes Saunders' first day at the old training ground at Trowse – sitting there, bare-chested in the pre-season sun, making it abundantly clear that you were either in or out. The door was over there. The same door is still there at Colney. De Waard and Derveld were the first through it.

'Every football club has passengers – even the best clubs. But at that time Norwich City had far too many passengers. I'm coming into the city, coming into the football club and all I can hear is "Costa del Norwich" and that's not for me. It's not for Doug; it's not for Steve.

'Hopefully the tag of "What a lovely place Norwich is for a holiday. You get a three-year contract and sit on your backside..." all that's gone. That's gone. Anybody that's been at this football club in the period that we've been in charge has worked hard, has had to work hard and will have to work hard. And if they don't, then they know where the door is.'

Walsh exited with a rather larger cheque attached after Hamilton's one-time skipper at Wigan Athletic failed to find either the kind of form or fitness that had made him such a magnificent leader of men at Leicester City.

'There's very little you can do in those circumstances as either a manager or a football club – just bite your lip and come to the best mutual agreement that you can come to. Not just with Steve but with other players, for me we've done very well on that side of things to keep it tidy, to keep the momentum going. And that's important – that you've got a healthy dressing room.' A good barrel – another lasting management lesson learned at a very early stage.

'I joined Sheffield Wednesday on 4 February 1984, in their promotion year into the Premiership as now, First Division as it was then. Howard Wilkinson agreed the contract, everything was sorted and he took me a few miles down the road from the ground to the chairman's offices.

'Funnily enough, in Sheffield, it was a steel business. I walked into his office and he was a lovely man, Bert McGhee, and he said: "How are you son?" I sat down and the very first thing he said to me – and I still carry it round with me – "I hope you're a good apple because it only takes one bad apple to sour the barrel..."

'And he said: "We don't have any bad apples!" And, as I say, that's something that has stayed with me from that day. And it's important.'

Survival was the name of the game in that first six months – the time to be big and clever would be the summer when you could set out your stall properly for your first full season in charge. For now, do whatever it took to stay up.

'That first season was all just about making sure we stayed in the division – very much so. Just stay in the league, try and tidy it up as much as you could in those six months and then get ready for a push. A big pre-season; good group of players; get everybody 100 per cent fit. And then you're off and running.

'But at that Christmas time, it was just: "We've got to run through brick walls!" We've got to get the ball up there – percentage play. Yes, it wasn't the prettiest, but it was effective. It did the job at the time.'

Needs must when relegation drives. Over the longer-term, however, the three men at the helm wanted to play the Norwich way – to go Bondy and play their way out of the division, but all on a platform of fitness, discipline and work rate that was pure Saunders. The middle way.

'The great thing that all three of us agreed was that we wanted to pass the ball. We wanted to play good football. We knew that the football club had a reputation for passing the ball and that was something that we were all very conscious of...And that's something that I think we can say that we've worked very, very hard on. And we're reasonably proud of.'

Courtesy of Brian McGovern's "huge" goal at Tranmere that gave the

Nigel Worthington

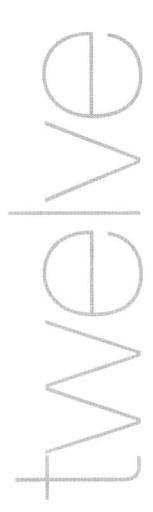

Canaries a crucial 1–0 win that April, Norwich would scramble to safety and would finally finish the season six points clear of the drop zone.

All eyes now turned to the summer and the chance to gear up for "the push".

'We had no time to say: "Right, we'll go away for six weeks, have a lovely break..." It was: "Stay up, right! Get ready for pre-season; what we want to do; how we go about it; then do it." And that's exactly what happened.'

One way they decided to do it was with a big, heart-of-oak, strapping centre-half in the shape of Malky Mackay – promoted out of the reserves to partner Craig Fleming in a new-look defensive partnership that had Stringer-Forbes written all over it. All of which left popular club skipper Matt Jackson out in the cold. Time to bite another bullet.

'Jacko was a big decision. A big influence in the dressing room. But people talk about sentiment in football – not for me. There's no sentiment in football.

'He'd been here whatever amount of time, very popular with supporters, but was getting older. I had a good centre-half in Fleming, and another in Mackay who found it hard getting into the team. I felt that rather than Jacko getting frustrated we could move him on and bring the other two into a partnership. That was the reason for it,' said Nigel, who would face a similar decision three summers later when it came to the prospect of handing long-time favourite Iwan Roberts a ticket to the Premiership after all his years of sterling service.

'It's very much like the Roberts scenario. Big personality within the football club and among the supporters, but the football club has got to continue to move forward. Players, managers, whatever. It's got to continue to move forward to be successful. Decisions have got to be made and I think we've made more right than wrong.'

It was Paul McVeigh's 86th-minute strike at Bradford City on 1 April 2002, that – for Nigel – set something special in motion as the Canaries made their belated push for sixth spot and a place in that season's play-offs.

Even a 2–0 home win over Stockport County on the final day of the season was no guarantee of the fun and games to follow; Burnley were still playing their game at home to Coventry and with the two sides tied on 75 points, it all came down to goals scored.

'The final whistle goes; are you or aren't you? We don't know because they're still playing. And then to get in by a goal...' said Nigel.

The next three weeks until the play-off final at Cardiff on 12 May 2002 will long live in the memory, as City booked their place at the Millennium Stadium courtesy of an epic play-off semi-final success against Wolves. Mackay, rising magnificently to the challenge and opportunity presented by Jackson's exit a year earlier, stole the show in the home leg at Carrow Road with a thumping header in the final minute to give Norwich a priceless 3–1 lead going into the away leg at Molineux.

Though on the day they lost 1–0 to a Kevin Cooper screamer, that trip to Molineux – with all that the Wolves faithful add to the party – remains one of the highest points of Nigel's managerial reign.

'How the lads performed in that hostile environment, with a massive crowd, on a huge occasion, was absolutely outstanding. Every player performed on that night and those sort of occasions live with you for the rest of your life.'

Through luck or design, Nigel's troops had lit the blue touchpaper in Norfolk and City were on a roll. The runaway train that took Jeremy Goss to Munich and Milan had once again left the station.

'You knew that the Club had gone through some lean times and, yes, you could feel the momentum because the place was filling up again. Not only here at Carrow Road, but at Barnsley, Bradford – the different away grounds.

'Wherever you went, all of a sudden you had 1,500, 2,000 and growing all the time. Absolutely magnificent. And great credit to them. And all of those supporters have had a huge part to play in what we've achieved in the last four years.'

Look at the team that boarded the plane to Cardiff that year and the management trio leading Norwich into battle – in a game billed as "the richest cup final in the world", given the estimated £25 million ticket to the top flight at stake – had got the very basics of team-building right.

From future England 'keeper Robert Green, through strapping Scottish braveheart Mackay and good, old-fashioned Yorkshire grit in Craig Fleming and on into the midfield legs of Gary Holt and up front the strength and experience of Roberts – who, alas, would only be able to start on the bench that day – Norwich had a spine. Not only that, but as they had proved at Molineux, they had backbone.

'I think the fine blend of experience and youth – ie legs – was a big thing,' said Nigel, with Peterborough full-back Adam Drury and Holt, the one-time army chef, proving particularly inspired signings.

'Drury – young, hungry, learning, good legs. Holt – got him in for £100,000 – great legs. And I think has improved no end from the day he came until now. Does a great job for you – week in, week out.

'Up front you had Robbo with all the experience in the world; a real handful. It must be horrible for centre-halves to be playing against. So there was a good spine to your team – goalkeeper, centre-halves, midfield and the forward.

'And then you've got people around it. You build around it. McVeigh coming in, Phil Mulryne, who'd had a very, very difficult time, a torrid time with injury, coming back into it and was a big part of it. And enjoying it.'

For 11 magical minutes, until Geoff Horsfield's 102nd-minute leveller wiped out Roberts' extra-time opener, Norwich were up. In the end, of course, they were denied by a penalty shoot-out. On that occasion, it wasn't meant to be. But what an occasion it was.

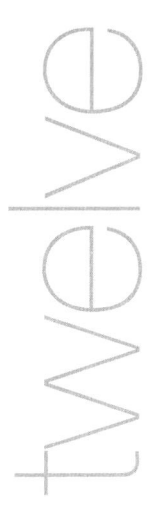

'People say we were unlucky, played well, must have been disappointing, whatever, but I'd have to say I was never disappointed. We travelled to Cardiff on the Friday; trained at Cardiff City on the Saturday morning, had the game on the Sunday and, from when we left Norwich on the plane until we came back on the coach, I enjoyed every single minute of it. No pressure. Just enjoyed it.

'The players enjoyed it. OK, we didn't get the result, but the way we went about our business and the credit that the players, the football club and the supporters came out with meant as much to me.'

As do the memories. 'The players are warming up, 40 minutes or so before the game, you've got green and yellow one end, blue and white the other and I've got to say my eyes filled up – just the sheer sight, the passion. Norwich City at the Millennium in a play-off final. And as a young manager you do – you take a deep breath.'

'Would I do anything different if I had my time again? Go a goal up; eight, ten minutes to go. Yes, experience might just go 4–5–1 for five minutes. See how you shape up. Calm the game down a little bit – but it's all in hindsight. And if you believe in fate, that's your destiny.'

Norwich weren't destined to win that final penalty shoot-out – no matter how hard they tried. 'There was a set five. We'd practised them but practice is nothing like the real thing.

'Maybe the little bit that didn't help was that it was at the Birmingham end. So they helped to suck the ball into the net and, from our point of view, they're blowing it out.

'But hands up – Birmingham took five good penalties. Ours weren't of the best on the day, but the one thing I always say is that a player who steps forward and puts his hand up to take a penalty, that takes a lot of courage. An awful lot of courage.

'Yes, it would have been a dream come true to have got promotion in that first year. It would have been the Iain Dowie of last year. Yes, we'd have loved to have done it, but with hindsight we were nowhere near ready as a team and as a football club to do it. We're now much more the whole, round package to try and establish ourselves in the Premiership.'

With the summer over, it was high time to banish those Cardiff blues with a spot of pure Big Ron – a trip to the sun ahead of the new season.

'I went to the Club and said: "Could I take the players to Marbella prior to the start of pre-season for five days?" It was light training – and it was a social. The boys can go out and enjoy themselves on the night. No pressure – as long as they behave themselves.

'I can remember the first couple of days were a little bit heavy, but after that, well, that kicked us off. The disappointment had gone; we're focused on the job ahead; Cardiff was history. That was one of the great decisions that – as a club, as a manager – we've made in the last four years. To do that – to get rid of what had gone and look into the future.'

The fact that Marbella didn't become a La Manga of Leicester City "fame" also says much as to the line the manager has drawn with regards to the players' behaviour.

'They know the boundaries – it's black and white. There's no grey areas as far as I'm concerned. Discipline in the football club is high – and equally so outside the football club. Because some football clubs – and football players – see themselves above the law.

'Not at this Club. We're the same as any other public figure. The players deserve respect – but they've got to earn that. And that's being on an equal footing. The rules and the laws are there, whether it be by the police, the government, whoever, and we've got to abide by them. And we're no different to anybody else. We're all on an equal footing.'

The following season never quite happened. 'You look back and getting to the final, the momentum and everything, eighth wasn't a disgrace – by no means. It's how you move on from there.

'Do you do a Sheffield United, a Nottingham Forest – you get there and bounce backwards? Or do you try and keep the momentum there? Take part of the jigsaw out and put a new piece in? And keep adding – gently, gently.'

No surprises as to what the missing part of the jigsaw was – the same piece that Dave Stringer had spent most of his managerial career scrabbling around under the sofa to find, a 20-goal-a-season striker.

'You can pick a centre-half or a full-back up for X-amount of £100,000 and they'll do you a good job. A striker who is going to guarantee you 20 goals-plus a season – or as near as damn it – each season costs a lot of money.

'It's not easy when most of the other parts are more or less filled in. It's not easy,' said Nigel, well aware of how far the Club stretched simply to bring Messrs Huckerby and Crouch into the building. To make the next step up striker-wise is, with the best will in the world, beyond Norwich's reach – unless the Club's academy can unearth another Chris Sutton, the second Craig Bellamy.

'There's no way that we were going to jump from a Peter Crouch/Darren Huckerby situation to a van Nistelrooy/Wayne Rooney situation. It's as simple and as straightforward as that. It's about building. Bit by bit. And we will not jeopardise the Club's position like a Derby, a Bradford or a Leeds because that's no good to anybody.'

Simply taking the next step on the ladder and getting to the Peter Crouch/Darren Huckerby situation was the key to last season's success, after an early exit to Northampton Town in the Worthington Cup found Norwich's strike hopes resting on the tender teenage shoulders of Ian Henderson and Ryan Jarvis.

'It was happening and I said to Steve, I said to Doug: "We've got to try and do something!" We identified Huckerby and Crouch as main targets.

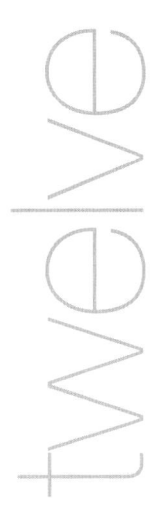

Expensive in terms of Norwich City's means, but I think the way that we were as a staff and as a football club was spot on. We did it on a three-month loan situation and that's how I sold it to the board.

'"Look, these two players are better than what we've got, will add quality and, hopefully, will take us forward. Expensive, but can we try and get them in?"

'It didn't put the Club at major risk financially. And it was on a short term. And it worked a treat. Momentum was growing; the two boys were in; we were getting results.'

Come November and the end of their three-month loan deals was looming over the horizon. With Aston Villa slapping a big transfer fee on Crouch's head, all eyes were on Huckerby, whose performances that autumn had put the Canaries firmly in the promotion pack. Like Jimmy Bone 30-odd years ago, Norwich had found their spark. Could they prise him out of Manchester City and keep the Canaries on course for the Premiership?

'He set the place on fire while he was here – we had to try. He was better than anything we had as an individual. He got bums on seats; he got bums off seats. And we had to try and keep the momentum not only with the team, but with the supporters.

'We had to try and capture his signature. I can remember myself, Neil Doncaster and Barry Skipper working on it on Christmas Eve – up till about 11.30, 12 o'clock that night. Endless phone calls. Agent, football club, manager, player. Back to the agent.

'And that went on from midday for about 12 hours. Non-stop. And eventually we got there. We got there.

'Not only for Norwich City, but for Nigel Worthington to get a player such as Huckerby to sign for me and for the Club was a big thing. He'd been with some big managers; some big clubs. And for me to capture his imagination, to get him into this football club on a contract was a great pleasure.'

Way up on the north Norfolk coast, a bottle of red wine was opened and a toast made – just in time for the clock to strike midnight. Christmas probably came five or ten minutes early in the Worthington household that year. For the Canary faithful, Christmas came rather later – on Boxing Day when Huckerby was officially unveiled to an ecstatic Carrow Road crowd ahead of the 1–0 win over Nottingham Forest.

Having gone top of the league at Portman Road five days earlier, life really couldn't get much better.

'In the back of your head you've got Huckerby on board. Knowing what he's done for you; knowing the type of lad; knowing how he fitted in; knowing what an honest boy he is. To have him in your club, to have him as something to build round was just a great pleasure. Not a relief, pleasure, because you're working with a good player.

Stringer, of course, played under Atkinson at Cambridge United. It was Atkinson's first job in management. He was just 35 years old when he took over at the Abbey Stadium in November 1974. He was, you presume, still finding his way as a manager. Picking up ideas and thoughts on how to play wherever he could.

Stringer first bumped into Atkinson at Trowse. As he watched Norwich City train. 'He used to come and watch us train because he liked Bondy, he loved Bondy,' recalled Dave.

'He liked his way of playing – and everything else. I think he would have had the blend as same as me because he had Ron Saunders at Oxford when he was there and then he saw John Bond and the way that they trained and played. I think he liked that.

'But having learnt from it, he also put his own stamp and authority on what he was doing. Like, I suppose, we all do.'

As Nigel Worthington certainly has.

But, somehow, it would be nice to think that the man who last summer led the Canaries into the bright and promised land of the Premiership owes a little bit of that success to a footballing family tree that stretches back to the playing fields of Saunders and Bond at Trowse. That there, in Norwich's rich past, lies an even richer future.